JESUS
SON OF GOD, SON OF MAN

KING OF THE JEWS

VOLUME 2

JESUS

SON OF GOD, SON OF MAN

STEPHEN HOUSER

A Novel by Stephen Houser

Lionel A Blanchard, Publisher

First Printing

Ltd. Ed. Hardcover ISBN: 978-1-7335858-1-1

Hardcover ISBN: 978-1-7335858-2-8

Cover Art and Design by Vincent Chong

Printed in the United States of America

This volume of my life of Jesus
is dedicated to my father and mother.
Despite everything they did to make sure
That I turned out right, I wound up being okay.

CHAPTER ONE

CALVARY WAS FILLED WITH DYING Jews. The Romans had been crucifying them here for a hundred years. And they were still killing them here a decade after the empire had leveled Judea. A half dozen naked men hung from crosses, their hands and feet nailed to the wooden beams. Jesus sat on his horse at the edge of the killing zone. He watched as the men on the crosses moaned, wept, and cried out in pain and misery.

Jesus knew exactly the kind of agony they were experiencing. He had been crucified here. His son Saul had been crucified here. And they both had been buried here. The area next to Golgotha had been a quarry in King David's time. It had been repurposed to house the wealthy dead in elegant rock-hewn chambers. A man named Nicodemus had donated his tomb for Jesus' burial. He hadn't stayed. Years later Saul was buried there. He had stayed.

Jesus rode on. He entered Jerusalem by the Joppa Gate across from Golgotha. After the Roman commander Titus had pierced the triple walls of the city, he killed the last Judean rebels and razed the capital. All that remained of Herod's great temple was an expanse of scorched earth littered with burned ceiling beams and limestone blocks ripped apart stone-by-stone. Jesus gazed upon the unholy ruins of God's house. The Lord may have given. But the Romans owned the taketh away part.

Now the Latins had apparently decided to perform the giveth part as well. Emperor Titus had specifically requested that Jesus accept the role of King of Judea, ruling it as a vassal state of Rome. Titus wanted it restored as a productive and tax-paying part of the empire. Titus knew and had long admired Jesus, having first met him when Nero was emperor. Vespasian, Titus' father, had been Nero's successor. Titus himself had become emperor after his father's death a year ago.

Jesus rode slowly through the wreckage. Little had changed since Jerusalem had been destroyed. Only a single commercial street had been restored. Leather shop. Clothing shop. Blacksmith forge. Furniture vendor. Clay and pottery works. Almost all of the city's homes still lay in ruins. The owners dead or never accounted for.

Jesus was looking for a particular house that he had last visited some fifty years ago. It had belonged to Elizabeth, his mother's cousin. Mary had lived with her, and stayed after Elizabeth died. Titus' tax officials in Rome had assured him that his mother was still living in the house. And more importantly, paying taxes on it. She would be in her nineties now. Jesus had no idea what her health or vitality would be like. He was sure, however, that her tongue would not have lost any of its vitality.

How often as a lad had he received her pointed and irritated lectures regarding his failure to talk or act like the future Messiah? Jesus had never gotten direct word or guidance about such things from God himself. But he had gotten thirty years' worth of painstaking direction from his mother. Even when she stood below his cross she still believed that the Lord would rescue his Son. He hadn't. Much to Mary's chagrin. But she moderated her irritation towards Jehovah after he raised Jesus from the dead three days later.

She had declined to sail to Gaul with Mary Magdalene and Jesus. And in the decades after, she had become something of a Grand

Dame to Jesus' followers. She hit it off especially well with Paul of Tarsus who had proclaimed Jesus the Christ, the suffering Savior who'd shed his blood for the salvation of all mankind. Mary not only converted to Christianity, she had begun addressing her letters to her son as Jesus Christ. She even drew a little fish under her signature. **Ichthys.** The Greek word for fish and containing the first letters of Jesus Christ, Son of God, Savior. The drawing functioned as a secret symbol for the early Christian community.

Sunset was near and the spring days were still short. Jesus rode on, retracing the steps he believed led to Elizabeth's house. He wished Mary Magdalene was here to hold his hand. She had often kissed his scarred wounds, whispering in his ear that they were medals of honor. Maybe. Jehovah hadn't mentioned that to him when the Roman soldiers were nailing him to the cross.

Mary Magdalene was gone now. His youngest son David was gone. And Saul, his oldest boy, was gone as well. Their bones eaten white. Shut in limestone boxes. David had been sweet as honey. Saul as violent as a curse from God. Yet they had both died young. Neither one spared to live out a full life. Like their mother, they had succumbed grasping dreams and hopes that would never be fulfilled.

Yet pagan Titus was alive and had received the approbation of Rome's rich and powerful families as the new emperor. Even the poor lauded him, cheering the daily gladiator contests he sponsored. They were staged in the huge Colosseum that he and his father had built using the slave labor of a hundred thousand Jews. Did God see what was happening in Rome, Jesus wondered? The good succumbed and the evil prospered. Of course, that was just as true here in Roman-occupied Judea. Maybe God just didn't look anywhere anymore.

Titus' agents had reported that Judas Iscariot was in the city somewhere, too. He would be ancient now, yet probably still agitating for Hebrews to avenge the destruction of Israel. Good God. Give it a rest, old man. There are no patriots left to hear your words of blood and sedition. Mere echoes against their gravestones. Jesus rode on.

Suddenly he heard the distinct cry of a lion in the nearby ruins. He had grown up in rural Galilee when lions had still roamed the hills and raided shepherds' flocks. Perhaps the great maned cats had taken to roaming Jerusalem, searching the abandoned wreckage for dead bodies. He heard the cry again. Fear? Pain? He reached for the sling in his belt and the small leather sack full of smooth stones hanging next to it.

He got off his horse and entered the ruins, wending his way through burned and broken houses tracking the lion's repeated cries. He found a small lot where two young men with swords were standing over a downed lioness. Jesus could see blood soaking her hide. The men took turns stabbing the fallen animal. She cried out in pain and misery.

"Leave the beast alone!" Jesus commanded.

"Mind your own fucking business!" one man shouted back. He was tall and swarthy. Filthy with matted brown hair. He turned toward Jesus and held his sword out.

Jesus placed a small rock in the flap of his sling.

"Back away and leave," he said. "You'll only get this one warning."

"Or what?" the man answered in a mocking tone.

His companion taunted Jesus as well.

"Are you going to *giant* us to death?" he asked.

Both men laughed raucously.

"I'm going to break your hands," Jesus answered. "Like this." He slung the stone. It hit the first man's hand. He screamed in agony and dropped his sword. In a moment Jesus had slung another stone. The second man heard the bones in his hand crack. He screamed and ran. Both men vanished into the wasteland of ruins. Jesus approached the wounded lion. She eyed him warily, but made no sound. The last of the lioness's blood left her body, and in moments the mighty beast closed her eyes and died.

Two very small lion cubs left their hiding place and approached their dead mother. The female had had her litter here and had been discovered. Jesus watched the babies nudge the fallen lioness. After a moment, he knelt and held out his hand. Both youngsters came over and looked at him. One licked his hand. Then the other followed suit.

"Well, boys. I am sorry about your mother," Jesus said. "But she brought me to you, so now you will be part of my family." He stood up and looked around. No one was present. He put the sling in his belt, then bent down and picked up the two baby lions. He held them close as he climbed out of the ruins.

Both lion cubs closed their eyes and purred loudly. He recalled his mother's words the night he and Mary Magdalene told her good-bye. That he better have grandchildren with him the next time he came knocking at her door. And now he would. Two lions of Judah. Bless them, or bite your tongue, Grandma.

— ⚜ —

Mary swung the wooden door open. She stared at her son standing in the doorway. Her face was lined and its skin hung loose. Her eyes, however, were inquisitive, and though her expression was one of *who the hell are you*, she knew who it was. She just hadn't expected her son to look exactly as he looked when she had last seen him almost fifty years ago.

"What are you selling?" Mary asked in an ill-tempered tone. "Wine? Pomegranate juice? Pineappleade?"

"Mom, it's me."

"I know it's *you*," Mary answered. "You haven't changed."

"Yes, I have."

"No, you haven't," Mary argued. "I should know. I'm your mother."

"May I come in?"

"Did you come all this way alone?"

"Yes," he answered. "My horse is tied over there." Jesus nodded his head toward a post on the street. "And I have these little fellows."

Mary squinted at the baby animals nestled in Jesus' arms. "What are those?"

"Lion cubs. Their mother was killed by some toughs in the ruins."

"What are you going to do with them?"

"I don't know. Keep them for now."

"Are you going to breastfeed them?"

Jesus smiled as if she was teasing. But he wasn't actually sure if Mary was joking.

"They'll drink from a bowl when they're hungry enough," he told her.

"And piss like crazy when they're done," Mary complained. "I've got some reed mats. We'll put them down and keep the cubs on them by putting chairs around them."

"Thanks, Mom." Jesus looked at Mary. She was wearing a dark blue robe with a light blue scarf across her breast and covering her hair. She looked very old, but she stood erect and did not appear disadvantaged in any way. "So how about a hug?" Jesus asked.

Mary smiled slowly. Tears formed in the corners of her eyes. Then she stepped forward and hugged her son, leaning her head against his chest and the baby lions. Both cubs began purring loudly. Mary stepped back.

"I never saw a lion this close before," she said.

"Want to hold one?" Jesus asked.

"No. Let's get them some milk and a place to pee."

Jesus followed his mother into the house and watched as she put down several mats and poured goat's milk into two bowls. He set the cubs down and they ran for the milk. While they lapped at it, Mary put several wooden chairs around the mats.

"Come sit by me," she told her son. "That bench is fit for two." She pointed at a long bench against a wall. It was painted white, but the seat had been worn down to the wood.

"I remember this bench," Jesus said sitting.

"Of course, you remember it. Your father Joseph made it."

Jesus watched Mary's face as she sat down beside him.

"What?" she asked noticing his stare.

"You called Joseph my father. Not stepfather."

"I said what I said," Mary responded. "He raised you well. Besides any idiot with a pair of eyes can tell who your *real* Father is. You look eternal. Eternal and everlasting. The spotless Lamb of God sacrificed for the sins of the world."

"You've been reading my palms."

"Don't be funny," Mary said irritably. She looked at the terrible scars in his hands. "Those holes declare that you are the Counselor, the Mighty God, the Prince of Peace."

"You forgot Wonderful."

"I didn't forget. I left it out."

Jesus shook his head and grinned.

Mary smiled.

"Actually, I did forget. You have always been wonderful. Except for arguing about this savior stuff."

"What would you like me to say?"

"I would like you to say that you are the Redeemer. 'Believe in me and thou shalt be saved.'"

"Do I have other choices?" Jesus asked.

"Quit that," Mary scolded.

She lifted up a gold chain fastened around her neck. It had a gold cross with the figure of a crucified man. She held it out for Jesus to see.

"John gave it to me."

"I haven't seen one of those before," Jesus said frowning. "Makes me feel odd."

Mary responded instantly.

"It is a revered symbol for Christians everywhere."

"It is a hated symbol for Hebrews everywhere," Jesus countered.

"You will live to change your mind."

Jesus arched an eyebrow. Nothing short of a visit to the woodshed with Jehovah himself would change his mind. He didn't like

Christianity. It was a hybrid religion combining Jewish blood sacrifice with Gentile notions of triumph. He'd read the Gospels. They were stories that pitted him victoriously against the unbelieving Jews.

He'd have to write his own account some day and lay out his true life's story. And his teachings. Obey God. Do good. Keep it up until you die. Ten words. Nothing fancy. *His* Gospel to the Jews. In a moment of unexpected clarity, Jesus suddenly realized why God had called him to be the Messiah. He had never been sure though he had chased the meaning of what it meant all of his life. Now he knew. There was no great emotional catharsis. No awestruck wonder. He just knew. *His destiny was to save the Jewish people.*

His resurrection had demonstrated to the Jews that Jehovah still cared about his prophets, his martyrs, and his people. And Jesus' rule on the throne of Israel would shine like a ray of hope to Hebrew people all over the world. Helping them maintain their identity, their lives, and their religion. Like a beacon of hope, Jesus would be there to help them prevail.

"Your pets need some attention," Mary said interrupting his thoughts. "That's not rain you're hearing."

"Well, at least they've figured out where they're supposed to go," Jesus said agreeably.

"Ha!" Mary snorted. "Let's watch what happens when they're *not* on the mats. Please pick up those wet ones and stack them outside. I'll wash them later."

"I can wash them," Jesus told her. "Can't be any worse than washing my disciples' feet."

Mary gave Jesus a sour look.

"You did that?"

"Only once. Women and girls do it all the time for their menfolk and houseguests."

"True. Because it keeps the house a lot cleaner, truth be told. Otherwise we probably wouldn't do it."

"As I recall, you made Dad and us kids wash our own feet," Jesus responded.

"Yep. Judea's most liberated mother," Mary commented.

"I've heard a lot of rumors over the years about just how worldly you were forced to be."

Mary gave Jesus a long look.

"Don't believe everything you heard."

"I don't."

"Don't disbelieve everything you heard, either," she added.

Jesus snapped his head back as if he'd been slapped. Mary stared straight at him. She smiled a thin smile. Jesus noticed that his mother had no teeth left.

"When did you lose all your teeth?"

"Who knows?" she answered flippantly. "They were there. Then they were gone."

"I actually had a couple of mine knocked out by the crucifixion detail back when," Jesus told her.

"And?"

"And they grew back." Jesus reached over and held Mary's jaw. He looked at her gums and felt her chin and jaw. "Can't guarantee anything, but it won't hurt to try," he told her. He closed his eyes and prayed silently. Mary squirmed while he held her face.

"Ow!" she cried. Mary pulled away and covered her mouth with her hands. "Everything hurts," she groaned. Blood leaked out between her fingers. She ran to a basin filled with water, dipped a cloth into it, then wiped her mouth, catching more blood as it flowed out. It took several minutes for the bleeding to stop. Mary sat down and glared at Jesus.

"What exactly did you do?" she asked accusingly.

"Go look at your reflection in the copper mirror on the wall," he told her.

She did. Mary gasped. Her jaw and very sore gums were full of perfect teeth.

"My Lord!" she exclaimed. "How did you do that?"

Jesus shrugged.

"I didn't do anything. God did."

"Well then, bless you both!" Mary cried. She looked her son in the eyes. "Can I have a steak?"

— ⚜ —

They were able to find an excellent inn that served local beef grown by Scottish Picts. They'd migrated to Judea thinking that the soldiers serving in the last Roman legion would have both the interest *and* the money to afford big slices of big animals. Mary ate a thick steak and Jesus had a fresh garden salad with vinegar and oil.

He had eaten very little meat since his son David had been murdered on a hunting trip decades ago in La Valdieu. And over time he had lost his willingness to see animals suffer and die in order to be his supper. Now he usually ate only grains and vegetables. They probably had fears and feelings too, he thought. But he had to draw the line somewhere.

Mary ate like a growing girl, consuming every bit of her steak and a whole loaf of fresh bread. No wonder she had managed to make it to ninety healthy and scrappy. Jesus carried the steak bones in his handkerchief for the little lions at home. No matter what *his* scruples were, it was very unlikely that the two cubs would opt to cut back on meat.

"How long have you been back in Jerusalem?" he asked Mary. They were sitting on the kitchen bench again, drinking red wine mixed with water from inexpensive glass goblets.

"I was with John in Ephesus for almost twenty years. Then I came back to take care of Elizabeth thirty years ago." she replied. "John watched over me. Unlike some other party I could mention."

"I sent you a fortune in gold every year, Mother," Jesus told her.

"Well, it didn't buy me off," Mary snapped. "Would have been nice to have seen you once in a while."

"You're seeing me now. Further, Emperor Titus has had a large palace erected in Jericho to serve as my headquarters and private residence. I would like you to come and live with me."

Mary scowled.

"I can't believe you accepted his offer to rule Judea," she complained.

"Would you prefer Latin governors?"

"I would prefer freedom."

"Let's not go there, Mother. The fact is I am a capable man and I will rule this *unruly* people effectively. I will use the empire's resources to rebuild the cities and towns and return our pastures, orchards, and farmlands to productivity."

Mary sipped her wine and remained silent. Jesus watched her for a few moments, then spoke again.

"What are you thinking?" he asked.

"I am thinking that you will make a good king."

"Thank you."

"For the Jews," Mary specified. "But how will you handle Christians?"

"Why would that be a concern?" Jesus asked.

"With you on the throne, Christians will stream here from all over the world. Maybe they will be satisfied with a pilgrimage. But maybe they'll stay. Maybe they'll even become the majority. In which case the day will surely come when they will wish to see you—or someone else—rule as a *Christian* king. What will you do then? What will the Jews do then?"

"I fail to see that that would ever be an issue," Jesus replied.

"Really? You don't have much imagination for a king, do you? Try hard to picture the day when the Roman emperor himself is a Christian and demands that every subject in the empire converts to Christianity. Including the Jews in *your* kingdom."

"Rome will never do that," Jesus protested. "It has allowed every subject nation to pursue its own preferred religion as long as its people pay their taxes. You are worrying about nothing."

Mary stamped her foot.

"You are in for some big surprises, my boy. I will be long gone when these things occur, but they *will* occur. Remember I warned you."

"I will be King of the Jews," he said. "Ruler of God's Chosen People. *That* is the role Jehovah has ordained for me as Messiah. *That* is the role I will have."

Mary looked at her son, not pleased.

"As hard as it is for you to believe," she said upset, "if you stand in the way of Christianity you will be scorned and driven from the throne. By Christians. They are the successors to the Hebrews. They are the *new* Chosen People. Jews will be considered heretics. And they will be expunged by the Christians."

Jesus stared at Mary.

"What a terrible religion you have chosen, Mother."

Mary did not reply. She got up and refilled their wine glasses.

"I can't believe we're having this conversation," Jesus observed.

Mary disagreed.

"God has abandoned the Jews," she insisted. "You fulfilled all the Hebrew prophecies, and now that religion will pass away. God himself will drive the destruction of the Jews." Mary's eyes narrowed. She spoke sternly, emphasizing her words and speaking her one last unarguable belief. "Maybe you've forgotten just how vindictive a deity Jehovah is?"

Jesus stared at his mother, and for the first time in the course of this surreal conversation about the future of the Jews, he felt afraid.

— ⚜ —

Jesus fed and watered his horse and the lion cubs. Then he talked with his mother long into the night. Eerie shadows flickered on their faces from the small oil lamp Mary had set on the table. Mary had showed him the tip. A cross was incorporated into the mold and stood out on the nose of the clay lamp.

He took blankets to sleep on the roof and Mary gave him fresh matts for the lion cubs.

He stretched the mats out and laid down on the blankets. The little lions snuggled up to his sides.

"You already have a name. I know that," Jesus told them. "The one my great grandpa Adam gave your kind when the world was new. But since you cannot tell me what that is," he said looking at one of the cubs. "I'm going to call you Alpha, after the beginning of all things. Earth. Sky. And heaven." Then he petted the second cub. "And you are clearly the thoughtful one. I will call you Omega, the word for the *end* of all things. Don't worry though. It wraps up happily with a new heaven and a new earth."

Jesus lay awake for a long time. He could not get his mother's harsh words out of his mind. Had Jehovah really turned away from the Jews? Would he actually allow Christianity to eliminate the Hebrews once and for all? Was such a thing possible? Even Rome hadn't been able to do that. Jesus closed his eyes. Better rule as fast as you can, Jesus of Nazareth, his mind warned him. The future is going to be mortal for everyone. Including you.

CHAPTER TWO

JESUS HAD A CALM AND pleasant sleep. He was surprised given the epic genocide his mother had prophesied for the world's Jews last night. He woke at dawn with both lion cubs licking his face. They had snuggled him all night. No one had slept at his side since his wife Mary Magdalene.

How many years ago had that been? More than twenty. She used to wrap her arms around his chest and put her head against his back. Now all he had left of her was the ring she had given him in Joppa the night they had exchanged marriage vows. And loved each other for the first time. Their one flesh had been torn apart by her death. It still hurt after all these years.

"Wake up, sleepy head," a male voice spoke mockingly.

Jesus sat up. A figure stood at the top of the outside stairs that led to the roof. In the early light, he could not make out who it was. The voice, though, was familiar. Of course. He knew exactly who it was. While the good died young, this evil person had endured on and on.

"It's Judas!" the figure called out to him. "It's me, Judas!"

Jesus stood up and watched his old disciple approach. He was alive, but he was as ruined as the land he dwelt in. He wore an eyepatch over his left eye. He was missing his right hand and his entire left arm was gone. Judas supported himself with a crutch. His legs and feet were intact, but they appeared weak. He moved slowly.

"You survived," Jesus told him.

"Mostly," Judas answered. "Though what remains of my flesh is not to be deemed robust by any means."

"Be tough to hang yourself this time around," Jesus commented.

"Ha!" Judas mocked. "I'd sure like to find the bastard who started that rumor."

"Yes, me too," Jesus agreed. "I'd shake his hand for the pleasure it gave me, no matter how brief."

Judas stopped a few feet away from Jesus and stared at him.

"Dear God," he murmured stunned. "You haven't aged a day."

"I get that a lot."

Judas smiled.

"I don't. Though folks do sometimes say I'm lucky to be around at all."

"You don't look so lucky."

"Oh, I don't know. I've outlived the rest of the Twelve except for John."

"Is that your measure of being lucky?"

"One of them," Judas insisted. "And not *dying* the way they did! Stabbed, flayed, crucified, beheaded—whatever! As bad as I look, I'm still breathing. But you! You look amazing. What is your secret?"

"I was brought back to life to serve Jehovah."

"Why didn't he just save you from dying?" Judas asked with a sneer.

"He was making a point."

"Eh?" Judas replied and smiled nastily. "That's a good twist."

Jesus gazed at Judas, but he did not respond.

"I want to serve you, Lord," Judas said suddenly serious.

"Pass," Jesus replied.

"You need me!" Judas insisted. "Not everyone in Judea is pleased that you are Titus' puppet. I will protect you against assassins."

"As long as you don't have to chase them."

"Ouch!" Judas said acting hurt, but then grinned. "I don't recall you being all that funny before."

"Maybe you bring it out of me."

"It doesn't matter how much you tease me," Judas commented. "My offer is bona fide."

"How do I know that you will not simply plunge your blade into *my* heart?" Jesus asked. "You're not a Christian, are you?"

"Oh, please," Judas said and groaned. "Do I look like a moron?"

"My mother is a Christian."

"There are exceptions" Judas said quickly. "Not many, however."

"So, who is out to murder me?" Jesus asked.

"Patriots."

"I wasn't sure there were any of those left. Are they in better shape than you?"

"Sons of the fathers murdered by Titus will paint a target on your back."

"Titus crucified my son."

"Everyone knows that. They revere Saul's memory. But it doesn't change the fact that *you* are a Roman toady." Judas wagged his head at the apparent irony. "If Saul was alive, he would try to kill you, too."

"But I would have you to intercept him."

"Ho, ho!" Judas exclaimed delighted at Jesus' repartee. "I'm going to have to get used to this witty new Jesus."

"Yes, you are," Jesus said and bowed his head. Then he pulled his sling out of his belt and held it out for Judas to see.

Judas was surprised.

"You use that now?"

"Yes," Jesus replied. "Against you as quickly as anyone."

"You are not the man I knew," Judas said shaking his head.

"I am not the man you betrayed for thirty pieces of silver," Jesus responded.

"You know that so-called betrayal was purely symbolic," Judas said getting angry. "Your arrest should have been the nation's tipping point towards rebellion."

"So, then the silver was just symbolic?" Jesus concluded. "There were whispers that you gave it back to the authorities."

"Another lie!" Judas denied, "Probably started by the same rumor monger who said I had strung myself up."

"You didn't return the silver?"

"I used it for the rebellion."

Jesus studied Judas' face. He couldn't read anything into his blank expression. As a young man Judas had stolen money from the disciples' treasury. Guess agreeing to take money from the Sadducees who had paid him to lead them to Jesus was no worse.

"Did you know that I fought beside Saul?" Judas asked.

"He never mentioned it."

"We fought together in Galilee. Your son was the greatest warrior I ever saw. He always led his soldiers into battle, unlike the Latin generals who stayed behind the lines. The only exception was Titus who led every single attack during the siege of Jerusalem." Judas held up the arm that had no hand. "I rallied the defenders behind the first wall and faced Titus at the head of the Roman charge. He cut this hand off, then lopped off my other arm. My men carried me to safety, staunching my wounds with cloth ripped from their own robes.

"Titus took the day, driving the Jews back and moving onto the next wall. I didn't witness that horror. I spent a week delirious and near death. By the time I began to recover, the Romans had breached the second wall and were building dirt ramps for their battering rams to break down the third and final wall."

"And what lessons did you—or anyone—learn from the revolt against Rome?" Jesus asked.

"That's an odd question," Judas responded. He stared at Jesus, blinking in confusion. "It's not like there will be another rebellion."

"The day may come when this battered people finds themselves facing another powerful enemy."

Judas arched his eyebrow and watched Jesus' face.

"Such as?"

"My mother is convinced that Christians are the successors of the Jews. And as their numbers grow, they will become their antagonists. In fact, Mary believes that the time will come when a populous Christendom will no longer tolerate Judaism at all and will actively suppress it."

"That sounds like religious genocide," Judas said stunned at Jesus' words.

"You're right," Jesus agreed. "Which leads back to my original question. What did you learn from the quashed Judean rebellion that might help us defend ourselves against another attempted extermination?"

"Don't fight the Roman Empire," Judas said abruptly.

"Ha! I thought you called yourself a patriot."

"Patriots can't be wise?" Judas asked.

Jesus rolled his eyes.

"Don't do that," Judas snarled. "I'm not an idiot. I watched two million Jews die in the revolt. I am not willing to contemplate that such a slaughter could happen again. The only way Judea could defend itself against Rome would be to raise armies that would be the *equal* of the empire's war machine. That's a quarter million soldiers.

"We entered the Patriotic War with forty thousand soldiers," Judas reminded Jesus. "The equivalent of four Roman legions. We won significant victories against the empire's best professional soldiers, wiping out two entire legions. However, as our own losses mounted, there were no men left in Judea to replenish the ranks. The Romans, on the other hand, possessed twenty-six more legions ready to fight and a population of young men across the empire from which to draw recruits. By the time Titus won, the emperor had sent ten full legions here.

"So, if Judea winds up having to face Rome's might another time," Judas summed up, "it has to build and maintain as many legions as it can, all the while encouraging the people to breed sons so they can replace lost soldiers. Only then will there be a truly leveled battlefield."

Judas nodded and went on.

"Another lesson. Don't simply defend the homeland. *Aggressively move against enemy territory.* Be it Rome—or any other power—invade their country, burn their crops, and destroy their towns and cities. Reduce their ability to supply their war effort. Such a strategy also would simultaneously protect and save Judea *by taking the war's destruction to the aggressors.* Judah would retain its capacity to grow crops and livestock. Certainly, the stuff of war as much as young men bearing swords."

Jesus pondered Judas' perspectives. It was clear that Judea would not be able to wage a war against Rome—or any other major power—for many years to come. However, it could become a formidable military threat *within a generation* if he focused its national attention and the lion's share of its economy on raising legions of fighters to match Rome's armies.

Jesus remembered declaring once that his kingdom was not of this world. Alas, such a position was no longer tenable. The broken kingdom of the Jews had been handed to him, and he was determined to heal it. To make it whole and precious in the sight of the world. And a blessing to Jehovah once again. Perhaps a nation of obedient Jews would mean as much to God as the Christian Gentiles dedicated to the cross. Enough so that Jehovah would reach out and save the Jews. Then again, maybe he would not. He hadn't done so during the revolt. All the more reason for Jesus to create a mighty army.

"Thank you, Judas," he said. "I will not forget what we talked about."

And he did not, taking to heart Judas' perspectives. Offered by perhaps the last surviving Jewish freedom fighter to have fought alongside his son Saul. And Jesus believed that he had no option but to take on the role of Israel's warrior king. Killing his thousands like Saul. Killing his ten thousands like David.

And never once in all the years that lay ahead in his long life did Jesus regret embracing that decision, though his final and greatest victory was achieved not with a sword in his hand, but with innocents in his arms and love in his heart. But that story is of another place and another time, two thousand years in the future.

Jesus and Judas went downstairs into the house. Judas visited with Mary while Jesus took up a goatskin filled with milk for his lion cubs. He poured it into their bowls and replaced the soiled mats. Once the cats had decided that the reeds were there for peeing and pooping, they raced around the roof every time they soiled them, having proved once again that they were truly the kings of the jungle.

Jesus washed the mats on the street, then laid them out on the roof to dry. He fed and watered his horse, then went back upstairs and picked up the lion cubs. He took them down into the house. He was surprised to see a fully-armored Roman Praetorian standing inside. The soldier wore a short-sleeved tunic, a pleated scarlet leather skirt, a steel chestplate with a gold embossed portrait of Mars, the Roman god of war, and a red cape. He was holding a steel helmet, topped with a general's vermillion horsehair crest.

The legionnaire had a grim visage and a large scar on his cheek. Jesus recognized the soldier's distinct features. He was a long-time confidant of Emperor Titus, having served under him when Titus had been the commander of the Praetorian Guard during his father Vespasian's reign as emperor.

The general's name was Atticus, son of Cato, one of the few senior officers in any Roman legion whose Latin ancestry stretched all the way back to the earliest Roman settlement on the Tiber River.

Today the majority of Roman soldiers were Spaniards, Goths, Gauls, Syrians, and Moors from North Africa. The Praetorians were such a mix as well, and Jesus imagined a day when they would decide *not* to support a new Italian emperor, but agitate instead for an African Taureg or a western Spaniard. And he thought, perhaps not so long after that they might even prefer a Christian emperor over a Roman one who still worshipped gods they didn't care about.

Jesus raised his hand and saluted the general. He saluted in return.

"Greetings, Atticus, son of Cato. I remember you and your devoted service to both Emperor Vespasian and his son Emperor Titus."

Atticus smiled in response to Jesus' acknowledgment and nodded his head respectfully.

"Greetings and salutations from the emperor, King Jesus. I bear a message from his highness."

"You found me awfully fast," Jesus commented. "I only got here yesterday."

"Well, actually not so fast," General Atticus replied amused. "I left Rome with six Praetorians when you sailed for Judea. Titus ordered that his missal be delivered to you as soon as you disembarked at Joppa. We raced on horseback to compete with the speed of your ship."

"Well, congratulations," Jesus said. "You accomplished a nearly impossible feat. And on top of that, you found me here at my mother's house."

"The emperor thought it critical to offer you protection," Atticus told him. "I am just sorry that we did not catch up with you yesterday before you entered Jerusalem."

"I am grateful, General. But as was likely reported to you, I was not bothered making my way here alone."

"Nonetheless, Highness, the emperor has asked that I escort you to Jericho and remain stationed there with my men as a small, but trustworthy personal guard while you select your staff and establish the mechanisms of your rule."

"Thank you, General. I accept your offer," Jesus replied. "You and your soldiers will be my honor guard until I can create a force with local men."

"Yes, Lord," Atticus replied. "And having served in Judea with emperor Titus, I am sure that you will find young men here who are brave and true and will be committed to your safety."

"Well and fairly spoken, Atticus."

The general untied a leather bag attached to his black cincture and handed it to Jesus. Jesus recognized Titus' wax seal affixed to its drawstrings. He broke it, opened the bag, and pulled out a parchment scroll. The emperor's seal secured it as well. Jesus broke it in half and unrolled the scroll.

To: Jesus of Nazareth, King of The Jews
From: Titus Flavius Augustus, Emperor of Rome

Greetings!

Peace be to you my respected friend, who, by the desire of the emperor and the Senate of Rome will reign as ruler of the Province of Judea. Continuing prayers to the gods for your success.

I have decided to crown you king myself and will send word as to when the royal visit will occur to accomplish this event. Before any planning for that occasion, however, I will wait for General Atticus' word that you have properly settled into your official residence and that you are prepared to receive me. I am a man of simple needs, as you know, but I would appreciate having some good Greek red wine laid in for me as a welcoming gesture.

I must confide to you as well that I have a personal and longtime friendship with Berenice, half-sister of the late Herod

Agrippa II. She is not young and she is not beautiful, but she can talk politics better than any senator in Rome and will surely have the latest gossip about you! Would you be so kind as to make sure that she is invited to stay at your palace to coincide with my visit? She may share my guest quarters, leaving space for your other guests. Is my desire on this clear? I trust it is.

May Jehovah bless your rule, and I will sacrifice to both divine Vespasian and Augustus Caesar himself to honor your inauguration as King of the Jews. Please be aware that I have sent funds with Atticus to make any necessary restoration or improvement to your son Saul's tomb and gardens in Jerusalem. I do not know the state of the place where he rests, but I would not like to think that it was damaged or left untended as a result of the destructive conclusion of the Jewish War of Rebellion. I am sending additional funds as well to aid in your efforts to rebuild Judea.

I will look forward to our meeting and your coronation!

Always your respectful servant,

Titus

Signed in my own hand and sealed with my personal mark.

Postscript

If you think my letters are wordy, remember what I'm like when I'm drunk!

Jesus smiled. Titus' letters were always charming. Full of plans and dreams. Always alluding to sexual activities in one manner or another. Jesus had heard of Berenice as far back as when Paul of Tarsus had complained about her liaison with her half-brother Herod Agrippa II. At least twenty years ago.

From there she had gone on to charm Titus and he had taken her back to Rome where she lived openly with him as his de facto wife. After the empire's elite had been burned by Julius Caesar's affair with the Egyptian Queen Cleopatra and Antony's subsequent polygamous marriage to her, the powers of the empire—mainly the Roman Senate—witnessed Titus' behavior with dismay.

Suspicious of Berenice's political influence, the senators had insisted that Titus drop her as a condition of accession. He had complied publicly. He obviously had not complied privately. Jesus was not surprised—nor was he pleased—that Titus was prepared to use the occasion of his coronation to hook back up with Berenice. But there was no way to prevent Titus from doing what he wanted. Jesus would invite Berenice to the ceremony and offer her guest quarters in the Jericho palace. Titus could make his own way from there.

Jesus rolled up the papyrus scroll and spoke to Atticus.

"Thank you, General. May I ask that you return here tomorrow at eight in the morning to escort my mother and me to Jericho? Please procure a wagon with a seat for her."

"I will have one available for her use in the morning," Atticus replied. "A half dozen additional wagons will accompany us as well, bearing the gift the emperor mentions in his letter." Atticus bowed his head, saluted, and left through the front door.

Mary looked at Jesus.

"Please do a miracle and get rid of the asshole smell in my house," she said irritably.

"Dangerous request, Mother," Jesus told her with mock gravity. "Might remove Judas. And maybe even you."

Mary scowled at Jesus. Then she laughed a robust, hearty laugh for a ninety-year-old.

"Judas, I don't care about. But I've got a home service here tonight."

"A home service?"

"A Christian gathering."

"What do you do?"

"Sing. Pray. Listen to a word from the Lord shared by one of the men or women. Then we break bread and drink wine in remembrance of your last meal with your disciples, giving thanks for your life, death, and resurrection."

"Sounds very much like a synagogue," Jesus commented. "A fellowship of believers."

"Exactly. It is a quite a comforting experience."

"The Jews have been in agony over the loss of the temple," Jesus noted. "No sacrifice. Thus, no forgiveness. But Christians don't have a need for a temple, do they?"

"No," Mary said. "We live in a state of grace because *you*, dear son, took on our frailties and our sins and paid the price we owed Jehovah. You were the sacrifice offered once for all."

"The whole cross thing," Jesus said without enthusiasm. It made him feel awkward to hear his mother speak like this.

"Yes," Mary affirmed. "Your shed blood propitiates our trespasses. We live because you died for the sins of the world."

"Where do you get that kind of talk, Mom?"

Mary frowned impatiently.

"*Christians* get it from the Word of God."

"Good, because they didn't get it from me," Jesus responded stubbornly.

"You doubter," Mary chided. "You remind me of Jonah. He did everything he could to avoid God's command to preach repentance in Nineveh. Even sailed away from Israel on a ship. But the sailors threw him off and a big fish swallowed him up and spat him out right in front of Nineveh. Relenting, he preached, but then went into a despondent state when the pagans listened and converted. And that's you! Thousands of Christians around the world have been born to a new life because of you, and all you can do is pout."

Jesus shook his head.

"I am not going to argue," he said. "I was sent to bring God's love and hope to his Chosen People, the Jews. You were the one who taught me that. Yet now, you have joined up with *non-Jews*. I am not and never have been part of *any* mission to the Gentiles."

Mary answered angrily.

"Well, according to John's Gospel, we learn that 'God so loved the world that he gave his only begotten Son that whosoever believeth in him should not perish but have everlasting life.'"

Jesus shook his head.

"I never made such a promise to anyone. Not even to the Jews. Everlasting life?"

"Oh, don't get on your high horse," Mary snapped. "The message is still true. Christians live in God's forgiveness, poured out from your obedient sacrifice. And in the future, we shall—even as Job confessed—awaken in these very bodies and see God with our own eyes."

Jesus decided not to argue with his mother any more. Her new faith focused her on being saved and going to heaven. Judaism, on the other hand, was about caring for your neighbor in *this* life. Being obedient to God in *this* life. It was practical and real. It was only about the present. And it was all that Jesus wanted to believe.

Mary silently fixed dinner. Baked fish, herb sauce, bread, and olive oil. She served Jesus, Judas, and herself. They ate in silence. Jesus gave the lion cubs the leftover fish—minus the fine bones which he carefully removed—and went to bed early on the roof again. Later he could hear Mary's gentle singing in the company of her fellow believers at her home service.

He could feel the cubs snuggled up on either side, adding a warmth that kept him from getting chilled in the night air. Whatever would happen next, Jesus felt a calmness and a wholeness that he had not experienced ever before in the land of his birth. Thank you, Father, he prayed. Bless my mission. Bless my hopes. Bless my future.

Or don't get in my way.

CHAPTER THREE

THE PALACE IN JERICHO WAS *not* a palace, at least not to Jesus' eastern eye. It was a Roman villa with three large limestone wings configured in a U-shape and built near the Jordan River. It had red adobe roof tiles and a huge granite-tiled courtyard in the center. Planters filled with flowers, bushes, and miniature palm trees had been sorted everywhere, giving the courtyard the appearance of a luxurious oasis.

A defensive stone wall surrounded the palace. It was fifteen feet high and ten feet thick with stations for sentries every dozen feet along the top. There were massive wooden gates at the front and back, constructed three feet thick out of cedar from Lebanon. They were covered with two-inch thick sheets of iron bolted on with crisscrossed bars of iron. Above each gate rose a three-story stone watchtower large enough for several archers to engage an approaching party.

Jesus was not pleased. The king was supposed to rule his people, not hide from them. Then he remembered once again that the Judeans were still digging out a decade after the Roman defeat. It would take time for the survivors to acknowledge that Rome had put Jesus in charge, let alone find it in their hearts to accept him as king.

General Atticus and his Praetorians began to unload the things that Mary had brought in the wagon. Jesus had packed only a few parchment scrolls in his saddlebags. Mary had invited Judas to come along, and he'd brought nothing at all. The villa was decorated in a minimalistic military style. There were few furnishings, though what was there was luxurious.

The formal dining room held a large rectangular marble table with semi-precious stones inlaid on top. There were also eighteen chairs made of thyine, an African wood highly prized by the Romans. The great room next to it was furnished with a dozen reclining silk coaches, copper end tables, iron lampstands, and a huge, open-pit fireplace with a hole in the roof to draw the smoke. There was a marble pedestal painted black featuring the armored torso and bust of Emperor Titus. Still keeping an eye on the Jews, Jesus figured.

There were numerous rooms for the administrative staff furnished with marble desks, thyine chairs, and cedar bookshelves. A large private study had been reserved for Jesus next to his bedroom. It featured the Egyptian olivewood desk that Miguel had shipped all the way from La Valdieu. There was an olivewood chair for the desk and three more for guests. The room had built-in cedar shelves lining three of its walls. Good. Home for his collection of parchment scrolls and papyrus books.

All of the rooms and hallways had granite tile floors covered with woven carpets from Asia and additional black pedestals bearing sculptures of Vespasian, Julius Caesar, and Augustus. The palace had at least twenty bedrooms, the largest of which was reserved for Jesus. Each bedroom had marble toilets with piped-in flowing water to remove the waste. There were personal marble writing desks, chairs, and oil lamps. There was a large kitchen in the palace, and a small one next to a private royal dining area furnished with a round marble table and a circular marble bench that seated six.

There were dozens of rooms for servants, supplies, and storage. The largest room in the palace was the throne room. It had high ceilings, clad-marble walls, granite tile floors, and colorful silk banners representing the twelve tribes of Israel. It had a marble throne for the king. The room clearly bespoke the absolute power granted to Jesus by Emperor Titus and the Roman Senate to rule a people who historically did not like being ruled.

This imperial presence was brought home by dozens of Roman soldiers stationed throughout the house and grounds and atop the walls surrounding the compound. Jesus wondered where all the legionnaires had come from. They stood motionless as Jesus and Atticus passed them. Jesus wasn't even sure their eyes followed him and the general.

"How many soldiers are here?" Jesus asked.

"A century has been brought in from Caesarea," Atticus answered. "It is the largest Roman posting in the eastern Mediterranean. A full legion of soldiers is permanently stationed there. Joppa is the international harbor. Caesarea is the military port. General Septimus Agricola is the legion's commanding officer. He will be a great ally in rebuilding the nation."

"And why would that be?" Jesus asked, curious as to why *any* Roman officer would care about captive Judea.

"His mother is a Jewess," Rufus answered. "Descended from Hebrews who are longtime citizens and live in Rome itself. Septimus is also fluent in Aramaic. He is not married, as that is not to his taste. He likes being single. He served in Caesarea during the revolt and is probably the toughest—and no doubt the strongest—soldier serving in Judea today."

"Then we'll have to promote the spectacle of Septimus and Titus meeting in an

arm wrestling match," Jesus responded. "I have never seen the emperor's equal in sheer physical strength."

"I agree," Atticus said and smiled a bit.

"What?" Jesus asked noticing the general's smile.

"We just have to make sure that both men know that the contest is limited to arm wrestling," Atticus explained. "And remind them of that before the wine flows too freely."

"Septimus likes men?" Jesus asked.

Atticus smile turned into a mischievous grin.

"He likes emperors, too."

Jesus shook his head.

"Well, good luck to Septimus," he remarked. "I understand that Titus has already invited the person he intends to bed."

"Yes, he has," Atticus said nodding. "The emperor commanded me to send a messenger to Berenice once you arrived here."

"You know about his plans?"

"Yes. Titus wants her settled in before he gets here."

"So, your messenger is inviting her here?"

"My messenger is *bringing* her here."

Jesus frowned. It was like hosting another Cleopatra in the guise of a Jewish asp. He looked at Atticus who was quietly observing him.

"Have you met this woman?" Jesus asked.

"I have. She was in Rome with Titus while Emperor Vespasian reigned. She is quite a charming socialite."

"Which accounts for Titus's interest?"

"Ha!" Atticus snorted loudly. "Even though Berenice is at least forty, she is built like a brick shithouse. Emperor Titus likes that. Can't say that I blame him."

"So, you're not face men, leg men, or breast men?" Jesus teased.

"No. We're both brick shithouse men."

Jesus and Atticus laughed. It was pleasant male banter. Jesus' first disciples had been young men who had talked endlessly about the pretty women who came to hear Jesus speak. They were careful, however, *never* to include Jesus in their idle conversations about the females they ogled.

"Sire, I don't know if Emperor Titus mentioned it in his letter to you," Atticus continued. "He will be accompanied by his younger brother, Titus Flavius Caesar Domitianus. He goes by Domitian." The Praetorian's eyes narrowed. "He is not to be trusted."

"Titus did not speak of him," Jesus answered.

Atticus' continued in a noticeably quieter voice.

"Domitian has carried many posts in Rome, but he has never wielded real power. His greatest desire has always been to lead troops to war. But both his father Vespasian and his brother Titus had concerns that Domitian was not cut out to be a military commander. His skills lend themselves more to bureaucratic enterprises, *not* leading men into the breech. He is also a bit of a soap box orator preaching adherence to Roman practices and traditions. He and Titus will surely butt heads over the fact that Berenice will be here. Domitian gets apoplectic on the topic of extramarital sex. He finds it *unRoman*."

"May I be bold enough to presume," Jesus asked, "that since he is accompanying his brother—newly ascended to the throne of Caesar Augustus—that someone or some party has asked Domitian to monitor his brother's conduct?"

"Yes. Specifically, in regards to Berenice," Atticus affirmed.

"But what in the world can Domitian do when he discovers that Berenice will already be here waiting here for the emperor?" Jesus asked.

"Kill her."

Jesus scowled with dismay.

"Truly?" he asked.

"Yes," Atticus answered. "And what can the emperor do about that?"

"Strike his brother down?" Jesus ventured.

"The emperor would never kill his own brother."

Jesus gazed at Atticus who looked at him in return.

"And that's the *real* reason Titus sent you here," Jesus stated. "*You* will strike down the royal brother if necessary."

"Just following orders."

"Without any emotions?"

"Oh, there are emotions, my Lord," Atticus said. "I don't like Domitian."

"Does he know that?"

"I didn't say *obvious* emotions."

"No, you didn't," Jesus noted. "And presupposing that in the future my rule turns out to be an embarrassment, or even worse, at direct variance from Titus' will, is it likely I will see you again?"

General Atticus looked straight into Jesus' eyes.

"You would once again have the pleasure of my company."

"Not sure if *pleasure* is the word I would choose."

"Right of you to be suspicious, my Lord."

"But you'd just be following orders."

"Indeed—and *only* the emperor's orders—for I have to admit that I personally have become charmed by your manners, worn humbly by a man acclaimed to be the only Son of God."

"Thank you."

"Why don't we just keep our eyes focused on Domitian for now, my Lord?" Atticus suggested diplomatically.

"All right. May I ask that no matter what happens to either Berenice or Domitian that above all you keep Titus safe?"

"A prudent request. You value your mentor."

"A blunt analysis," Jesus responded. "But accurate. I believe the emperor is truly interested in the restoration of this land. I need him to live and prosper so that Judea may do the same."

Atticus nodded solemnly.

"From your lips to Jupiter's ears," he said.

Jesus stared at the general.

"I don't think you have that quite right," Jesus corrected him. "That's what Jews say about Jehovah."

"I know," Atticus replied. "I was just hoping to pray to someone who might actually answer."

Jesus watched a slow smile form on the general's lips.

"Prudent, to use your word, General," Jesus responded. "Prudent indeed."

— ⚜ —

General Atticus bivouacked with his Praetorians in guest quarters located in one of the palace wings. Jesus, Mary, and Judas shared dinner on the round marble table in the private dining area. The room was small—perhaps twelve by twenty feet—and not particularly cozy. None of the palace rooms were. Jesus decided that he needed to have Miguel come visit from La Valdieu and use his decorating genius to make the palace warm and inviting. Miguel would have fun and it would be so wonderful to see him again.

Jesus and his two guests sat down to a table set with platters of roast lamb, boiled potatoes, buttered peas, pickled cabbage, garlic herb dip, and fresh rye bread. There was also a silver flagon of red wine mixed with water and a half dozen uncorked bottles of dark beer. Jews didn't drink much beer, but legionnaires marched on it, so it would likely be served with every meal here in the palace.

"Good vittles," Mary commented, lifting little bits of lamb to her mouth on top of broken-off pieces of bread.

"But where are the cooks and the servers?" Judas asked.

"I haven't met any kitchen personnel yet," Jesus answered. "I guess they'll appear when our meal is finished."

"It's weird that no one introduced themselves *first*," Judas insisted. He ate by pushing food off his plate into his mouth with his amputated forearm. It wasn't pretty. But then neither was Judas.

"Maybe official servants prefer not to be noticed," Jesus said. "Not seen *and* not heard."

"Or maybe they're pissed off Jews who'll stuff you then stab you," Judas commented.

Jesus put his piece of bread down and looked at Judas.

"Are you serious?"

Judas nodded vigorously.

"I told you before that this country is filled with young men whose fathers, brothers, uncles—and almost every adult male they knew as kids—were killed by the Romans. And you, Jesus, are Rome *incarnate*, waiting to be murdered by any one of a hundred thousand of those young men."

"There are that many?"

"More than a million Jews were killed in the first years of the revolt," Judas replied. "And another million men, women, and children were slaughtered in Jerusalem at the end. That leaves maybe a million survivors, of which at least a quarter are male children, all of them orphaned. So, yes," Judas said. "There are a lot of young men in Judea who think they owe you a knife in the chest."

Jesus ruminated on those numbers while Judas tried a beer. Mary was kind enough to hold the bottle up to his lips. Jesus had not known about it until recently, but she and Judas had spent a lot of years surviving in Jerusalem together. Judas protected her from thieves and deserters from the Roman legions. She cooked and fed him, often putting the food in his mouth and holding up wine or beer for him to drink. True, he had betrayed Jesus to the authorities, but she understood his action long ago in dark Gethsemane.

Like Judas, she had believed that it would take betrayal and maybe even imprisonment itself to get Jesus to stand up against the Romans. Of course, now he was King of the Jews, but it was not the same. In her mind he'd gone Roman. She hated that Jesus served at the will of Emperor Titus, but the long and terrible revolt had taken a lot of the bile out of her.

Too many dead. Too much disease and hunger. Judas had gone to see Jesus in Gaul before the revolts, and Mary herself had met and embraced her grandson Saul when he came to fight in the rebellion. For years Jesus had invited her to come and live with him and Mary

Magdalene in Gaul, but she had steadfastly refused. She was a Jew. Not a Frank.

Now Jesus was *here* for good. Or for as long as he could stay alive. She and Judas both believed he would be assassinated. Not that Mary wanted that. He was still her son. To help protect Jesus, she carried a weapon for Judas in her bag. It was a sleeve made from an iron cuff that could be pushed over the stub his amputated arm. It had a Sicarii blade securely welded to the front.

"Judas," Jesus asked. "If these young men you talk about were offered a chance to be molded into soldiers in *Jewish* legions—not Roman—how many would join?"

"Most," Judas guessed. "Some are lucky enough to have a trade or a small farm to occupy their lives, but the vast majority have nothing. Would they be paid?"

"Double what Roman soldiers receive. Five hundred silver pieces a year. Thirty-year contract. And when they retire, a farm in Israel."

"You mean Judea?" Judas corrected.

"I mean Israel," Jesus repeated. "It may take time, but I intend to restore the Holy Land to its original size as deeded by Jehovah after Joshua's conquest."

Judas gazed at Jesus without speaking.

"Further,' Jesus continued, "I intend to create an army equal in the size to Rome's. I will do it slowly—being careful not to flaunt it in the emperor's face—while the population recovers from the revolt, stabilizes, and grows. And produces children." Jesus looked directly at Judas. "As you have taught me, I will need replacement soldiers for the legions."

Judas was stunned.

"Truly, you have changed, Lord."

"Truly, I have, and I hope that you live long enough to see this plan put in place."

Judas smiled.

"I'll make every effort to keep breathing for as long as it takes."

"And what are you going to do with all those legions, Son?" Mary asked. "Send the Romans home?"

"Perhaps," Jesus answered, a pensive tone to his voice. "Or maybe we'll march on Rome itself."

"And how do you propose to build your army under the emperor's watchful eye?" she asked.

"By putting it at his disposal until it is large enough to be at *my* disposal."

"You think your Jewish recruits will stand for that?"

"Actually, I expect them to eagerly sign up for that," Jesus answered confidently. "Fighting for Rome will hone their skills and strengths. It is the best way for troops to learn how to fight. Of course, they'd prefer to kill Romans. But killing Egyptians, Persians, and Greeks will settle a few other old scores."

"Ha!" Judas cried. "Jehovah be praised!"

"Don't talk donkey duty, Judas," Mary railed at him. "Jesus be praised is more like it. When's the last time you saw Jehovah do anything? My son is about to embark on raising dozens of Jewish legions." She turned to Jesus. "Do you have access to that kind of money?"

"I do. From the emperor himself."

"Good God!" Judas exclaimed.

"More like good *gold*," Jesus responded.

"What's with you two bashing Jehovah?" Judas cried in frustration. "The day will come when you'll need him, and he'll turn a deaf ear."

Jesus and Mary looked at each and burst out laughing.

"Been there, done that," Jesus told Judas.

"You can never leave God out." Judas said holding his ground. "Never."

"I'm not an atheist, Judas," Jesus reassured him.

"Well, I should be," Mary declared. "Though I do believe in *you*, son."

The table fell silent. Judas stared past Jesus at the entrance to the room.

"Put my knife on," he told Mary. She took the cuff out of her bag and pushed it onto Judas' amputated arm. Judas quickly hid his arm under the table. A young man entered the room dressed in a plain white robe. He had an olive complexion and tussled black hair. He approached the table and bowed toward Jesus.

"My Lord, I am Nathan, son of Amos. The food you and your guests were served was cooked by slaves brought here by the Romans in anticipation of your arrival. Alas, they are mostly Spanish Jews, so they know little about *real* Jews. What we have suffered. What we must do to avenge those who hunted us down like vermin."

"You don't work here," Judas challenged him. "How did you get in?"

"I deliver bread to the kitchen and chat with crew," Nathan answered. "Also, I volunteered to bring dessert when you were through so I could meet Jesus."

"Really?" Judas asked, then jumped up and lunged for the young Jew. Stunned at Judas' move, Nathan stepped back and pulled out a knife concealed inside his robe. He was a fraction of a second too slow. Judas plunged the Sicarii blade into his heart.

Mary began screaming. Judas pulled his blade out of the assassin. Blood gushed onto Judas' face and robe. He pushed the wounded man away. Without a sound he fell onto the floor. Jesus knelt beside him. His heart raced as he watched the young man dying before his eyes. He was panting hard and his eyes were glazing over. For a moment Jesus thought of trying to heal the man, but he did not. He was now the king and would live now by the same code as this dying youth. Live by the sword. Die by the sword. You made your choice, Nathan, son of Amos.

Mary kept screaming as the panicked kitchen crew rushed into the family dining room. The servants stood staring down at Nathan's body.

"Does anyone know this man?" Jesus stood up and asked.

The cooks and servers said no and shook their heads.

"He entered this room ready to kill me," Jesus told them. "My life was saved by this man." He pointed at Judas. "His quick actions slew the would-be murderer."

He turned to Judas.

"Thank you."

Judas told the staff people to fetch General Atticus. They left hurriedly, fearful and bewildered.

Judas looked at Jesus.

"I know I nag you a lot about the attitude here," Judas spoke up. "But this proves my point. You need guards stationed everywhere in the palace."

Jesus nodded.

"I will ask General Atticus to post Praetorians."

"You can't trust *him*," Judas sneered. "Why weren't there guards here already? Tomorrow I will hire mercenaries to watch you and Mary. Canaanites from Phoenicia."

Jesus frowned hearing that.

"What are Canaanites doing in Jericho?"

"Killing whoever they are paid to kill."

"Not what I'm asking," Jesus said.

"They are freelancers. Hired by folks to kill Romans, Parthians, Persians, and other foreigners. They make a good living throughout Judea."

Jesus shook his head.

"No mercenaries. I'll accept help from Atticus for now. I have invited my estate manager from La Valdieu to visit. I'll ask him to recruit some of the younger sons of that kingdom's knights who wish to seek their fortunes. Only the best will be sent by RoxAnna, the Queen Mother."

"RoxAnna?" Mary repeated loudly. "Everything I've ever heard about her has been upsetting."

"She is a strong and resourceful woman, Mother," Jesus answered. "Most men and a lot of women find that disturbing. Who were you talking to about her?"

"Him," she said, and pointed at Judas.

Jesus looked at Judas. He and Mary were both standing away from the table, distancing themselves from the blood flowing over the floor tiles. Judas didn't look particularly repentant about whatever he had said about RoxAnna.

"I gave your mother my impressions," he said. "Plus, how long ago was that anyway? Fifteen, twenty years ago? I was in your kingdom at La Valdieu to ask Saul to join the uprising."

"And what, may I ask," Jesus said turning to Mary, "did Saul have to say about his wife when you met him out *here*, Mother?"

"He said he loved her." She shrugged her shoulders. "What else would he say?"

"And you didn't take your own grandson's word for his feelings about RoxAnna?"

Mary didn't answer.

Jesus arched an eyebrow and looked at his mother. Then he looked at Judas. Judas put a finger to his lips. Jesus stopped speaking.

General Atticus rushed into the kitchen followed by his Praetorians. He had his sword unsheathed and held it high as he surveyed the dead man on the floor. He lowered his sword and spoke to Jesus,

"Assassin?"

"Former assassin," Judas answered for Jesus. "Failed assassin, actually."

"I can see that."

"But after the fact, General," Judas said sarcastically.

"For that, I apologize," Atticus replied. "From now on, two Praetorians will be stationed wherever you are Lord Jesus."

"Thank you, General," Jesus acknowledged. "I would also ask that special attention be paid to my mother as well. Judas is probably better off without a guard. He'll be able to kill more people that way." Atticus nodded, wondering if Jesus' last comment was made at his expense.

General Atticus bowed his head toward Judas. So did his six Praetorians. Judas nodded at the tribute. He had lived a life of shed blood. And slaying this assassin without any hesitation was a lesson in the advantage of swift and relentless violence for the King of the Jews. It wouldn't be the last.

CHAPTER FOUR

JESUS HAD THE JERICHO PALACE expanded by Roman engineers. They built a fourth limestone wing and enclosed the courtyard and gardens. That shut off all access to the royal villa except for guarded entrances at the front and rear. The new wing housed additional work chambers for palace administrators, a dozen more guest bedrooms, and a larger royal office for Jesus. He furnished it with a massive marble desk and a marble chair, with three smaller marble chairs for guests.

He had considered having Miguel bring some of his books from La Valdieu. But Judas told him that scores of books were available from Sadducee families who no longer had a scholar in the house. The Sadducees had comprised the hereditary priesthood of the Jerusalem temple and had been widely regarded as liberal thinkers at best and as atheists and pantheists at worst. These relatively enlightened Jews had been deemed dubious patriots by the Zealots during the revolt, and few Jews mourned when every remaining Sadducee was murdered during the final days of the siege of Jerusalem.

Jesus authorized Judas to hunt for available books and provided substantial monies for their purchase. He instructed him to buy Greek philosophy and drama composed in both ancient and contemporary Greek. Roman history and biographies in Latin. Hebrew commentaries on the Scriptures. And a complete multi-volume set of *The Jewish War*, written in Latin by Josephus, son of Matthias. He was the Jewish general who had abandoned the Galilean army he commanded and surrendered to the Romans. Vespasian had spared Josephus' life and attached him as a personal translator to his son Titus while he led the Roman legionnaires in the conquest of Jerusalem.

Josephus had been in Titus' tent when Saul had been invited to parlay with Rome's commanding general in an effort to save the city. Josephus had stabbed Saul in the back when his discussions with Titus came to blows. Saul had survived the wound, but Josephus' attempted assassination had cost him his own family. His Sadducee father, his mother, and his wife all perished in Jerusalem when the destruction of the city could not be averted.

Jesus had already read the part of Josephus' lengthy account of Hebrew history leading up to the revolt against Rome. Jesus had learned Latin during his decades in Gaul and found that Josephus' use of the Roman tongue was elegant and immanently readable. He'd very likely perfected it as a young man sent to study in Rome. While Jesus himself had been pouring cement and building homes for rich Romans in Galilee.

Hours and hours into that volume, Jesus ran into a passage that discussed the period when Herod the Great's lesser sons sat on the thrones of a partitioned Judea.

> *About this time there lived Jesus, a wise man, if indeed one ought to call him a man. For he was one who performed surprising deeds and was a teacher of such people as accept the truth gladly. He won over many of the Jews and many of the Greeks. He was the Messiah. And when, upon the accusation of the principal men among us Pontius Pilatus had condemned him to a cross, those who had first come to love him did not cease. He appeared to them on the third day restored to*

life, for the prophets of God had foretold these things and a thousand other marvels about him. And the tribe of the Christians, so called after him, has still to this day not disappeared.

Jesus dropped the parchment on his desk stunned. Who had provided Josephus with this information? He had been Saul's commanding officer. Had Saul shared these stories about his father? Or had they come from Josephus' own father who had been a young priest in the temple during Jesus' ministry in Judea? He would actually have been an eyewitness at Jesus' trial, and heard the judgment sentencing Jesus to death.

What surprised Jesus the most, however, was Josephus' almost casual reference to his being the Messiah and that the Hebrew prophets had predicted this role as well as his resurrection from the dead. Curiously, Josephus did not mention that Jesus had departed Judea to live in Gaul, and that he was, in fact, still alive at the time of his writing. He did offer a surprising—if lukewarm—affirmation of Jesus' life and ministry by saying that Christians were still active, a cursory acknowledgment of something that most readers would already likely know. It also seemed odd that Josephus did not identify the Christians as Hebrews. Was Christianity already seen as a Gentile religion?

Jesus read the paragraph again. Josephus had carefully tailored the ending of his brief comments by noting that Christians had not disappeared. It wasn't really an endorsement of Jesus *or* Christianity. He wondered what Josephus' readers would think of this paragraph millennia from now. Would Jesus be remembered at all? Would Christians have disappeared? Idle thoughts. Useless speculations. A more urgent concern for Jesus was whether there would be any *Jews* left in the future. Or would they manage to get themselves killed off by pagans, barbarians, Romans, and the Christians themselves?

"Lord, you have guests."

Jesus looked up from his reading. The Praetorian who announced the visitors stepped aside allowing another Praetorian soldier to enter.

"My Lord?" the legionnaire asked, waiting for the king's acknowledgment.

Jesus stood up. He was wearing the scarlet Persian pantsuit his wife Mary had given him ages ago. Its bottom was threadbare now, but he still wore it. Who was going tell the king what he could or could not wear? Besides, no one should be looking at his butt.

Actually, Miguel might challenge him about what he wore. He had written to say that he'd arrive in Jericho in four or five months with a complement of young men from noble families in La Valdieu. Roxanna was selecting them and told Miguel to warn Jesus that the men would most likely be blonde and blue-eyed. They wouldn't look like Jews *or* Romans. Fine, Jesus thought. At six-foot-six with red hair and freckles he didn't exactly look like any of the locals either.

"What is it that brings you here?" he asked the waiting Praetorian.

"Two noble ladies have arrived, Majesty. One is named Berenice, the daughter of King Agrippa of Judea. The other is Salome, the daughter of Queen Herodias, herself the daughter of Herod the Great."

Berenice, the seductress of Titus' heart was here. *And* Salome. The infamous stepdaughter of Herod Antipas who had ruled a divided Judea with his three other brothers. Herod had married Herodias, his own half-sister. He had been condemned quite vocally by Jesus' cousin, John the Baptist. Which was not unusual. John was quite vocal about *everything* he didn't approve of. This particular tirade, however, infuriated Queen Herodias herself.

Salome had performed an erotic dance for her stepfather at a drunken court affair, and Herod promised her whatever she wanted. Her mother Herodias told her to ask for John's head. She did. John's protest days ended with the presentation of his head to Salome. And now she was here. Salome couldn't be more than sixty-five or so, but might be an even worse terror than Jesus imagined her cousin Berenice to be.

"Show them in," Jesus told the Praetorian. "Please instruct the kitchen staff to prepare a light lunch for the three of us. Do you know if anyone offered to wash the women's feet when they arrived?"

The Praetorian looked confused. He was evidently unaware of the Jewish custom that dictated that guests' feet were to be washed when they entered the host's home covered with dust, a traveler's bane in the country's dry climate.

"Have someone bring me a basin of clean water and some towels," Jesus told the legionnaire.

The Praetorian bowed his head and left. Almost immediately a young male servant appeared carrying a large basin of water with white towels tucked under his arm. He bowed towards Jesus.

"Put it on the floor by the chairs in front of my desk," Jesus said pointing.

The boy did so, leaving the towels on one of the chairs, then exited after another bow.

General Atticus himself led the two princesses into Jesus' royal office. Daughters of kings. Sisters of kings. Wives of kings. Lovers of kings. Expecting well-dressed temptresses, Jesus was surprised. The two women were dressed in black linen robes with thin white collars and black scarves covering their heads and surrounding their faces like widows in mourning. Both women wore heavy gold chains with gold crosses. When they saw Jesus, they fell to their knees. He walked over and gently touched each one on the shoulder.

"Arise, noble daughters," he said gently. He offered his hand to one, and she took it. She stood and gazed up at him, a middle-aged handsome woman who was clearly sensual and made little effort to hide it. "Berenice?" Jesus guessed. She nodded. Standing, she was no more five foot tall. But even wearing a loose robe, it was obvious that she was indeed a shapely woman.

Jesus offered his hand to Salome, looking at her face as she stood. Tall and very thin, she was much older than Berenice. Her once beautiful face was lined and unhappy, marking a lifetime of troubles.

"Your highnesses," Jesus said. "Welcome. A luncheon is being prepared, and in the meanwhile, I will have the honor of washing your feet."

Berenice was appalled. Salome shook her head, no.

"It is we who should be washing your feet, my Lord," Bernice said.

"No," Jesus said gently. "My home. My rules."

Both women stood speechless. Jesus swept his arm towards the chairs and the water basin on the floor.

"Please," he said.

The ladies walked gracefully to the chairs. Their carriage was genteel and their bearing elegant. Jesus was reminded of Lazarus' sisters, Mary and Martha. Long gone, those two women had exuded beauty and charm the equal of their brother's graciousness.

Jesus knelt at Berenice's feet. He lifted them one at a time, untied the leather straps at the top of her calves, then slipped off her sandals. He placed her feet in the basin in front of her chair and gently washed her feet. They were white and soft, pampered as only a rich woman could afford. Then he dried them with a towel.

"Where do you live?" he asked her.

"Caesarea," Berenice replied. "My grandfather Herod built a palace there when he ruled. I received it when he died, and the Romans have always honored it as my heritage."

"Is that where you met Emperor Titus?"

"Yes. I met him while I was his father's mistress."

Jesus was startled. He never heard that part of the tale.

"During the rebellion?"

"Yes. Please do not condemn me, Lord. I was alone and Emperor Vespasian protected me."

"I am not one to condemn," Jesus replied. "My own mother has faced unkind tales her whole life that she serviced occupation legionnaires in order to survive as an orphan girl. You did what you had to do."

Bernice put her sandals back on as Jesus moved the basin beneath Salome's feet.

"Thank you, Divine One," Salome whispered softly.

Jesus looked up at her. The old woman's eyes were closed. Her fingers were grasping the golden cross on her chain, and her lips were moving soundlessly. She opened her eyes and gazed at him with open adoration. He removed her leather slippers and washed her feet in the basin. "These are very famous feet if I may say so," he told her.

"Alas, they are, Lord Jesus," Salome replied. "Sad puppets would be the proper description, I'm afraid. They danced for but a single purpose on the night for which they are remembered. To please my stepfather and then use his promise to fulfill my mother's wish. The beheading of John the Baptist. I have lived in shame every day since."

"It was a great tragedy," Jesus shared honestly.

Salome began to weep.

"I have prayed all my life for forgiveness," she moaned.

Jesus dried her feet and stood up. He put his hand on her head. "Your sins are forgiven, Salome. Rise and shed your shame."

Salome stood up and put her feet into the slippers. She pulled back the sleeves of her black robe and held out her arms for Jesus to see. There were long scars in the soft flesh of their undersides.

"I tried to pay the price for my sin," she told him. "But Berenice told me that you had already paid the price. I wanted to believe her words, and today I accept with my own heart your saving grace. Oh, thank you, Jesus!" Salome dropped to her knees again.

"You don't need to keep doing that," Jesus told her kindly and offered his hand. She took it and stood up again. Salome held onto Jesus' hand and gazed at the hole in his palm. She kissed it and thanked him again and again. Jesus invited her to sit. She did. Then he sat down behind his desk and faced his guests.

"You are both Christians?" he asked.

Berenice nodded. Salome nodded as well, once again clutching her gold cross with its crucified figure. It was identical to the one Jesus' mother wore. Mary called it a crucifix.

"Why do you carry that?" Jesus asked.

"It humbles me to be reminded of the price you paid for my sins," Salome answered.

Jesus looked at Berenice who had converted Salome.

"And who reached out to *you*?" he asked Berenice.

"The commanding officer of the Caesarea garrison," she replied. "His name is Septimus Agricola."

Jesus and his two female guests were escorted to the large formal dining room for lunch. It was huge with tapestries on the marble-clad walls, Oriental carpets on the floor, and a long marble table with a top decorated with an inlaid mosaic of lapis lazuli, carnelian, turquoise, silver, and gold. The room itself had little decoration, but boasted a large field stone fireplace at the far end.

Jesus sat at the head of the table in a high-backed thyine wood chair with a silk cushion. Berenice and Salome sat on either side of him. Individual serving plates and handcloths had been set for each person, along with golden goblets for water, wine, or beer. Servants brought in platters of roast pheasant, goose, and duck, boiled carrots and beets, hot breads and rolls, plus fresh raw onions, lettuce, cabbage, pickled green olives, vinegar and oil, and garlic herb dip.

The women accepted wine, and Jesus took water. It had been drawn from deep aquifers and tasted as pure and delightful as the water of Galilee had when he was a boy. Galilee was a fresh water lake, but was so large the locals had always called it a sea. Oddly, not a lot of Romans or Jews drank water, believing that in some way it was unnatural to consume it. It was meant to grow food and provide a proper bath. But drinking? Goodness, no.

Palace staff served Jesus and his guests. Jesus wondered where all the food came from. He knew that much was grown on the verdant land surrounding Jericho's oasis, but the roasted birds were rare and not frequently available. And there was an overabundance of everything.

"What is done with uneaten food from palace meals?" he asked one of the servers, a trim handsome man with a hook nose. A Latin?

"It is given to the servants, Lord," he answered. "And anything leftover is thrown away."

"From now any remaining food beyond what the servants take is to be given to any poor who gather at the palace entrance to receive it."

The server frowned nervously.

"Sire, I am not allowed to do such a thing without General Atticus' approval."

"You have *my* approval, son. If the general questions you, tell him the king ordered it."

The youth smiled boldly at the thought of contradicting the Praetorian officer. Jesus saw his delight. He was not Latin.

"What's your name?" Jesus asked.

"Solomon, son of Jeremiah."

A Hebrew.

"How did you come to work here, Solomon?" Jesus asked.

"I am a slave belonging to the master who has the contract with the Romans to provide,
prepare, and serve your food, my Lord."

A slave?

"What is the name of your master?"

"Albanus, son of Cornelius."

"Are there other slaves who work in the palace?"

"*All* of the servants are slaves, Majesty."

"Thank you, Solomon."

The young slave bowed low to Jesus and then stood in a corner of the dining room ready to attend to the king's needs or the needs of his guests.

"Sorry for the interruption, ladies," Jesus told Berenice and Salome.

"Are you concerned that the young man is a slave?" Berenice asked, having heard Jesus' exchange with the servant. "He is well-treated, has shelter, and does not go hungry. I doubt that the Jewish slaves taken to Rome fared so well."

"I agree," Jesus told her. "But those souls are beyond my help. As of here and now, I will not have slaves serving me in the palace."

"You will break a contract over that?" Berenice asked surprised.

"No," Jesus answered. "I will buy the slaves from their masters and employ them as free men."

"They'll run off," was Berenice's sour response.

"To where?" Jesus asked. "I believe that they'll stay and be all the more hardworking."

Berenice arched an eyebrow at Jesus' optimism.

"You don't think so?" Jesus asked.

"Most of my life I've found that I couldn't trust anyone," Berenice answered. "Romans or Jews. Now I feel safe only trusting other Christians."

Jesus gazed at Berenice for a moment. He wondered how Titus would fit now into her believer's life. He and his guests talked through lunch as though they had known each other all of their lives. Both Berenice and Salome were bright, verbal, and used to being treated as the equal of any man. The women wanted to know about Jesus' life and the events of his passion—his suffering, death, and burial—which by now had become almost legendary among Christians.

They also wanted Jesus to talk about his parents' flight to Egypt to avoid Herod the Great's massacre of innocents. And the personalities of his disciples. His confrontations with the religious authorities. His triumphant ride into Jerusalem on what Christians now called Palm Sunday. And so much more.

In turn, he asked Berenice and Salome about what kinds of people were converting to Christianity. How did it affect the way that they led their lives? Did they know if there were any Jews anywhere who still practiced his own modest original teachings? He knew that his brothers James and Jude had maintained a fellowship of believers built around Jesus' homilies and prayers. Caring for each other and living together as a family. For their loyalty they had been singled out and martyred by Herod's ruling sons.

Berenice described what she had witnessed concerning Jesus' early followers.

"The Pharisees worked hard to get that small community of believers banned as heretics. But all that did was to make people sympathetic towards them. Their numbers flourished. Eventually, Judea's kings began to persecute them claiming they had rejected formal Judaism. They murdered many of the leaders, including James and Jude. But at that same time, the Apostle Paul's teachings began to be find universal acceptance. Converts began to appear all over the empire.

"Romans tolerated the new religion until Christians refused to acknowledge Emperor Caligula as a self-proclaimed deity. That sparked the first widespread persecution. After that, emperors used Christians as scapegoats for everything from deadly plagues to fires in the capital city. The outbreak of the Jewish revolt caused most Christians to flee the Holy Land. Today only a few believers remain in Judea, but across the Roman Empire they number in the tens of thousands."

Jesus shook his head. He knew Paul's teachings. His obedient death on the cross had become the apostle's sacrifice of the Lamb of God. And Jesus' shed blood had become the agent whereby believers had their sins washed away.

At some point in the conversation, Salome fell silent. Jesus noticed, and so did Berenice.

"What's wrong, dear one?" she asked. "Was it something we talked about?"

Salome shook her head slowly, but she was obviously burdened by whatever had caused her to go quiet. She spoke softly and with great emotion.

"I just realized after all these years that John the Baptist's head is still buried up in Machaerus."

"Wasn't his body taken away by his disciples?" Berenice asked.

"Yes. But not the head. I took it—still bleeding onto the silver platter—and found a quiet place to bury it. I think I should retrieve it and have it buried with his body."

"His body was buried secretly," Berenice responded. "No one alive would know where it's at." Berenice put a hand on her friend's shoulder. "Plus, the Romans tore down all of Herod's fortresses. Masada, Herodium, *and* Machaerus. The palace, the courtyard, the soldiers' barracks—everything was were demolished and left in ruins. How would you ever find the place where you buried the Baptist's head?"

"I hear what you're saying," Salome responded. "But I know I can find it. I buried it in a place where I would be able to locate it again no matter how long it lay hidden. Even when I put it in the ground, I thought of returning someday to retrieve it. I can find it. I have no doubt."

No one spoke. Salome's anomalous desire seemed truly strange. John was mortal. His body had decayed. Any remains of his skull had to be fragmentary at best. And what would be the purpose of retrieving it after all these years?

Jesus asked Salome exactly that.

"You've been forgiven for John's death," he told her. "His body has gone to dust. Little can be left of his skull. What would you do with such a strange and unlikely relic if you did find whatever remains of it?"

"I will keep it and care for it," Salome answered. "Forever. No one owes fealty to that sad token of the Baptist's life like I do. I will venerate it until the day I die."

Jesus and Berenice stared at Salome without speaking. Souls buried and waiting for the resurrection didn't care about their bones. Why should Salome care about John's? Then Jesus remembered for the first time in decades that his mother had hidden away relics from *his* earthly life. Not bones, thank God, but Lazarus had given her the sign that Pontius Pilatus had ordered nailed over his head on the cross. Jesus of Nazareth, King of the Jews.

Lazarus had also given her the twisted vines that had been plaited into a crown of thorns and forced down on Jesus' head. A crown for the king the soldiers had jeered. What had she done with those things? There would be other Salomes who would want them. Collect them. Venerate them. Jesus felt his blood go cold.

Although, to be honest, he had his own memento as well. He had been given the silver chalice he had used at the last supper with his disciples. He kept it hidden, only rarely looking at it. When he did, he remembered that the meal had been confusing and upsetting. His followers were in denial over his upcoming martyrdom. Even as his betrayer sat next to him. Christians had made that night into a pious remembrance of his last hours with his disciples. In truth it was a bitter prelude to his crucifixion and death.

Salome looked into Jesus' eyes.

"Will you go with me to find John's skull?" she asked him. "It would mean the world to me to recover it and bring it back. Will you help me?"

CHAPTER FIVE

IT WAS A SMALL GROUP that set out from the palace, but one that drew attention. People stopped what they were doing and stared as it passed. Two fully armored Praetorians on horses led the way. Jesus followed riding a donkey, wearing a white robe and a red-and-white Idumean keffiyeh on his head. Idumea was the homeland of Antipater, the father of Herod the Great. Had Jesus worn it to show honor to the famous ancestor of both Berenice and Salome? He didn't say. But the women noticed and felt complimented by the homage shown to their royal line by the King of Jews himself. They followed on donkeys wearing black robes and black scarves over their heads.

A half-dozen palace servants rode donkeys as well, pulling another six laden with portable military tents, food, drink, and water. The ruined fortress of Machaerus was thirty-six Roman miles away, high in the mountains on the eastern side of the salt Sea of Sodom. The trip there and back would require a minimum four-day journey. Bringing up the last of the group and providing a rear guard were two more Praetorians on horseback.

Jesus had spoken to General Atticus about Salome's desire to visit the site of John the Baptist's martyrdom. Atticus provided the king and his companions with an armed escort and camping supplies brought down from the Roman legion in Caesarea. The general even briefly considered going himself. But a trip through the desert *and* a climb into the mountains—all just to view a bunch of ruins—had no appeal. And to have forced himself to go anyway would have required more wine than could be practically carried by Jesus' group. Atticus remained behind, wishing Jesus a successful journey.

With stops to eat, drink, rest, and take care of their animals, the day passed comfortably for the travelers. They covered almost twenty-four miles in fourteen hours, making the next day's journey shorter and that much more manageable. The servants—all young Jewish men who had had their freedom purchased by Jesus—set up camp.

There was an individual tent for Jesus. Another tent for Berenice and Salome. And one for the four Praetorians who would rotate their sleeping shifts to make sure that there were always two legionnaires on watch. The young servants would sleep under the stars. The day had been hot, but the night would be cool.

Dinner was adequate and abundant. The servants prepared food from the provisions carried by the pack animals. Dried fish, olives, nuts, dates, currants, fresh bread, butter, and honey. There was water, beer, and wine. Jesus drank water. Everyone else, including the servants, drank alcohol.

A large campfire was kindled from dead wood. As it grew dark, everyone drew near to the fire except for the Praetorians who had taken the first watch. They stood at opposite ends of the small encampment, eyes adjusted to the dark, fully aware of their responsibility to keep the king and his friends safe.

There was little conversation as everyone felt their hours in the saddle. Except for Berenice. She had things she wanted to talk about.

"Lord Jesus?" she spoke softly.

"Yes?" Jesus answered and looked at her. Berenice's face was illuminated by the campfire, and for the first time since he had met her she had taken off her scarf and combed out her long dark hair. It made her look younger. Berenice wore make-up in the Egyptian style. Pink rouge on her cheeks and thick black eyeliner which redefined her eyes into stylized almond-shapes, with horizontal strokes drawn almost to her ears.

"Titus still regards me as his mistress," Berenice began. "He had me fetched by Atticus because he still thinks I'm his strumpet."

"Was that your status before?" Jesus asked.

Berenice was silent for a long moment. Then she answered.

"Titus loved me, and I loved him. Though we were not married, he treated me with the love and honor due a true spouse. I had trouble seeing our relationship as illegitimate."

"It wasn't."

"But we weren't married."

"That doesn't null your love or void your relationship," Jesus said.

"But I am a Christian now," Berenice said. "Sex is a sacred act saved for marriage."

"Who taught you that?"

"All the early believers held that view. As a group, they agreed that premarital sex was wrong."

"So, Christian morals are subject to a group vote?" Jesus asked.

"The Ten Commandments also forbid it."

"No, they don't. God specifically says that he does not approve of *adultery*."

Berenice frowned and looked at Jesus.

"Are you telling me that having sex with Titus was not wrong?" she asked.

"I am saying it was not a sin."

"What about sleeping with him now?"

"It's not adultery."

"You're not very strict, are you?" Berenice asked.

"I obey the will of God, not men."

"And God invented sex," she added. "Not men,"

"I think you're starting to get it," Jesus told her.

"Did you have sex before you were married?" Berenice dared to ask.

"No. But I had it as soon as possible *after* I was married."

"Ha!" Berenice laughed. She looked at her handsome companion and dared tread a little deeper into Jesus' private business. "Have you had sex since your wife died?"

"No."

"Lack of interest?"

"Partly. Also, lack of candidates. Who am I to choose from? Servant girls? Young maidens waiting for husbands?"

"Do you think sex requires a relationship?" Berenice asked.

"I believe that sex *benefits* from one. At least for me."

"And my relationship with Titus?"

"Do you still love him?"

"Yes."

"Then there's your answer."

"Sometimes, the way you talk confuses me."

"Yes," Jesus agreed and smiled. "People tell me that I'm somewhat famous for that."

"Why do you do it?" Berenice asked.

"So that people have to make up their own minds."

"But isn't there one answer for every situation?"

"What do you think?"

"Probably not."

"That sounds like a response I'd give," Jesus said and smiled.

Berenice grinned.

"You seem to be a rather liberal thinker," she said.

"I prefer to consider myself flexible," Jesus replied.

"How about situational?"

"Even better. Life is nothing *but* relationships. Every relationship and every situation calls for a wise choice."

"I think that is very Christian," Berenice remarked. "And it sounds a lot simpler than Judaism. Jews have a lot of rules and not a whole lot of choices."

"It's not *that* bad," Jesus disagreed.

"No, I suppose they can pick *which* commandment they want to break."

Jesus laughed. Now it was his turn to question Berenice.

"When you referred to the Jews, you spoke as if you did not include yourself."

"Being a Christian makes being a Jew irrelevant," Berenice answered. "I am no longer beholden to Abraham, Moses, or John Hyrcanus. I am only beholden to *you*."

"You are only beholden to people in need."

"You know what I mean."

"But do you know what I mean?" Jesus asked. "Feeding the hungry. Clothing the naked. Comforting those no one loves. Those are the activities that flow from a heart that understands good, be it Christian or Hebrew.

Berenice fell silent.

"No one talks like you."

"I thought that last subject was pretty clear."

"Yes, it was. Not much matters to you except doing the right thing in the eyes of God, does it?"

"*And* doing the right thing in my own eyes."

"Isn't that the same thing?"

"Often. But not always."

"How can you say such things?" Berenice asked surprised. "You would disagree with Jehovah?"

Jesus shrugged and smiled.

Berenice wagged a finger at him.

"God puts up with a lot from you."

"Yes," Jesus conceded. "And I put up with a lot from him."

Berenice's expression was both entertained and flabbergasted.

"There's a lot of stuff about you that didn't get put into the Gospels," she commented.

Jesus smiled.

"God expects to be your best friend," he responded. "Despite having flaws and issues just like you do."

"You could be describing Titus."

"Jehovah is a perfect parallel to the emperor. Boyish. Violent. Innocent. Forgiving. Charming. Wielding unlimited power. And when he's in the mood, using it right in your face."

"Or in my nightie."

"That, too. At least for Titus."

Berenice blushed.

"Paul told me that Jehovah isn't male or female," she said. "Sometimes I wish Titus was not so male."

"Really? I have the distinct impression that you are looking forward to sleeping with him."

"Yes. I suppose that has been in my heart all along. I didn't want to die before I could hold him in my arms again." Berenice shook her head slowly. "What would be worse than that?"

"Living forever."

Berenice stared at Jesus. She had nothing to say.

Neither did he.

— ⚜ —

The next day's journey was completed by the middle of the afternoon after a short but arduous ride up to the mountain summit where Machaerus was perched. Or rather, had been perched. The majestic fortress had been torn apart by the Romans during the Judean revolt. Its huge building stones and majestic pillars were strewn all over the mountain top.

The servants started setting up camp while Salome went wandering through the ruins, orienting herself by her memories. Berenice joined her. Jesus waited in the camp. His mind was full of memories of John and him as boys. Running ahead of their families on the way to Passover in Jerusalem. Marching along the top of the city walls imagining themselves triumphant Maccabees. Sneaking away from their parents to stare in horror at the crucified men on Golgotha. Such a long time ago. John had been dead for fifty years, and now the woman who had arranged his murder was here seeking his skull.

Salome led Berenice through the litter of stone blocks heading for the edge of the ruins. She was careful to watch for the snakes, scorpions, and poisonous centipedes that commanded the desert peak. Berenice was following her, but stopped to gaze at the vast Sea of Sodom in the distance. The Dead Sea as the Romans called it.

A distinct haze rose from its surface, and she remembered swimming in it as a child. It was so salty she had floated, paddling around like she was sitting in an invisible chair. She'd heard that some enterprising Phoenicians were selling small bottles of its rich bottom mud, declaring it to be a marvelous facial restorative. Jewish women wouldn't be stupid enough to purchase any. But plenty of the rich women she'd met in Rome would ante up the money to buy it.

Salome walked back to her.

"I think I found the spot. But I didn't bring anything to dig with."

"I'll go back to the camp."

"And bring a trowel?"

"Better than that," Berenice answered her eyes turning mischievous. "I'll bring a couple of those nice young men to help."

And she did, rounding up two teenage servants who brought knives for digging. Two Praetorians came as well, realizing that Salome and Berenice had ventured well beyond where they could be observed. Salome led everyone to the spot she remembered. There were foundation stones half-buried, half-exposed.

"This was the corner of the entertainment hall. I came out here to bury the Baptist's head. The ground was soft and I dug a hole with my hands and covered the head over."

"The ground was soft?" Berenice asked. "If this spot has gotten wet on a regular basis the skull is long gone."

"Let's find out," Salome answered. She pointed where she wanted the servants to dig for the artifact she had buried so long ago.

"Careful," she told them. "We are looking for something fragile."

"Ma'am, can you tell us what we are searching for?" one of the young men asked.

"A human skull," Salome told him.

The servant nodded, and he and his companion began digging carefully where Salome indicated. A generation ago, young Hebrew lads told to go digging for a skull would never have seen one. *These* teenagers had seen them everywhere in Judea, as ubiquitous as the fallen stones, wild cactus, and feral cats in the country's sprawling wreckage.

As Jesus had witnessed when he returned to Judea, the land was still mostly a macabre morgue, memorializing the hubris of the Jews who thought that the Romans could be defeated. It had been like making war on the sun. Death by heat, fire, and burns. Rome, one. Jews, a million zeros.

Digging only a few inches down, one of the boys' knives touched something in the soil. He carefully dug around it, brushing away the dirt. It was the crown of a skull.

"Stand back," Salome told him. She got down on her knees and used her hands to push away the soil and reveal the entire skull. It was flint black. She touched it gently. It seemed sturdy, if perhaps softer than bone should be. Salome could tell it had indeed been affected by periodic rains. Its surface was spongy, though the bone had not disintegrated. Salome carefully lifted it out of the ground. The lower jaw had disintegrated, but the rest of the head was intact. She held it in her hands and gazed at it.

"It could be anybody now," she said wistfully. "I alone know that it is the Baptist." Salome's present disappeared into her past as she relived the night of John's beheading. She was a barefoot girl again, wearing sheer dance garments and carrying the head of a man who'd been alive only moments before. She'd dug a shallow hole and laid it inside. The Baptist's eyes were open and staring at her. Yes, yes, I deserve your censor, she had muttered. "Stare at the one who asked for your death!" she abruptly cried out loud. "Guilty, guilty, guilty!" Suddenly a hand clamped her mouth shut.

"No time to be raising your voice," a man hissed behind her. Salome managed to turn her head far enough to glimpse a figure dressed in rags. He had one hand around her waist and the other hand over her mouth. Two more men appeared. They had ambushed the two servants and the Praetorians, putting arrows into their backs.

Berenice screamed. One of the men hit her on the forehead with a hammer and another slammed his sword handle against Salome's temple. Both women sank to the ground. The leader,
a small, sinewy man—filthy and stained—knelt down by Salome and pulled up her robe to reveal her undergarments. He ripped away the cloths binding her breasts and female parts. Another man dropped his bow and quiver of arrows—a short bone-thin man with an unruly head of gray hair—and pulled Berenice's robe up over her head binding her arms. Then he stooped down and drew down her undergarments.

He pulled his own robe off and stroked his penis. His ringleader was already kneeling naked between Salome's legs. It was the position he would die in. A stone pierced his temple and flew into his brain. Without a thought or a sound, his life fled his body. The man who was standing over Salome stared at the blood spurting from his partner's skull. Another stone traveling at the speed of death entered *his* forehead and burst out the back of his skull. He grunted and fell over.

The third and last man quickly notched an arrow to his bow and aimed it at the giant running toward him. Two Roman soldiers in armor followed him. The brigand considered his situation, then threw down his bow and reached for his dead partner's sword. He dropped its tip on Salome's bare breast and shouted at the approaching men.

"Come any closer and the woman dies!"

Jesus stopped, holding his loaded sling in his hand.

"Spare my life and she lives," the marauder cried. "I walk away and that's that."

Jesus whipped his sling back over his neck and threw the stone at the ruffian. It entered his mouth as he finished speaking and smashed into the back of his throat. His sword dropped and he fell, collapsing on Salome's body. The Praetorians yanked him off and Jesus pulled her robe down. He did the same for Berenice.

"The other outlaws are dead, Lord Jesus," one of the soldiers said. "This vermin is the only one who still lives." The Praetorian pointed at the man who'd been hit in the throat. He was lying on his back. Blood was flowing out of his mouth. His eyes watched Jesus as he knelt beside him. Jesus spoke in Latin. They were in Roman Transjordan.

"Did anyone send you?"

The man shook his head no.

Jesus rose and looked at the legionnaire next to him.

"Put your sword in his heart."

The legionnaire drove his sword into the man's chest. His body slumped, dead, even as his eyes watched the soldier withdraw the sword that killed him.

"Bring me water and clean cloths to revive the women," Jesus said. The soldier took off his canteen and wet his handkerchief. Jesus gently wiped Berenice's face. She opened her eyes. Jesus helped her sit up. He did the same for Salome. Both women got to their feet, stunned at the carnage surrounding them. Jesus spoke to them.

"You will have to seek some privacy to secure your underthings."

The women picked up their modesty garments and walked off. Berenice looked back at Jesus.

"Did you kill all the men who attacked us?" she asked.

Jesus nodded. Then he watched the two ladies disappear into the ruins. He had indeed been responsible for the deaths of all three raiders and did not have a hint of regret. Then or now. If they had been hungry, he would have fed them. Lonely, he would have invited them to share fellowship. Naked, he would have found clothes to cover them. But as the bastards had only wanted to satisfy their lust, he had meted out justice as he'd seen fit. On God's behalf? On the law's behalf? It didn't matter. The point was moot. No one challenged his executions. And the dead were not eligible for an appeal.

— ⚜ —

The servant boys were buried and Jesus sang the Kaddish, the Jewish song for the dead. It honored their lives and united them with all the Jews who had gone before. The bodies of the Praetorians were washed and wrapped in blankets. Tomorrow their corpses would be carried to Jericho over the backs of their horses. The malefactors were left for the birds and wild beasts. Salome had wrapped John the Baptist's skull in linen cloths and held it in her lap. Everyone ate a quiet dinner and went to bed early. One of the remaining Praetorians retired and the other guarded the camp.

Early the next morning the travelers left for home. Berenice rode beside Jesus, convinced that if anyone could get them back safely it would him. She marveled that the Son of God who she worshipped was so different in person than in the stories she had been taught. He put no credence in the efficacy of his death to save sinners, saying rather—with some wry amusement—that his crucifixion had been his private 'Come to Jesus' meeting with Jehovah. He had asked God to spare him, and Jehovah had refused.

Jesus talked in terms of living a meaningful life and above all else striving to be a faithful Jew. Those teachings did not make him the Christian savior. What they did make him was the last and greatest of all the Jewish prophets who had cried out that God's Chosen People were still his pride and possession. Berenice chewed on these things riding back to Jericho feeling both confused and joyful at meeting the marvel of a man named Jesus.

The party camped the second night in the same place they had used on their outbound journey. While the servants were setting up tents and gathering wood for a campfire, a handsome middle-age Roman soldier in full armor and a general's plume in his helmet approached the camp followed by a dozen Roman legionnaires.

Berenice ran to greet him. The general got down off his horse and embraced her. Holding his hand like a school girl, she took him to meet Jesus. The king was struck by the commanding presence of the handsome officer. The Roman was, in turn, clearly stunned by the size and appearance of Jesus.

"My Lord," Berenice told Jesus. "This is General Septimus Agricola. He has been my kind and protective friend," she said. "Septimus, this is Jesus of Nazareth, King of the Jews."

Septimus immediately knelt, his head bowed.

"Please," Jesus told him. "Arise and let us be friends."

Septimus stood, took off his helmet, and smiled at Jesus. The general had even masculine features with thick curly black hair and a well-trimmed beard. He kept staring at Jesus, amazed at what he saw.

"Lord Jesus," he finally spoke, "Emperor Titus has arrived in Jericho. I was dispatched to check on your progress. He is most interested in having you join him as soon as possible. He was escorted by ten centurions and ten centuries. His younger brother Titus Flavius Caesar Domitianus has also accompanied him."

"A very large name for the much lesser son of Vespasian," commented Berenice.

General Septimus did not acknowledge her remark and continued speaking to Jesus.

"The emperor sends you his warm regards, Majesty," he said. Then he looked at Berenice. "And conveys his deepest affection for you, Princess."

"Do I need to interpret those words, *deepest affection*, for you, dear Septimus?" Berenice teased.

The General blushed and shook his head, no. He spoke to Jesus again.

"We brought fresh provisions for your party, and we will stay the night offering protection and security. On the morrow, with your permission, we will escort you the rest of the way to Jericho."

"Thank you," Jesus replied. "You are most welcome."

"It is my honor, Lord," the general responded. "I must confide that after you have supped, I have the highest hopes that you will allow me to experience the fulfillment of a lifelong dream of mine."

Intrigued, Jesus had the temerity to ask the general what that cherished expectation was.

"I would very much like to hear you explain some of the parables I don't understand," Septimus answered. "They are multi-leveled stories, as you, of course, know. And often they seem ambiguous to my struggling mind. It's especially hard for me to correlate the earthly story with the heavenly meaning. And to top everything off, they often end with a puzzling twist."

"Which parables are you referring to?" Jesus asked.

"All of them."

CHAPTER SIX

A LONG, BUT UNEVENTFUL DAY OF travel brought Jesus and his group back to Jericho. The party dismounted outside the palace walls and servants hurried to take care of the caravan animals and the war horses ridden by General Septimus and his men. There was great dismay that two of General Atticus' Praetorians had been killed. Their bodies were gently carried inside the villa where Atticus and his soldiers were billeted. As Jesus, Berenice, and Salome walked towards the palace entrance, Emperor Titus came out to greet them. He was wearing a white toga and a purple cape. Jesus bowed and Berenice and Salome fell to their knees.

Titus took Salome's hand. He helped her stand again. Then he did the same for Berenice who stood and held onto Titus' hand. They looked deeply into each other's eyes without speaking.

Then Titus asked her, "Who is your acquaintance?" nodding at Salome.

"She's a royal relative of mine," Berenice answered. "From the line of Herod the Great's daughter Herodias."

Titus smiled at Salome.

"That makes you somewhat of celebrity in these parts then, does it not?" he said.

"No, Majesty," Salome replied seriously. "The few remaining relatives of King Herod have been disgraced, and all of his mighty works have been overturned."

Titus studied Salome for a moment, then turned his attention back to Berenice who was still holding his hand. He looked at her somber dress, her head covering, and the chain and golden crucifix hanging down on her breast.

"Jesus give you that?" he teased.

"Hardly," Berenice answered her tone frosty.

"Quite right, darling," Titus replied ignoring her chilly manner. "Everything I know about Jesus suggests that he has a greater affinity for downtrodden Jews than ascendant Christians." Delivered smoothly, Berenice did not miss the fact that Titus had slapped her right back.

"You might want to tuck that token inside your robe when you see my brother Domitian. He's got this Roman pride thing going right now. Roman traditions. Roman values. And, oh yes. Roman gods. He does not particularly like Christians. Says they're not Romans at all. That they don't give a damn about the empire. Undermining Rome's unity and solidarity, he claims."

Titus looked at Jesus.

"What do you think?"

"Christians look beyond this life to God's heavenly kingdom," Jesus replied. "That may make them seem aloof from the empire's traditions, but people who sing, pray, and dedicate their lives to the pursuit of good deeds are hardly a threat to Rome."

"Well said!" Titus exclaimed. "Remind me to have you repeat that to my brother. Like you, he drinks only moderately. So, by the end of the night, you two will probably be the only ones still making any sense." Titus chuckled, imagining that, and turned back to Berenice. "Cover up the cross, darling," he said firmly. "You need not be showing that to Domitian. He already bears a less than friendly attitude towards you."

Berenice looked instantly alarmed.

"Does he know that you invited me?"

"Of course. His spy network puts mine to shame." Titus grinned. "What a waste of money. The only time spies pay off is when they warn that an assassination is in the works. And as far as I know, no emperor ever had a network *that good*."

"What should I do?" Berenice asked as she tucked the cross inside her robe.

"Sit by me at dinner," Titus replied. "And fuck me when it's over."

Berenice, to her credit, blushed. So did Salome, Jesus, and General Septimus.

"My duty is to obey," Berenice answered.

"A woman's woman," Titus replied. He smiled mischievously and gave Berenice a peck on the cheek. "Thanks for coming. I won't pretend that you have forgiven me for dismissing you in favor of my father's throne. But I haven't forgiven the Senate who demanded it, either. Therefore, we both carry some bitterness in our hearts."

Titus beckoned General Septimus to draw near.

"How were the two Praetorians lost on this trek?" Titus asked. He had commanded the Praetorian Legion for ten years while his father Vespasian ruled the empire. He was fond of the elite legionnaires, and as the emperor's personal bodyguards he had personally rewarded them with his admiration *and* paid them generously from his own personal wealth.

Septimus addressed the emperor's question.

"I am told that the ladies were exploring the ruins of Machaerus under the protective eye of the two Praetorians. Two other legionnaires stayed back to guard the king. Three brigands ambushed the legionnaires who were watching the women and slew them with arrows. Then they assaulted the ladies with intent to rape. Before such craven deeds could be accomplished, however, Lord Jesus himself took out all three men with his sling. He brought the bodies of our soldiers back and left the dead outlaws to the whims of the wild."

Titus turned and faced Jesus.

"You killed three men?"

"One way or another," he replied.

"The Son of God now takes life?" Titus truly looked astonished. For the entire time he had known Jesus—almost two decades now—the righteous Jew had always eschewed violence. The only time he had ever done physical harm to anyone was when he had taken Titus' sword and performed the coup de grace for his own crucified son, Saul. Yet *now* he had killed three men. He stared at Jesus, not knowing what to think.

Jesus was not about to explain. He had no regrets. The men he killed had been judged, sentenced, and executed for their misdeeds. And in ending their evil lives Jesus had learned that taking life was the most significant act a man could perform. It would have been nice to believe that loving, forgiving, and restoring were, in fact, life's most profound actions. But they weren't. Taking away a person's life was. God had used it to solve problems since the first days of Creation. Didn't make it an ideal action. But it was completely effective without a doubt. There would be other men who would lose their lives at the hand of the King of the Jews.

"God's will was done," Jesus finally spoke.

"Well and good, my friend," Titus responded. "But based on what I know of your Hebrew God, I would guess that it was *your* intervention that saved the ladies." Titus gazed at Jesus. He just did not know what to think.

Titus realized that he was still holding Berenice's hand. He raised it to his lips and kissed it. He looked back at Jesus. "Thank you, Jesus of Nazareth."

Jesus bowed his head.

"Welcome to my home."

— ⚜ —

The large marble dining table was laid out for Jesus' guests. Titus. Berenice. Salome. Generals Atticus and Septimus. And if he chose to attend, Domitian, the emperor's younger brother. Rumors among the army of servants working in the royal kitchen—circulated by both the Jewish servants and the Roman slaves travelling with the emperor—suggested that Domitian had come with Titus to see whether or not his brother had arranged a rendezvous with Berenice.

Odd, that this should be of *any* interest to Domitian. Titus had complied with the Roman Senate's requirement that she be removed from his house and his life in Rome. And she had been. More than a year ago. If she and Titus had an assignation on the occasion of Jesus' coronation, who was Domitian going to tell?

Titus' younger brother hated the Senate. A bunch of rich, pompous asses he was sure, who mistakenly thought that actual power resided in their assembly. The fact was that the true power of the Roman Empire resided absolutely and *only* in the person of the emperor, backed up by the Praetorians. Domitian had already spent much of his inherited wealth—the equivalent of one third of the entire annual expenditure of the empire—bribing the Praetorians to support his elevation to Caesar Augustus if and when, the gods forbid, anything should happen to Titus.

Some of the emperor's slaves spoke in hushed tones to the palace servants that they suspected Domitian would use Berenice's presence to stir up a tempest between Titus and himself. They believed that Domitian would initiate this clash as a pretext to kill the emperor and have the Praetorians in Rome declare him his brother's successor. Some of them even placed bets on who the goddess Fortuna would confirm or condemn.

Currently the big money to be made was on Titus being assassinated by Domitian. There were also lucrative odds offered on an alternate scenario where Domitian would murder Berenice. Some of the slave boys risked their money on that latter possibility. There were always a few mystics who bet on the underdog.

All of the men at dinner were wearing white or cream Roman togas except for Jesus who wore a white cotton robe. Berenice and Salome had on colored blouses and linen skirts. Much more cheerful and feminine than the solemn black robes they had worn earlier. Berenice's blouse was cut low and exposed much of her ample breasts. As though reminding Titus that the evening's pleasures need not be limited to food and drink.

The servants filled everyone's wine goblets, asking each guest if they wanted wine mixed with water, or undiluted. The latter choice was the drunkard's style according to the sniggering servant boys. Straight undiluted wine was preferred by Titus, Atticus, and Salome. A servant bearing a small bowl of toasted bread crumbs followed the wine servers. He used a silver spoon to shower crumbs into the goblets of those guests who chose to add them. This practice had been introduced in Republic times by early vintners trying to reduce the acidity of their wines. The empire added the Greek tradition of saluting guests, and thus was born the Roman habit of *toasting* one another's health and fortunes.

When everyone's goblet had been filled, Titus stood and held his out toward Jesus. Every guest spontaneously stood and lifted their goblets towards Jesus. Titus spoke slowly, seriously, and with genuine emotion as he looked at Jesus.

"Over the course of my life," Titus began, "I have had the fortune of observing some of the world's greatest men close hand. I count my father, Vespasian, in that number. And I count Jesus of Nazareth in that number as well. He is *unquestionably* a god dwelling among us, strong and mighty, yet compassionate and forgiving.

"I know not his equal. *I* am not his equal. My divine father was not his equal. How fitting that he has accepted the task of restoring Judea. Making it a leaven to all the world as it is blessed by his presence. To you, Jesus, Son of Jehovah, King of the Jews. Live holy. Live long."

Titus drank from his goblet as did Jesus and everyone else. Everyone sat down, but the toasts continued. Titus offered a second one to Berenice in praise of the size of her breasts. The guests laughed. Berenice thrust her chest out. Everyone drank. The servants brought the first dinner course. A thick stew made of wheat, millet, and corn. Long a comfort food of Romans in every station of life, the cook had added fresh-water sardines from the Sea of Galilee.

Hot rye bread was served with the stew, along with goat cheese and a garlic sauce. Bowls of the stew were placed in front of guests. Silver spoons were offered to those who wished to use them. Most Romans drank soups and stews directly from the bowl. All other foods were eaten with fingers, though iron knifes were available to those who wished to cut their meat into smaller pieces.

Part way through the first course, a tall man in a toga walked into the dining room. He was handsome, of regal bearing, with piercing brown eyes, a shapely nose, full lips, and a high forehead made more prominent by thinning black hair. He scanned those who were present even as Titus rose to welcome him.

"Dear friends and colleagues, please greet my beloved brother, Domitian."

Goblets were held high, but Domitian ignored the guests and simply beckoned Titus to join him outside the dining room. Titus scowled at Domitian's rudeness. He excused himself to the group and followed him out of the room.

Jesus noted that no one seemed disturbed by Domitian's decision not to join the dinner, although he saw that Atticus had stopped eating and watched for the emperor's return. It was customary for royal families to interact without bodyguards near them, but the general's Praetorian instincts were on alert nonetheless.

Titus truly loved his younger brother, ignoring what others said about Domitian. Mainly that he was openly envious of Titus' role as emperor. Domitian's servants in the slave boy gossip network had shared that he often complained that Titus had loose morals and failed to set an imperial example by declining to marry and have children.

The servants cleared the dishes and food from the first course and set fresh plates for the second. Fried hare. Roast pheasant. Poached geese. Fried lamb sausages. Boiled mushrooms, cabbage, and turnips. Plus, raw radishes, onions, and ripe black olives.

Wine goblets were perpetually refilled, and the guests ate, drank, and conversed. But after a while, everyone began to watch for Titus' return. At last, General Atticus rose and left the dining room taking a pair of Praetorian guards with him. The servants outside the dining hall told the general that the emperor was in a nearby bathroom and pointed toward it.

Atticus entered the room, done in marble-clad walls and granite flooring. There was a row of toilet openings in a long marble slab beneath which running water was continually flushed. Standing at a pedestal bearing a basin of water was Titus. He was holding a damp cloth against his right cheek.

"Are you all right, Sire?" Atticus asked.

Titus turned and showed the general his check.

"That bastard had the nerve to slap my face," he said furious. Atticus frowned deeply. "He's pissed because Berenice is here, and I told him that it was none of his business. At which point, he slapped me and stormed off. I came in here to try and get some of the red to go away." Titus turned back to the basin of water, dipped his cloth, and reapplied it to his face. "Snotty little son of a bitch," he muttered.

Atticus watched the humiliated emperor apply the wet cloth to his face. Striking a Roman emperor was a crime punishable by death. It didn't matter that Titus' brother was the perpetrator. The Senate had passed the law. Of course, the emperor could offer clemency to whomever he wished. But in this case the pardon was more likely going to be Titus' silence about what Domitian had done.

Titus dried his face and spoke to Atticus.

"Is my cheek still red?"

"Only slightly. My guess is that most of the guests have drunk enough wine to have earned equally red cheeks."

"Don't try to make me smile," Titus complained and then smiled. "My asshole brother told me that he is going to kill Berenice. Not handing it off to anyone else, he says. He's going to do the deed himself."

"I don't think he's ever killed anyone, has he?" Atticus asked.

"Not to my knowledge. He is army trained and often use to ask our father if he could lead a legion fighting in England or Germany. Vespasian never acceded to his requests. He knew Domitian was not a soldier. He might prove to be a killer though."

"Killing an unarmed woman in a foreign king's residence?" Atticus said, offended at the thought. "For his all of his patriotic rhetoric, that would be a heinous crime for any Roman to commit."

Titus nodded and walked down the hall to the dining room. He strode in energetically, full of smiles. He noticed that Berenice observed him carefully when he took his seat next to her. He leaned over and gave her a long kiss on the lips as if to say there was nothing to worry about. When he withdrew, she noticed the faint outline of a hand on his cheek and realized there was everything to worry about.

Servants immediately brought both main courses to Titus. He drained his wine first, then pointed at what he wanted from various platters while his goblet was refilled. He drank it down again and thanked the servant who had remained close by to fill it yet again. He motioned for the boy to leave the wine flagon by his place. It might be a breach of dining etiquette, but who was going to tell the emperor that?

After dinner, and after dessert—fried bread crusts covered in honey—and after a lot more wine, Titus raised his goblet and proposed another toast. His companions stood and raised their goblets.

"To the honored dead. Praetorians ambushed and slain by cowards. May those men be reclining in the company of Rome's heroes at this very moment." Titus paused and looked at Atticus. "What were their names, General?"

"Adrianus, son of Oeneus," Atticus answered. "And Philippus, son of Bernardus. Both men were Greeks who earned citizenship during their decades of service in the Praetorian ranks."

"Alas," Titus said softly. "I personally knew both of them. Fine men. Fine soldiers. May Jupiter bless their shades and prosper their bereft families." The emperor drank down his wine and the others drank from theirs. Everyone sat, somewhat subdued. The dining hall was silent. Titus looked at Salome sitting at his side. Drunk enough to put aside his customary good manners toward women, he addressed her.

"Princess, I am told that your journey into the mountains rendered a treasure that you brought back." Titus looked into Salome's golden eyes. "I would like to see it."

Salome's face flushed and she choked on her reply.

"Come now, dear," Titus cooed. "Your prize cost the lives of two of my Praetorians. For their sakes, I ask you to reveal it to this group of friends and relatives."

Salome's eyes darted to Jesus across the table. He had found this banquet to be a long and tedious meal. How could Titus stand attending these over and over again? Jesus had not thought it necessary to speak all evening, but he spoke now.

"Titus, Emperor and Lord. As a young woman Salome was responsible for the death of my cousin John. As a penitent decades later she went in search of his skull which she had buried long ago in order to spare it from abuse or destruction. In seeking to recover it, her intent was to pay respect to the martyred man."

Titus stared at Jesus.

"I have never heard this story," he said. "Pray, tell it to me."

Jesus did.

"Many years ago Israel was ruled by the famous king, Herod the Great. He reigned during the years of Augustus, and upon his death he divided the land into four kingdoms, designating his sons as tetrarchs. Rome approved the symbolic role of these petty kings, but actually ruled the Jews with Roman governors and legionnaires.

"One son, Herod Antipas, asked his new wife's daughter, Salome, to dance for him. Her mother, Herodias, a daughter of Herod the Great himself, had divorced her lawful husband to marry her half-brother Herod Antipas. John was a public preacher who repeatedly condemned the king's acts of incest and adultery. The king imprisoned him.

"After Salome's dance, he granted her a wish. Her mother provoked her to ask for John's death. She did. The Baptist was executed and Herod presented his head to Salome on a platter. Driven by guilt and fear, she buried it at the fortress of Machaerus to prevent it from being dishonored." Jesus paused. Then he finished. "That is the story."

Titus raised his eyebrows and remained silent for a moment.

"A beautiful and solemn tale," he said slowly. He turned to Salome. "How odd that you are both the villain *and* the heroine in that story. And after all this time you went to retrieve the dead man's skull. What I fail to grasp is why did you bring it back?"

Salome teared up, and Berenice held on to Titus' arm as if to say don't be harsh. Titus pressed on anyway.

"Is it an icon to your piety?" he asked. "A relic to grant you forgiveness? Or is there some baser possibility at work? Has repatriating the dead's man's head done homage to the once-upon-a-time young girl whose beauty was enough to have a man killed at her request?"

Salome broke down and began to weep. Berenice knelt by her chair and comforted her.

Titus still persisted. Maybe he wanted to bully the Jewish woman, an old royal castoff whose self-pitying antics had cost him the lives of two of his prized Praetorians. Or perhaps his behavior was a petty and perverse way of recovering his pride after being slapped by his own brother. Titus emptied his wine goblet and filled it himself from the nearby flagon.

"Show me the skull," Titus commanded Salome. No one moved. No one spoke. "Now."

Salome left the room without a word. Titus nodded at Atticus who followed her. The emperor drank and waited. In minutes, Salome returned with an object wrapped in a red satin scarf. She stood by Titus who gazed at her without responding.

"May I help?" Jesus spoke up.

Titus nodded.

Salome walked around the table and put the wrapped object in Jesus' hands. She retreated to her place at the table, and Jesus slowly undid the scarf. A black skull was revealed. Eye sockets empty and its jaw long gone. Jesus stared at it. He remembered the man who it belonged to well enough. The Baptist had been tall and dark, with long uncombed hair, a wild beard, blazing blue eyes, and a lean serious face.

A natural showman, he had worn animal skins, publicly baptized penitents in the Jordan River, *and* cussed out the wicked, whoever they were. This fearless bravado had led to his execution at age thirty. Jesus still loved John, but thought he might have served God better if he'd possessed even just whiff of a sense of humor.

Jesus thought he would be emotional seeing this remnant of John. But actually, holding his skull in his hands, he only felt a slight sadness. This was not John the Baptist. This was not John his cousin. This was a pitiful relic to which he could not relate. He placed the skull on the table facing Titus. The emperor gazed at it.

"I have to say that I am a bit bored by all of this," Titus said. "No magic. No curse. No *anything!* Just bone and dirt. Salome, return this macabre souvenir of your youthful misbehavior to your quarters." The emperor stood and everyone else rose as well. He waved to the men and women with whom he had dined.

"To all of you, dear guests, may you sleep well tonight and rise tomorrow full of happy vigor, ready to celebrate the coronation of our ally and friend, Jesus of Nazareth, as the King of Judea. Goodnight! Goodnight!" Titus cried waving his hand. With that he grasped Berenice's hand and led her out of the dining hall. She smiled and followed him willingly. She knew that someday she too, would be shrunk to nothing more than John the Baptist's remains. Reduced to one last piece of bone. But not yet. Not tonight. She looked at Titus and smiled again.

CHAPTER SEVEN

A WOMAN'S SCREAM WOKE EVERYONE IN the palace. Jesus knew it had to Berenice. He rushed to Titus' guest room. The door was blocked by two Praetorian guards. Jesus commanded them to step aside and they did. He looked inside, but it was too dark to see. Titus was shouting at Domitian and his brother was shouting back. Jesus couldn't see either one of them. He couldn't see Berenice either. Had she been murdered by Domitian? No. Domitian would be dead now. Instead, he and Titus were shouting in Latin so loud and so fast that Jesus' own Latin failed him. He ordered one of the Praetorians to fetch some oil lamps.

The soldier returned quickly with two large bronze oil lamps with the wicks lit. He held one out to Jesus who took it and entered the black room. What he saw was even more bizarre than he imagined. Berenice was lying naked on the bed. Domitian—fully clothed in a white toga and sandals—was kneeling beside her on the bed with the tip of his short sword pressed against her throat. Titus stood next to him on the bed, naked and furious, with the tip of his own sword thrust at the side of Domitian's neck. Titus had been wounded. Apparently by Domitian. He had a large puncture wound in his chest that was bleeding profusely. No one moved. The two brothers kept shouting at each other.

"Titus!" Jesus cried. Titus did not look at Jesus, but he did respond.

"This stupid bastard tried to kill Berenice!" he yelled. "Fucker missed and stabbed *me* in the chest!"

Domitian did not respond. He did not move. He just watched Titus. His life depended on it.

"Domitian, you need to put your sword down," Jesus told him. "Or you will not survive. I am going to bring in archers."

Domitian did not respond. Jesus stepped out of the bedroom into the hall. Septimus was standing there with a handful of legionnaires.

"Did you hear what I told Domitian?" Jesus asked Septimus.

He nodded.

"I ordered a pair of archers to be fetched immediately," he replied. "Does Domitian harbor a hope that he may one day succeed Titus?"

"He does," Jesus replied. "Apparently supported by most of the Praetorians."

"Then why did he get himself into this predicament? Is killing Berenice worth losing the throne?"

"He likely thinks that the act will be seen as Roman discipline meted out to Titus and that it will resonate favorably with the people."

"And if Titus puts his sword through him?"

"The population will approve the emperor's action. Self-defense."

Two Roman archers arrived at a run and saluted General Septimus. Wearing only loincloths, they hadn't taken the time to dress. Admirable, Jesus thought. Plus, they'll fit right into the madhouse in Titus' bedroom.

Septimus looked at Jesus.

"These men are yours to command."

Jesus addressed the archers.

"Inside this room, Emperor Titus has his brother at sword point. Domitian in turn has *his* blade at Princess Berenice's throat. Your only concern is to draw on Domitian and let loose if I, *and only I*, command you. Do you understand? The men cried aye together. "Follow me then," Jesus told them. "Take your stance. Pull on Domitian and wait for my command."

Jesus led the archers into the dimly lit bedroom. They quickly positioned themselves, drawing back their arrows and aiming at Domitian.

Jesus spoke to Titus' brother again.

"Domitian, my lord, a pair of archers has drawn on your person. If purifying your brother's bed is that last great Roman deed you wish to redound to your glory, then kill Berenice now. But if you wish to tell Emperor Titus that your zealous heart erred in making his business *your* business, then apologize and drop your sword. In ten seconds, the archers will put their arrows in your heart."

Domitian spoke up immediately.

"Brother Titus," he said loudly and with obvious fear. "You have always loved and honored me. I was wrong to try and separate you from the woman you care for, no matter what the Senate has decreed. I ask your forgiveness and I throw down my sword." Domitian took his sword away from Berenice's throat and tossed it to the floor. It rang as it hit the granite tiles.

Titus lowered his sword and stepped off the bed. He commanded Domitian to step down and face him. Domitian did, standing taller than his naked, infuriated brother. Jesus waved the archers to lower their bows.

"Stupid, stupid, stupid!" Titus hissed in Domitian's face. "What were you thinking?"

Domitian shook his head, eyes cast down to the floor.

"Someday, you will rule in my place," Titus spat out. "Until then, *behave*! Or I swear you will be banished from the empire."

Drawing his hand back Titus slapped his brother hard on the cheek. Berenice slid across the bed with a cover pulled around her. She stepped up to Domitian and raised her hand to slap him as well. Titus blocked her hand with his arm.

"No," he said.

Berenice glared at him, then grabbed her clothing from a chair and marched through archers, generals, Praetorians, and a crowded hallway full of gawkers to head for her] room. Titus—naked and bleeding—followed her. Domitian, humiliated, left for his own room. Everyone else just watched, wondering exactly how the Roman Empire was going to survive the last rulers of the Flavian dynasty.

— ⚜ —

Jesus went back to bed. But he couldn't sleep and got up again. It was hours till dawn. He asked a servant to fetch him a mug of mulled cider and bring it to his study. He left his bedroom and went to his private office. Two Praetorians followed him and stood outside. He sat down at his desk and lit an oil lamp.

Last night's dinner had been an altogether bizarre occasion. Titus drunk and flirting with Berenice. Domitian boycotting the dinner and then trying to murder her. Titus' bullying behavior toward Salome bringing her to tears. And then, of course, the Emperor demanding to see John the Baptist's skull—that strange and terrible symbol of his beheading—torn out of the past and placed on the dining table. Cruel. Humiliating. Pointless.

"Want some company?" Judas asked from the doorway.

"Sure," Jesus told him looking up. "If you'd like some mulled wine, wander down to the family kitchen and tell the servant to bring an extra mug for you."

Jesus looked at Judas supporting himself on his crutch.

"I'm old, and you're young," Judas complained. "I don't have any hands, but you've got a mostly good pair."

"Yes," Jesus said. "And your point is?"

"What?" Judas cried appalled.

"I've been reading the works of the Athenian Sophists," Jesus explained. "I'm attempting to reason and talk like them in my role as King of Judea. Afterall, I will be the royal arbiter of countless legal cases ahead."

Judas frowned.

"Can you translate that into something I can understand?"

"I'm learning how to bend any verbal exchange to my own advantage," Jesus told him.

"And?" Judas asked.

"Go get your own mug."

"What?" Judas cried again.

"You heard me," Jesus said.

Without another word, Judas left to find the kitchen servant preparing Jesus' wine. Jesus watched him leave and allowed himself a smirk. By the time Judas returned, his mother Mary had also appeared. Jesus suggested that they all break their fasts together. Jesus took Judas' mug and carried it to the family dining room.

The sun came up as they sat chatting and eating whole grain muffins with honey, scrambled eggs, and fried mullet. Jesus looked at his plate. This fare was a distinctly different kind of morning repast. Was the cook a Pict? A blue-tattooed fish eater from the frozen moors of northern Britannia? Or just a new hire from who knew where with no idea what folks here had for breakfast?

Mary waved a crust of bread to get Jesus' attention.

"Can an old woman and longtime despiser of all things Roman ask what the hell was going on around here in the middle of the night?"

Jesus arched an eyebrow.

"How could *you* hear anything?" he asked. "Your bedroom is in a whole different wing."

"I got up and made my way to where I could see the party-goers working off their alcohol."

"You were snooping?" Jesus asked.

"I was *investigating*," Mary corrected him.

"Domitian insulted Titus' mistress Berenice," Jesus told her. "And he and the emperor got into a fight."

"No manners."

"It all turned out okay though."

"I thought I heard a slap at the end of all the brouhaha."

"That you did."

"Sort of a spanking for grown-ups," Mary decided.

"Yes," Jesus agreed. "Probably not Titus' favorite kind of spanking. Both he and Domitian wound up with red cheeks."

"I can't believe that I have spent my entire life being subject to the idiocy of Romans," Mary said disgusted.

"What you really mean is the idiocy of its *rulers*," Jesus suggested.

Mary scowled.

"You, my boy," Mary responded in a disagreeable tone, "like to think that the most profound question in the cosmos is why does God allow the Jews to suffer? For me, it's why does he allow the jackasses in Rome to run the world?"

Jesus laughed and shrugged.

Mary offered her list of Latin offenders.

"Tiberias the pedophile. Caligula the madman. Claudius the moron. Nero the incestuous. Vespasian the Jew killer. And now Titus." Mary scowled. "The prick who refuses to grow up."

"Yes," Jesus said. "Reminds *me* of Saul the coward. David the adulterer. Joshua the Canaanite killer. Herod the sycophant. And the four sons of his body who ate, drank, and made merry while the Zealots dug a big hole and watched Rome bury a million Judeans in it."

Mary grimaced and folded her arms.

"Your point?"

"Oh, c'mon, Ma. Roman or Jewish, there isn't really much difference between how petty kings *or* powerful emperors rule. The authority they wield is often corrupted by self-interest, including showering special favors on their relatives and friends."

"I hope you lean toward that latter propensity, son," Mary replied.

"Yes!" Judas pitched in.

"Ah," Jesus said. "Agreement at last amongst my family members."

"It *is* fun to think about," Judas declared. "And I'll bet you're enjoying *this* meal more than the one last night with your *other* family."

"They aren't my family," Jesus said tersely.

"Well then, how nice that you have us!" Judas remarked happily. "Drinking sweet booze and fretting about the problems of the kingdom."

"Plus, you live in a nice place now," Mary added. "I think I'll stay."

"Not me," Judas said. "I'm not living under a Roman roof."

"Why don't we just consider it *my* roof?" Jesus suggested.

"I'd be all right with that."

"Ha!" Jesus said and chuckled. "The King of the Jews, breaking his fast with Judas on one side and his mother Mary on the other. Go figure."

"Yes," Mary agreed. "Let's do this every day."

"Can we go to a banquet sometime, too?" Judas asked.

"Only when it's with my Jewish supporters."

Judas raised his eyebrows.

"That's not going to happen anytime soon," he declared.

"Not in my lifetime," was Mary's take.

Jesus took a drink of his wine. Well, maybe during *my* lifetime, he thought. If someone doesn't manage to kill me first. He looked at Judas and then at Mary. The Lord giveth, and the Lord taketh away. Sometimes though you just had to wonder about what he giveth. In this case, Mary and Judas. Jesus shook his head. Blessed be the name of the Lord.

— ⚜ —

Titus found Jesus in his study reading the Egyptian story of Osiris. In a striking parallel to Jesus' own life, the god had been murdered and then brought back to life. In Osiris' case his sister, the goddess Isis, had gone looking for him after he'd been chopped into pieces and strewn all over the Nile delta. Crucifixion had been bad, but Osiris' fate was ridiculous. Jesus stood up and watched the emperor enter.

"May I interrupt?" Titus asked. He was freshly bathed. His hair was groomed. And his toga was wrapped perfectly.

"Of course," Jesus said and stood. "May I have food or wine fetched for you?"

"No, thank you," Titus replied. "I've already dined."

Titus sat down across the desk from Jesus. Jesus sat as well.

"What did you think of last night's dinner?" the emperor asked.

"Good conversation, but it ran a bit long."

"Are you kidding me?" Titus asked surprised. "Real Roman banquets run so long that people eat, sleep, and fornicate. Right on their couches."

"Fornicate? Are you pulling my sandal?"

"I'm serious," Titus insisted. "Romans are not terribly modest. During gladiator contests in the Coliseum, you can get your thirst, palate, or cock serviced."

"Right in the bleachers?" Jesus was amazed at such unrestrained behavior.

"Yes," Titus answered. "My father introduced the practice. Did the same stuff in his royal box."

"Somehow, I don't think your brother Domitian would approve," Jesus commented.

"That little shit?" Titus scowled. "You're absolutely right. Squeaky clean walloper would never screw a woman in public, but thinks nothing of trying to kill one in the middle of the night."

"Have you seen him today?"

"No. He left at dawn for Caesarea with Septimus and his legionnaires."

"Afraid to face you?"

"Probably."

Jesus looked into Titus' eyes.

"You know he intends to kill you."

"And I intend to live forever, so we're going to have a problem."

"I'm serious," Jesus said. "He wants your throne. And he has support. You did, of course, note that the Praetorians at your bedroom door did not stop him from entering with a sword *and* didn't take one step to intervene when the conflict started."

Titus nodded and changed the subject.

"What are your priorities for Judea?" he asked.

"Abolish slavery. Restore commerce and agriculture. And build an army as large as Rome's."

"Whoa!" Titus exclaimed. "Should I be worried about you?"

"No. But Domitian should be."

"Living or dead, I intend to support your rule," Titus told Jesus. "I sent five million gold aureuses when you first took up residence in Jericho. Even as we speak a half dozen wagons are being filled at the Joppa with five million additional aureuses. And *another* ten million are being delivered to Miguel at La Valdieu. For safekeeping. For you."

"Exceedingly generous, my Lord," Jesus said gratefully.

"I can afford it," Titus replied. "And if Domitian succeeds in his nefarious dreams to take my crown, you will still have what you need to grow Judea into a magnificence that it has not known since the days of King Solomon." Titus gave Jesus a small smile. "Call it my penitence."

"For destroying Judea?"

"No," Titus said. "For crucifying Saul."

Jesus looked down.

"How I wish that I could undo that deed," Titus said quietly. "It is the one mistake I will rue until the end of my days."

Jesus gazed at Titus.

"I forgave you long ago."

"Thank you. I think I knew that. Now spend that money and remember me." Titus paused, never having been this honest and intimate with another man. In a moment he recovered and changed the subject.

"This is supposed to be the day you are crowned," he told Jesus.

"How about if we just *say* we did it," Jesus suggested.

"Or how about if we actually do it, but keep it low key?" Titus countered.

"What do you have in mind?" Jesus asked.

"I'll pronounce you King of Judea."

"Right now?"

"Yes."

"Want me to kneel?"

Titus shook his head amicably.

"No, no. Stay comfortable. I pronounce you King of Judea." Titus waved both hands as if making the words take effect.

"Was that magic?" Jesus.

"More or less," Titus said. "But this will make it official." He pulled off his signet ring and tossed it to Jesus. Jesus caught it. It was superb likeness of Titus' face carved into orange carnelian and set in gold. "Wear it with my compliments."

"But you'll need it," Jesus told him.

"I have a dozen more."

"Thank you, Emperor. May you live long and prosper,"

"From your lips—" Titus paused. He looked questioningly at Jesus. Titus felt a deep pang of sadness that he would likely not live long enough to share another time like this with Jesus. "*You* will live long and prosper, Jesus," he said earnestly. "I have no doubt about that. As for me, this is probably as good a time as any to say farewell."

Titus and Jesus stood. Jesus gave Titus a firm hug. Titus hugged him back. Then he turned and started for the doorway.

"Goodbye, Titus," Jesus said his sadness evident.

The emperor turned and glanced back at Jesus.

"Will you take care of Berenice for me?"

"I will," Jesus said.

"Goodbye, Jesus of Nazareth, King of the Jews. Remember me. I will never forget you."

Titus looked at Jesus for a long moment, then left. The two Praetorians stood apart to let the emperor pass, then watched him walk down the hall. Jesus thought back to the first time he had ever seen Titus. At twenty he was already a general and his father's aide. He had ridden from Rome to La Valdieu and Saul had tried to unhorse him. Saul was the one who had been knocked down. By Titus. And by fate. Now it appeared that it was Titus' turn. Jesus stared out the doorway.

Judas suddenly appeared. He looked flustered.

"Can you come with me right now?" he asked urgency in his voice.

Jesus frowned.

"What's wrong?"

"Just come," Judas insisted. "There is something you need to see."

Jesus followed Judas through the palace into an adjacent wing where Princess Salome was lodged. Berenice and Mary stood next to the bed where Salome lay unmoving. Jesus walked over and looked down at her. The soft undersides of her arms had been cut again and again. Blood soaked her robe and the silk bedcover. Salome lay dead with her eyes open staring at the ceiling. Wherever she had gone, she was not coming back.

Berenice was dry-eyed and calm. Mary was respectful and silent.

"Maybe last night's humiliation was too much for her," Berenice ventured.

"We shall never know," Jesus responded. "I'll arrange to have her washed and prepared for burial. Leave her eyes open. If anything remains in that broken soul, I want her to see how we cared for her at the end."

Jesus looked around the room. He walked over to a small table and picked up the black skull of John the Baptist.

"This is mine now. It will be my talisman and my beacon. Always reminding me that just like John, death waits for me and will not be dissuaded." Jesus looked at the skull. Then he spoke to Berenice. "Titus crowned me this morning. My first act as King of Judea is to offer you sanctuary in my house. Titus asked me to care for you. I granted it."

Berenice knelt.

"Thank you, Lord Jesus."

He looked at Judas and Mary.

"You are my welcome guests as well."

"Thank you, son," Mary said humbly.

Judas spoke, stretching his remaining arm toward Jesus as if to beseech him.

"I thought we already settled this at breakfast?"

Jesus shook his head, amused. Raised from the dead. Eighty-three years old. King of Judea. And this was his family. Jesus shook his head again. Who knew?

CHAPTER EIGHT

Two years later Jesus was interrupted by a Jewish legionnaire who announced that General Septimus was at the palace entrance. The soldier had found Jesus in his private study declining arcane Chinese verbs out loud. The painted symbols of ancient Cathay were so numerous and so difficult to memorize that Jesus thought he might actually *need* to live forever to learn to read The Analects of Confucius in its original language.

"I'll come with you," he told the legionnaire, rising from his cluttered desk. He followed the soldier and was in turn followed by his bodyguards. Atticus and his Praetorians had long since departed and had been replaced by Jesus' own Jewish guards. He also employed more than two hundred palace servants that Judas had vetted to replace all of the servers, cooks, maids, gardeners, smiths, wrights, and livery personnel who had been brought in by the Romans. Some were Latin. Most were Jews. And none were slaves.

One wing of the Jericho palace was dedicated for his personal use. Three wings had lodgings for guests, rooms for palace housekeeping, his throne room, and office spaces for government workers, scribes, historians, tax collectors, and so forth. Judas had also overseen the construction of a sprawling military complex next door to the palace, with legionnaire housing, kitchen and dining facilities, equestrian barns and corrals, and vast training grounds for the army of new recruits.

More than a thousand of the men had come from La Valdieu. They were bright and brave. Born Franks, they had nonetheless immigrated to Judea to make careers and marriages. They added a fresh and vibrant quality to Jesus' kingdom. Some of these knights had converted to Judaism. Others had remained loyal to their Celtic, Druid, and Nordic gods. There was also a considerable number of Christians.

Jesus had decreed—in keeping with imperial law and tradition—that any religion could be practiced in Roman Judea. Not that religion was foremost in the newest men's thoughts as they searched for brides and waited for the day when Jesus granted them knighthood, orchards, a farm, or grazing lands where they could put down roots in their new land.

Even as Jesus welcomed other men from all over the empire, he had been actively seeking out young Jewish men who had survived the wholesale Roman slaughter of Jews during the revolt that had ended twelve years ago. As well as vigorously building a Jewish army Jesus had also spent the last two years personally overseeing the restoration of the great Hebrew defensive strongholds built during Israel's thousand-year royal history. Megiddo, Hazor, Lachish, and Jerusalem. He had also begun reconstruction of the fortress palaces Herod the Great had built at Masada, Herodium, and Machaerus. Triumphant Jewish citadels that would once again be manned by Jewish legionnaires.

All of these mighty bastions had been cleansed of the dead—the ancient remains of patriots slain and the latter-day victims of the Jewish uprising—and massive funds from Jesus' treasury had been expended on their renewal. Most of the construction crews had been brought in from Egypt, Phoenicia, and Greece. And the artistic finish work was being performed by the world's premiere artisans from Byzantium, Indus, and Cathay.

Miguel had visited him three times in the last twenty-four months and had turned Jesus' palace home into a luxurious domicile truly fit for a king. He had furnished Jesus' personal rooms and private work areas to look very much like his old manor house in Gaul, filling his study, bedroom, and family dining area with hand-loomed knotted Turkic carpets, fine thyine and mahogany furniture, and premiere grade cedar from Lebanon for bookshelves. Silk banners and streamers from Asia hung everywhere, and stunning masterpieces of Greek, Roman, and Egyptian sculpture adorned the halls, the public rooms, and all of the offices and bedrooms.

Miguel had also redone the throne room, incorporating a giant, elevated marble throne and a half-dozen imposing marble pillars set in a semi-circle around its back and sides. It looked exactly like a Greek or Roman temple, stating boldly to all who entered that the King of Judea was as powerful as any pagan god.

Jesus walked out of the palace doors and found General Septimus waiting in the courtyard with a half-dozen legionnaires. A detail of Jewish soldiers guarded the entrance. They wore steel breastplates, conical helmets with pointed tops, and carried round shields three feet in diameter with black steel faces displaying huge golden Stars of David.

The Jews were respectful of the Roman soldiers attending Septimus, but the Latins themselves could not take their eyes off the Hebrew shields. Most of them didn't know or recognize the Star of David. That would change in the years ahead as Jesus raised his own twenty-five legions to match the military manpower of the empire.

In fact, over the course of the decades it would take him to create and maintain an army of a quarter million men—his standing army and active reserves—the whole world would learn about the soldiers of Judea and their national emblem. No one said it, but everyone knew it—including the emperors of Rome—Jesus intended that the Holy Land, *and Jerusalem in particular*, would never fall again.

General Septimus went down on his knees as Jesus entered the courtyard. All of the Roman soldiers and Judean legionnaires did as well.

"Get up, boys," Jesus declared. "I'm not the emperor."

Every stood.

Septimus greeted Jesus.

"Lord, I am escorting an envoy bearing an epistle from Emperor Titus. He may release it into your hands only." Septimus raised his arm and waved the courier forward. A young Roman officer wearing the armor of a Praetorian guard stepped forward.

While Septimus had the looks of a Greek god, the Praetorian courier resembled a woodcutter whose face had been pitted and flattened by wayward flying chips from his axe. He was obviously a valuable soldier though, earning a Praetorian officer's commission and having been hand-picked to deliver a letter from the emperor himself. He stepped towards Jesus and held out a long thin leather bag, its opening secured by drawstrings that were sealed in wax. Jesus took it. He recognized Titus' seal and thanked the soldier.

Jesus addressed Septimus.

"General, will you join me in my study?" he asked. "I will have food and drink fetched for your men."

Septimus bowed his head.

Jesus asked the commander of the Jewish legionnaires to have the Roman soldiers and their horses watered and fed, and to send a soldier to instruct the kitchen manager to have wine and a light lunch brought for the general and himself. Jesus and Septimus walked to Jesus' study. When they entered, Jesus' two full grown lions with their great manes and huge bodies approached and licked his hands. Septimus did not move.

"Have a chair," Jesus told him. "Alpha and Omega are harmless. They usually run around pestering the servants. I'm not sure how they found their way here today."

Septimus sat down slowly, keeping his eyes on the lions. Jesus turned his desk chair to face the general and sat. The big cats immediately took places on either side of his feet.

"May I?" Jesus asked holding up the bag containing Titus' scroll.

"Absolutely," Septimus answered. "And please accept my congratulations on the second anniversary of your coronation by Titus. Your reign has been peaceful and productive, devoted to rebuilding Judea and winning the confidence of the Jews. Titus is not the only person in the empire impressed with what's happening in Judea."

"I don't know why," Jesus replied. "There are no adventures here. It's quiet and boring and everyone does a whole lot of work."

"Most of us would call that *peaceful*, my Lord," Septimus replied. "Almost every one of my men in Caesarea desires to retire here."

Jesus looked surprised.

Septimus went on.

"Many Romans know that we are not just observing a Jewish king. We are admiring the work of the Son of God himself."

"Thank you, Septimus," Jesus replied. "The day that the Judeans in this country say the same nice things that you Christians do will be a day for personal celebration."

Jesus broke the wax seal on the drawstrings of the leather bag, opened it, and pulled the parchment scroll out. It was also sealed. Jesus snapped the wax seal in half and unrolled the letter.

To: Jesus of Nazareth, King of The Jews
From: Titus Flavius Vespasianus Augustus,Emperor Of Rome

Greetings, my Friend,

Peace be to you, who by the will of the emperor and the Senate of Rome rules brilliantly over the kingdom of Judea. Be assured of our continuing prayers to the gods for your success.

I have just completed three years on Augustus' throne and find the work appallingly political. Thank heavens there are small wars that break out here that save my sanity. I take to the battlefield and get the hell out of Rome while my brother Domitian spends all of his time bribing senators and Praetorians preparing for the day he will need their support to succeed me. Which will be whenever he manages to assassinate me. Mind boggling, eh? I could kill him, but I am actually convinced that he will make a better emperor than me, whenever that succession occurs. He is a born bureaucrat, and it turns out most of this job is shuffling scrolls here, there, and everywhere.

I am about to embark on a campaign in Britannia. The locals need to be slapped around a little, plus I'll feel much safer there than here! I would like it very much if you could meet me at La Valdieu after the campaign is over. I will make it a point to pass through your old kingdom when my legions return to Rome. It is important for me to see you again.

Don't answer, just come. It will take you four or five months on horse, so why don't we plan on meeting in La Valdieu the first day of summer and bask in the mutual respect and admiration we've always had for one another?

Your respectful servant,

Titus

Signed in my own hand and sealed with my personal mark.

Postscript: Please bring Berenice with you. I have largess to keep her safe and happy for the rest of her life.

Jesus held the scroll out to Septimus. Titus wanted to meet in La Valdieu. It would not be the same place he remembered from his first visit twenty years ago. It had grown prosperous and was no longer the little rural kingdom where Saul had ridden down from the castle to challenge him.

And bring Berenice along, he had requested. He had largesse for her. Right. Largesse inside his toga. Old goat. No, Jesus realized. It was actually *he* who was the old goat at eighty-five. Titus was just getting old-goatish at forty. Berenice herself had become increasingly moralistic these days, and Jesus was not sure that she would even consider meeting Titus at La Valdieu.

Maybe he could bargain with her. She and the Christians of Jericho were ever hopeful that Jesus would allow them to build a church. He was actually more interested in rebuilding the temple. Solomon had built a temple. Hezekiah had built a temple. Herod had built a temple. Each one had been turned to ash and rubble. First. Second. Third.

Number four would likely be put off for decades though, until the Jews could be persuaded to worship without animal sacrifice, treating the new temple like a great national synagogue. So, he'd satisfy himself by offering to build local synagogues in the meanwhile, and sooner or later, a church for the Christians in Jericho. He had not made peace with the Christian movement, but he no longer felt alienated by its interpretation of his life and passion.

Septimus read the scroll, rolled it up, and handed it back to Jesus.

"Your impression?" Jesus asked him. Septimus waited to answer as three servants entered Jesus' private office together. A young man in a white robe removed the general's sandals, then washed and dried his feet. Two teenage girls held basins for Septimus and Jesus to wash and dry their hands. Then all three youngsters retreated.

Immediately afterward several male servants entered with trays bearing golden goblets, silver flagons of wine mixed with water, and a large ceramic plate filled with lamb roasted in garlic and butter, boiled sweet potatoes and carrots, fresh figs and dates, and pomegranate chunks dipped in sugar. Jesus and Septimus were given silver plates filled with food. They ate and talked about Titus' letter.

"I think the man has a death wish," Jesus commented opening up the conversation.

"Maybe," Septimus agreed. "The emperor has had a rich life and achieved whatever he wished. His altruistic comments about Domitian ruling Rome seem a bit hollow. I mean, after all, his brother is not only setting himself up for succession as the next Augustus, but is blatantly trying to dispose of Titus. I already dread the day when he puts on the purple. Clever as a fox. Mean as a badger. Moral as a snake."

"No offense intended," Jesus replied, "but my mother would argue that you could be describing a host of emperors, not just Domitian. What does that say about the selection process for the world's most powerful job?"

"It says that the Senate is a bunch of horses' asses," Septimus replied. "But any one of those rich, pandering sycophants would make an even *worse* emperor. They're all soft and cowardly. Clutching at their wealth while pushing moron after moron toward the throne."

Jesus just shook his head. There was something about great wealth that made its owners cowards. And there was something about ruling royalty that had the reverse effect, engendering rulers who puffed their chests out like narcissistic demi-gods, refusing to accept counsel or correction. Titus was the exception. Yet now, all *he* wanted to do was give the emperor's responsibilities to Domitian.

Jesus ate some lamb and conversed with Septimus.

"Why did you become a Christian, General?"

Septimus looked at Jesus and answered.

"I longed for a relationship with the true God. So-called Roman gods and goddesses are fickle deities. They do not care about anyone or anything except themselves. Their stories are sordid tales of palace intrigues, petty disputes, and endless sexual games. Opposite that is Jehovah. He is forthright, concerned, and passionate about my wellbeing. And willing to accept and forgive me as a repentant sinner because the blood of his Son has washed me clean."

Jesus nodded. Christianity certainly preached about a God who wanted to draw close to those who desired his presence. Didn't make it true, but it was a nice message. He suspected that Christians would find out in the long run that being embraced by God was a lot more traumatic than they could now imagine. Fifty years ago, early Christians were Jews and knew about God's mercurial nature. Today, most Christians were Gentiles and didn't have a clue as to the disastrous history of the Hebrews trying to get along with Jehovah. Good luck with that, he couldn't help but think.

"I'll need to prepare for the journey to Gaul this week," Jesus told Septimus. "I will talk to Berenice, and I would like you to consider traveling with me as well. You have a full complement of experienced officers who can handle things while you're gone."

"Yes, but do you?" Septimus asked.

"Actually, if I am absent no more than two seasons, I believe that Judas can sit on the throne in my place."

Septimus raised his eyebrows.

"The Zealot?"

"The Zealots are dead."

"And isn't the man something like eighty years old?" Septimus said incredulously.

"Eighty-five. Just like me."

"But *unlike* you," the general protested, "Judas still hates the Romans as much as ever."

"Yes, and as such he is criticized by some for deigning to serve in my court. With me gone and Judas ruling, there are those who might think it the right time to assassinate him."

"Really?"

"Yes, really."

"Then I'll go to La Valdieu with you and hope for such an outcome."

Jesus smiled, both men drank, and kept their thoughts to themselves for the rest of the meal.

— ⚜ —

Jesus asked Berenice to spend a few minutes with him in his study. He sat behind his olivewood desk. Bernice sat across from him. She wore a blue robe and a white headscarf. He wore a scarlet robe and padded about on his bare feet.

"I am planning a trip back to La Valdieu," he told her.

"Yes, I know. The servants can't talk about anything else."

"I'm going at the request of Titus." Berenice's eyes opened wide. *That* piece of information neither she nor the servants knew. "Would you like to read the letter he sent me?" Jesus asked her.

Berenice nodded. Jesus picked up the scroll and handed it to her. She took it and read it. Then she rolled up the parchment and handed it back.

"Why should I go?" she asked.

"I can't tell you that," Jesus answered. "All I can do is convey the emperor's request and wait on your decision."

"He wants to sleep with me," Berenice replied with a tone of disgust.

"Obviously," Jesus agreed. "But why you? Titus could have any woman in the empire. Young and willing. From Asia Minor to Britannia." Jesus gazed at Berenice. "So again, why you?"

Berenice stared at Jesus.

"Your thoughts?" Jesus persisted.

"Maybe he has some regard for me, even after all these years," Berenice answered quietly.

Jesus nodded.

"It seems to me I remember that he almost lost his life two years ago trying to save yours. That speaks of more than simple regard. That sounds more like love."

Berenice shook her head.

"Whatever he feels, it wasn't strong enough to keep me when the Senate demanded he get rid of me."

"You're a Jew," Jesus told her. "In fact, you're Jewish royalty. After a war in which tens of thousands of Roman men died fighting Jews, it was a relationship that could not be allowed. Which Roman anywhere would have tolerated the birth of a half-Jewish heir to the emperor's throne?"

"If he loved me, Titus would have kept me," Berenice insisted.

Jesus didn't respond.

"I am not going with you," Berenice said. She looked flustered, but determined. "There is also a higher consideration. That which is pleasing to God."

Jesus' face remained expressionless.

Berenice went on.

"Christian women are required to be pure, just like Jewish women are required to be chaste. Your own disciples levied *some* laws for Gentile converts."

"I remember we talked about this before," Jesus answered. "No eating meat sacrificed to idols, and no sex outside of marriage. So new Christians could be trusted with every moral choice except whether to eat pagan meat and have sex?"

"You make it sound idiotic," Berenice mused.

"No. But such rules fly in the face of personal freedom. It's exactly like the Pharisees. They made rules where a believer's common sense should have been allowed to prevail."

"Well, I'm not going," Berenice repeated. "I will not be Titus' mistress any longer."

"Whatever you choose is fine," Jesus told her. "I am departing in a few days. If you change your mind, you can tell me any time before that." Jesus looked into Berenice's eyes. "I am truly sorry Titus hurt you. Is it in your heart to at least entrust a letter to me?"

Berenice hesitated a long time before she nodded.

"Think of him kindly if you can," Jesus told her. "As I recall, one of the tenets of Christianity is to forgive those who have hurt you."

"*You* commanded that," Berenice answered.

"All the more reason then for you to practice it then. You live in my house, and you're my friend."

"I will give you a letter for Titus. But I will not go with you."

Jesus nodded, a bit disturbed that Berenice and other church women would allow men to once again set rules for their behaviors in life. What were his disciples thinking when they insisted on preserving Jewish law for Christians? He himself had preached the end of all that, simply asking his followers to love one another and abide together in forgiveness and tolerance. Yet *despite* that there were Christian rules. He suspected over time that there would be a *lot* of Christian rules. He shook his head. That was not his responsibility. He was a Jew with only his people's needs in his heart. So, he would live. So, he would rule.

"While you're thinking things over," Jesus finished up, "I am open to hearing what you and the other Christians in Jericho desire by way of a church."

Berenice stared at Jesus. Was he offering to change his mind if she would do the same?

She bowed and left, more fascinated than ever by the complex man occupying the throne. She wondered how long the trip to La Valdieu would take?

— ⚜ —

"All you're doing is setting me up to be killed," Judas complained. He, Mary, and Jesus were having breakfast together in the family dining room. The servants brought dark bread, goat cheese, orange jam, pomegranate jelly, and calda, a heated wine served with spices. Mary didn't drink calda. She only drank water now, having become recently convinced in her old age that it was *the* overlooked key to health and longevity.

"Why do want *me* to watch over things while you're gone?" Judas asked.

"You're capable. You're fair. And you're expendable," Jesus answered.

"What?" Judas cried.

"I know you're old," Jesus responded. "But you really should work on developing a sense of humor."

Jesus winked at Mary.

"I didn't think that was funny," she said.

Jesus turned back to Judas.

"All that will be required of you is to grant official status to petitions, arbitrations, and appeals. I will hear the cases when I return."

"That's all?" Judas asked.

"Yes."

"Can I sit on your throne?"

"Yes. And no one will be allowed into the throne room without being searched by the guards."

"The guards are all Jews."

"Yes?"

"And a lot of Jews don't like me."

"*I* don't like you."

"But I'm useful," Judas protested.

"And you saved my life once."

"You could just reward me for that and let your mother sit on the throne while you're gone."

Jesus shook his head.

"There still are a lot of Romans in this land. I don't want Mary to start another war."

"Well, someone should," Mary grumbled. "Perfect time to get rid of them."

Jesus ignored his mother.

"Judas, you will be a surrogate legal presence in my absence. That's all I'm going to say."

"I am not happy about it," Judas said. "But I'll do it." He picked up his goblet and drank the rest of his wine. He put the cup down and looked at Jesus. "Can I wear your crown?"

CHAPTER NINE

JESUS SELECTED A DOZEN KNIGHTS to escort him to La Valdieu. General Septimus decided to remain in Judea in case Judas ran into difficulties. Titus had once journeyed from Rome at Emperor Nero's request to bring Jesus to the imperial capital. He had traveled by himself. Of course, Titus was a brilliant soldier. Easily able to defend himself. And he was little known outside of Rome.

Jesus, on the other hand, was still hated by many Jews as the puppet King of Judea. Wouldn't be hard to assassinate him crossing his own kingdom. Twelve loyal knights would make a good entourage. Plus, the men Jesus picked had parents and close relatives in La Valdieu. So, it would be a splendid reunion for them while he met with Titus.

The overland journey would take four or five months. Jesus planned to bypass Rome. Titus was finishing his campaign in Britannia having left his brother behind in the capital. Jesus would have to meet with that puff pastry after Domitian stole the throne. He'd even have to swear his fealty to him as the new emperor unless he had Jesus killed first. But for now, he didn't have to see that pretender. So, he wouldn't.

The journey was quiet and without incidents. Occasional travelers on the road stopped and stared at the soldiers with their black shields inlaid with the Stars of David. Jesus and his legionnaires stayed in travelers' inns frequented by merchants and Roman army officers. Safe abodes with excellent food and clean beds.

He had sent word to RoxAnna that he was journeying to her kingdom. He requested hospitality for himself and a dozen knights and told her to be prepared to provide shelter and food for Emperor Titus who would be journeying to meet him in La Valdieu with at least a century of soldiers. He sent his affections to her and his grandson, King David. And to Miguel, faithful servant to the crown.

Months of riding together generated a closeness among Jesus' soldiers and a respectful familiarity with him. Over shared dinners many of the men were bold enough to ask Jesus about his extraordinary life. What had his ministry been like? Why had the Romans executed him? How did it affect him to never grow old? Did he ever regret that had he left his European kingdom to return to Judea? And since all of the men had spent their childhoods and young adult years in La Valdieu, they had their own stories to share about the land where Jesus had spent more time than anywhere else in his life.

The young soldiers expressed admiration for the Queen Mother RoxAnna, the regent of the boy King David. But several shared concerns about the young monarch. An adult now, he had been very high-strung as a youth, possessing an explosive temper that he exploited to cow his subjects. Particularly boys his own age. His adolescent goals seemed to have been less about learning how to rule than defeating every young man in one-on-one combat.

He had also been heard to frequently lament that La Valdieu was subject to Roman rule and taxation. And he had been so rude to imperial tax collectors that RoxAnna had received a series of visits from Roman officials in Marseilles regarding threats David had uttered against tax agents and the empire itself.

However, since David had still been a youth and subject to RoxAnna's authority, the Romans had refrained from punishing the king. But they had given RoxAnna stern warnings that David needed to be taught to hold his tongue when the days of his majority came and he reigned as sole ruler of La Valdieu.

Jesus' son Saul, David's father, had been a man of ferocious emotions, hating Romans with a passion that had cost him his life. He once told Jesus that his violence was because God's blood flowed in his body. The fervor of his bloodlust was such that he had raged against the Empire until that very blood had gushed out of his crucified body.

Was David like his father Saul? Passionate to the point of madness? Utterly possessed by his hatred for Rome? If so, then Jehovah's violence had dominated yet another generation of males sprung from Jesus' and Mary Magdalene's union. How odd that their gentle souls had produced such savage offspring. It indeed had to be the blood of the Hebrew God coursing through their veins. A jealous, hot tempered, endlessly narcissistic deity if ever there was one.

And though long repressed, was it now Jesus' turn to burn with the violence that was at the very core of Jehovah's being? He could only hope so.

A day's journey from La Valdieu, Jesus sent one of his knights ahead to announce their imminent arrival. The following morning day Jesus and his legionnaires entered the lands of La Valdieu. They left the sturdy Roman highway they had followed for months and turned north onto an immaculately maintained stone road that led to the heart of La Valdieu.

Hour after hour Jesus waited to see the manor house once so lovingly decorated by his wife Mary. Before he was near enough to make it out, he was struck by the sight of the huge castle on the cliffs overlooking the central valley of La Valdieu. Begun by Saul, it had taken forty years to complete. Jesus had never seen a larger fortress anywhere. Look at me and despair, the castle seemed to declare, with its towering walls and countless turrets.

As Jesus marveled at the mighty fortress a party rode down from its heights onto the main road. Three of his knights moved into lead positions while the rest deployed to protect his sides and form a rear guard. All of the knights wielded spears or swords. There was no question that they were prepared to die in order to keep their king from harm.

As the approaching company drew near, Jesus could see that the leader was a head taller than anyone else and was accompanied by a petite rider. King David and his mother Queen RoxAnna? There was only a handful of knights with them, clearly signaling that the intercourse between the two groups was intended to be peaceful.

As the group approached Jesus saw that the tall rider wore a helmet with a thick golden crown. He was sure now that the rider was none other than the King of La Valdieu, David, son of Saul. The smaller rider next to him wore a golden robe and a conspicuously tall gold crown. RoxAnna. Their escort was composed of bare-chested knights wearing plaid Celt skirts and leather sandals strapped up to their knees. They wore the conical, pointed helmets that Druid folk preferred, with exotic bird plumes affixed to their tops. The two groups stopped with no more than a dozen feet of road separating them. Jesus' herald called out to the approaching troop.

"Hail, King David, son of Saul, Lord of La Valdieu. Jesus of Nazareth, King of Judea, requests the courtesy of a visit with you and your kin."

David immediately dismounted and walked towards Jesus.

"Are you talking about my Grampa Jesus?" he called out cheerfully. David was

well-built and at least six foot in height. Not as tall as Jesus, but a lot taller than his mother RoxAnna. David pulled off his helmet, looked at Jesus, and grinned. He was the image of his long-deceased father Saul. "Who's the old man who came instead of the king?" he asked.

Jesus laughed.

"Criticize *me*, young man," he responded. "But respect the white locks. I earned those the hard way, if you'll recall." Jesus' hair had permanently gone white after his crucifixion.

"Granted!" David cried. "Come down and give me a hug."

Jesus dismounted and ordered his knights to do the same. David knelt at Jesus' feet.

"Up, up, up," Jesus said. "I thought we were talking about hugs?"

"Only after you bless me, Lord."

"May God bless and keep you, David, son of Saul."

David stood and hugged Jesus hard.

"Wow. I felt that right through my chestplate," Jesus joked.

"Ho!" David chortled and looked at Jesus' chestplate. "I may have dented one corner of your temple. Sorry!" He winked. Jesus looked at David's chestplate. It bore a large gold cross with a crucified man. Jesus looked at his grandson's face.

"I am a Christian, Grandfather," David told him.

"And just in the nick of time," a female voice interjected. RoxAnna walked over and gave Jesus a long embrace. She was now in her late middle age, but was still beautiful. Her complexion was unblemished and her hair was long and blonde, though perhaps her locks had had some assistance besides earnest prayer. "The boy was a monster until he accepted you as his Savior this year," she said. "Now, he has become the ideal man. Only missing a wife and family to be complete."

Jesus knew that this moment was the perfect time to be supportive. But what to say? Evidently, David's conversion had miraculously changed his life. But whatever he had done he hadn't really taken *Jesus* into his life. He had taken the Christian *story* of Jesus into his life. A placebo if ever there was one. Yet it had worked. Goddamn, Jesus thought, never having sworn before in his entire life.

"Have you become a Christian, too, RoxAnna?" he asked.

"No," she said emphatically. "I am still Druid through and through. *Someone* has to hate the Romans. I've given up on David." She gave him a sharp glance.

He shrugged.

"Mother wants me to get revenge on Rome for the execution of my father. I, on the other hand, have learned to pray for my enemies. And the Romans are at the top of that list, trust me."

"What does praying for your enemies entail?" Jesus asked curious.

"Reminding God that there really is a hell and that every Roman deserves to die and go there."

Jesus laughed.

David was surprised.

"Why do you find that funny, Grandfather?"

"I'm sorry, David. It is, in fact, the perfect prayer for one's enemies."

"I believe that it is," David said with a triumphant tone in his voice. "I don't want a single Latin to convert and be saved. No, thank you."

"I'd like to see the bastards slaughtered right now," RoxAnna added. "Send them on their way as quickly as possible."

"It's okay, Mother," David commented. "As long as they wind up down under sooner or later. We can rely on God to keep his promises. 'The righteous will rejoice when he sees the vengeance. He will wash his feet in the blood of the wicked.'"

Jesus arched an eyebrow.

"Is that from the Scriptures?" he asked.

"Isaiah."

"Are there verses like that in Christian writings?"

"A lot of them. But I like that one from the Hebrew testament best."

RoxAnna jumped in.

"So, Lord Jesus, when the time comes that you see me walking around with red feet, you'll know just how happy I'll be!"

A horse's whinny pierced the air. One of Jesus' knights reached down and petted his animal.

"I think the horse is asking about lunch," David offered. "Grandfather, please have your knights follow us to the castle where both they and their mounts will dine in style."

The castle's great inner courtyard was filled with the cheering relatives and friends of Jesus' knights, thrilled to be welcoming their young men back to La Valdieu. There were tears and laughter as parents greeted sons, sisters welcomed brothers, and hundreds of men and women welcomed back their prized acquaintances. And who could not help but admire the handsome King of the Jews himself? He had once been the Lord of this place and was now the ruler of the world's most famous domain. The Holy Land.

As Jesus watched the joyful reunions, he spotted the one figure he had been searching for. Miguel, his friend from the time they had met during Jesus' last days in Judea. Both he and Alejandro left Lazarus' home to emigrate to Gaul with Jesus and Mary Magdalene. Miguel had managed their manor house here in La Valdieu for five decades while Alejandro made the land flourish, married RoxAnna, and began to build a castle.

Miguel came forward now, old and lined, walking slowly with a wooden cane. He was dressed elegantly nonetheless, in cinnamon-colored silk pants, a white blouse, and pointed leather shoes with tassels on the toes. His appearance reminded Jesus of Lazarus. Art collector, wine connoisseur, bon vivant, and a woman's most charming suitor. He had been Miguel's first employer and Jesus' truest friend. The gayest straight man in Judea. Jesus remembered that Miquel probably *was* gay. He had never married. And he always had the prettiest twenty-something young males working with him. Good for him. Dapper and happy his whole life. No messy divorces. No disrespectful kids. No relatives here, there, and everywhere.

Miguel dropped to his knees before Jesus could greet him.

"Imagine my delight when I heard you were coming, dear Lord," he said with affection.

Jesus offered his hand.

"Get up, my friend. You haven't become a Christian, have you?" Jesus teased.

"Oh, no, no, no," Miguel replied accepting Jesus' hand. He stood up slowly. "Knees just gave out," he teased back.

Jesus smiled and embraced Miguel. Miguel hugged him, then stepped back and looked in Jesus' eyes.

"I don't have to be a Christian to honor the greatest man I've ever met," Miguel said. "But speaking of converts, have you been informed of one particular person's dramatic change?"

"You mean David?"

"Indeed. He had a terrible fever during the winter and swore to a Christian priest that if God spared him, he would convert and imitate the pious and righteous life of Jesus the Savior."

"And he has?"

"Oh, my, yes. Truly a new man. A saintly man. Full of good humor and generosity." Miguel blinked and smiled a wicked little smile. "I think RoxAnna really hates him now."

Jesus raised an eyebrow.

"Are you serious?"

"Pretty much."

"Judging by David's reputation before his conversion, you'd think his mother would be deliriously pleased."

"She actually liked the before product much better than the after result," Miguel confided. "RoxAnna has spent her entire time as La Valdieu's steward trying to inspire David to hate Rome and all things Latin. He was a good student. But he's done with that now, even if RoxAnna is not. David still loves and reveres his brilliant and powerful mother, but he is no longer obsessed with reviling the Romans.

"He rules La Valdieu wisely and puts the wellbeing of his people first. He has also begun to nurture a new ambition. To unite all the

Franks into a nation independent of Rome. It would be a vast kingdom, and he sees himself as its crowned head. Christian, spiritual, yet capable of protecting its saints against the dark forces of the secular world. As close to heaven on earth as the world has ever seen."

Jesus listened to Miquel's glowing description of his grandson David, but couldn't get past worrying about Miguel's weak and tired appearance.

"When can we talk more?" Jesus asked him. "Somewhere private. Just the two of us."

Miguel nodded.

"That can be done easily enough. It's late summer now. Days are still long and before tonight's welcome dinner it will still be light enough to allow us to lay flowers at Mary's tomb and chat."

"That would be perfect," Jesus said gratefully. "Do you take flowers for her often?"

"Every day." Miguel put his hand on his heart, remembering how very long ago he had laid the first flowers at her tomb.

Jesus thought back to when he and Mary had watched the flower beds being planted around the manor house. Alejandro had worked with Miguel for weeks to create a floral paradise. Wonderful Alejandro, gone now forever. Mary, too. Their bones gathered and placed in limestone boxes. A sad doom, no matter how familiar.

The heaviness of their absences weighed on Jesus. The burden the living carry for the dead who go before. He looked at the valley spread out as far as he could see. He breathed in the air heavy with the smells of La Valdieu. Apples. Wheat. Grapes. Life in ascendance. But his soul smelled the rest. Human decay. Rotting bones. Stone boxes filled with yesterday's lives.

"I take flowers for Mary," Miguel said. "But I also periodically lay a bunch of wine grapes to honor Alejandro. And a piece of a deer's antler to please our little hunter David. I leave a new sword every year for RoxAnna's mighty son Arduous. And last, a finely aged, blue glass bottle of our best wine for Lazarus."

"Fitting and wonderful, Miguel," Jesus said quietly. "Alas, Saul's bones lie alone. Resting in a tomb hewn from the bowels of the limestone hill on which Jerusalem sits."

"Your tomb," Miguel remembered.

"Yes. I am sad to confess that I did not visit my son when I first returned to Judea. More than a year passed before I went. Every tree, every bush, and every flower that had graced the area around the tomb had been cut down to the ground. Savage behaviors by the Roman victors."

"It's a miracle they didn't roll back the stone and desecrate the tomb."

Jesus nodded.

"Miguel, will you have Saul's bones brought back here for burial? Use money from the gold you have hidden. I will sign any document necessary for you to carry out the task. Explain to David and RoxAnna what I am asking and secure their blessing. Please also mention that I have come into possession of the skull of John the Baptist, my cousin. I would like two limestone boxes prepared. One to hold that skull. And one to hold *my* bones."

"Yes, Lord," Miguel spoke. "It is customary for the box makers to use the tip of their trowel to scratch the name of the departed on one of its sides."

Jesus nodded.

"Have them write 'John the Baptist. The Greatest Man Born of Woman.' And 'Jesus of Nazareth."

Miguel looked at Jesus.

"Is that really all, Lord?"

Jesus nodded.

"Let's see what the future holds before I feel brave enough to add any more." Jesus looked into Miguel's eyes. "Where do *you* intend to be buried, my dear friend?"

"In the ground," Miguel answered tersely. "No marker. No memory."

Jesus frowned.

"I would prefer that you would choose to rest with me, my family, and our truest friends."

"Thank you, Lord, but no," Miguel replied. "I would like my ashes buried in the flower gardens of the manor. Absorbed into the soil. Every time the flowers bloom, so will I."

Jesus nodded, touched by Miguel's wise and humble desire. The thought of this wonderful person returning with the flowers every spring diminished the pain he felt anticipating losing him, his oldest and most selfless friend. But not by much.

Weeks later, when the limestone boxes had been constructed for the Baptist's skull and Jesus' bones, Miquel had John's limestone chest carved with his name and epitaph exactly as Jesus had requested. And he had Jesus' box carved *almost* exactly the way he had been instructed. The inscription read, "Jesus of Nazareth. Son of God, Son of Man. King of the Jews." That box—the size of a small bench—would go unused and forgotten in one corner of the tomb for more than nineteen hundred years. When it was found, the lid was raised and the devoted friends of the greatest man who ever lived laid his bones to rest at last.

CHAPTER TEN

JESUS WAS DRINKING WINE WITH Miguel. They sat in camp chairs servants had carried outside the castle walls for them. Enjoying a panoramic view of the valley and the manor house as the sun set. Jesus knew that someone still lived in the house. A person with whom he had lost touch. Miquel told him earlier that his daughter Mary, now in her forties and never married, stayed there with a few loyal servants.

Miguel had given her a large sum of money at Jesus' direction years ago, and RoxAnna had granted her the use of the manor house for as long as she lived. Mary handled all of its affairs. Supervised the maintenance and budgeted funds for its upkeep. She also saw to all of her own personal needs.

Jesus loved his daughter and had initially stayed in touch with her after returning to Judea. But events had pressed him. And he had only realized on his return to La Valdieu that he had not sent her a personal note for a year. Or two. Or more.

"What does Mary do with her days?" Jesus asked Miguel.

"She reads," Miguel answered Jesus. "And she tutors children who are learning to read. She also carries on correspondence with scholars in Gaul, Spain, Italy, and even in Egypt and Arabia. She is enthusiastically conversant on every topic imaginable."

Jesus was pleased with what he heard. He had had the good fortune to be around powerful and bright women all his life. His mother Mary was a natural debater and to this day liked nothing better than an argument. His wife had been sweet, but intelligent and direct. Lazarus' sisters Mary and Martha were so smart and so verbal it was probably what prevented them from finding and marrying run-of-the-mill dolts in Bethany. He was also impressed with Berenice, Titus' longtime love.

For sheer grit, determination, and brilliance however, there was no match for RoxAnna. How Alejandro had loved her! And how his own son Saul mourned having given her up to join the Jewish revolt. Jesus knew that it was said to be a man's world. But she was easily the equal of any king who ruled.

He wondered if he could persuade his daughter Mary to return to Judea with him. It was not verdant and beautiful like La Valdieu, but it was stark and magnificent. And Jericho was a lush and bountiful oasis. Maybe he could be the good father that he longed to be. He'd pray on that. Well, no, actually he wouldn't pray on that. He had learned in these later years just to move forward with what needed to be done. If God didn't like that, he hadn't said so.

"I would like to see my daughter, Miguel," Jesus said. "Would you help arrange that?"

"It won't be an issue," Miguel answered. "Mary is not unhappy with you. Just a bit disappointed. Which is probably natural, eh?" He looked at Jesus.

"Yes," Jesus agreed. "I don't know why I allowed myself to grow apart from her. Maybe I was afraid that she would die young, too."

"Well, thank the Lord she didn't. I'll set up an occasion for you two to meet."

"Thanks, old friend. Would it be too much to ask you to gauge what interest she might have in returning to Judea with me?"

Miguel shook his head.

"That's for you to ask."

"I'm afraid she'll say no," Jesus replied. "Maybe you could soften her up a little bit."

Miguel laughed and slapped his head.

"You are funny, Lord. If she says no, *you* talk her out of it."

Jesus raised his eyebrows in surprise.

"Manipulate her?"

"*Win* her. Just as you did with Mary Magdalene once upon a time."

"I can't take any credit for that. Mary had already made her mind up about us."

"And good thing she did," Miguel said a bit wistfully. He had truly loved Jesus' wonderful wife. "The point is, you have charm. Use it."

"Thanks for the advice," Jesus said. "I'll chew on it. May I ask, by the way, where you are keeping the gold Titus sent?"

"A thousand bags are hidden inside the family tomb. Another nine thousand bags have been invested with Jewish moneylenders in Marseilles."

Jesus' face looked stunned.

"You *invested* my money?" Jesus said. He was incredulous that Miguel had decided to trust private bankers with ninety percent of his fortune. "You *risked* my money?" Jesus said getting upset.

"You didn't say not to," Miguel replied in his own defense. "It seemed prudent to put *some* of the money to work."

"And *how* did you make the money work?" Jesus asked trying to sound sarcastic.

"I instructed the moneylenders to give preference to merchant marine enterprises," Miguel responded calmly. "Import and export voyages. So far, such investments have more than doubled the invested money. You now have *nineteen* million aureuses instead of the original nine."

Jesus sat quietly, too embarrassed to speak.

"I'm sorry I doubted you," he finally murmured.

"No issue," Miguel responded kindly. "The merchant ships were loaded with salt purchased cheaply from Judea's Sea of Sodom, then sold throughout the empire—ounce for ounce—at the same price as gold."

"Take ten percent of those earnings for yourself, Miguel," Jesus told him, "and invest it to your heart's delight."

"What would I do with almost two million aureuses, Lord?" Miguel protested. "I have one foot in the grave."

"Then *give* it to whom you will," Jesus replied. "It is wealth beyond imagining. The lifetime wages of thousands of workers."

Miguel fell silent for a moment. Then he asked the question that had been on his mind for a long time.

"Why did Titus give you all that gold?"

"I don't know, Miguel," Jesus told him. "I want to believe that it was restitution for the destruction of Judea. It is, in fact, enough money to resurrect the farmlands, rebuild the villages, refortify the cities—"

"—And still have millions of aureuses left over," Miguel interrupted. "Yes. But *why*?"

"It might also be that Titus wants to keep that wealth out of the hands of his brother. Domitian is intent on assassinating him and taking the emperor's throne. If he succeeds, then Titus will have significantly shortchanged his inheritance."

Miguel nodded.

"That makes sense. Entrusting his wealth to you ensured that it would not be wasted. But it is still a remarkable amount of cash to spend on the Jews."

"Perhaps it's not just for the Jews," Jesus responded. "Titus knows that my longevity will provide opportunities to use that money for years to come. Perhaps even picking up the pieces if and when the empire collapses or is conquered. It would be enough money to help rebuild the entire imperial world into something better and more useful."

Miguel shook his head, amazed at Jesus' distant imaginings.

Jesus went on.

"It might also be that we are witnessing the hand of Jehovah in all of this, my friend. He moves mysteriously and without any conversation. It appears that he has willed his Son to live a long time. So perhaps *he* has provided me with enough wealth to gets things done far into the future."

"Or it's just a damn fine piece of luck," Miguel said resisting Jesus' religious argument.

"Having doubled the gold here," Jesus said, "you have definitely earned the right to your own point of view. But I think you misjudge the guile and manipulative nature of my Father in making all this money available."

"Now *that's* the God, I know," Miguel said. "Good thing you'll be spending it and not him. He causes enough trouble as it is."

"My," Jesus remarked. "You don't sound very religious anymore, Miguel." He winked. Miguel knew full well that Jesus wasn't all that religious either.

"Well, I'm not very *pious*, that's for sure," Miguel agreed. "Not after witnessing a world full of mischief and woe unchecked by *any* supposed god or divinity. You, however, are different. If anyone can change the world for the better, it will be you. Half God, half man, you are the best of both. So, I say who cares how you came into this wealth! Spend it and make us proud."

Jesus looked at eighty-year-old Miguel and felt tears come into his eyes. The Lord giveth and the Lord taketh away. But once in a while he let someone live out their full four score and ten years, blessing everyone they know by the quality of their lives. Without saying anything he reached forward and hugged Miguel. Unembarrassed, Miguel hugged him long and close. Jesus smiled. His precious friend was gay for sure.

— ⚜ —

King David and RoxAnna hosted a formal dinner that evening to welcome Jesus. A dozen knights and their wives attended, dressed in fine robes and elegant jewelry. The women wore heavy eyeliner in the same Egyptian style that Berenice preferred, and had their hair up, sculpted into buns and coils. David wore a golden robe and a gorgeously-worked gold crown. Vines, leaves, and grapes in golden profusion. RoxAnna, in contrast, wore a plain white cotton shift that fell to her ankles, and a thin circlet of gold on her head.

Miguel had laid out some elegant outfits for Jesus to choose from. But Jesus had dressed in the ancient Persian pantsuit that his wife had given him. Miguel made a face when he saw Jesus wearing it.

"That is *so* old," he told Jesus.

"I like it."

"It looks worn and shabby."

"I like it."

"It's ready for the trash."

"Shut up, Miguel."

"Wear one of these other costumes, please!" Miguel begged.

Jesus looked at what Miguel was wearing. He was dressed in tight silver pants, a sapphire-colored silk blouse, and silver sandals.

Jesus looked him over.

"I'll wear what have you have on."

"It won't fit," Miguel told him fussing. "You'd look like a sausage stuffed with barley."

Jesus frowned imagining that.

"I don't care," he told Miguel.

"Now *you* shut up," Miguel said irritably.

"We're not getting very far," Jesus commented.

"You don't think?" Miguel said and gritted his teeth.

"Look, my friend," Jesus said. "How about I wear what I have on? If you really want me to give it up, then have an outfit identical to yours tailored for me." He pointed at Miguel's silver pants and sapphire blouse.

"I can do that," Miguel said grudgingly. "But it won't help how you look *tonight*."

"I guess I'll just have to get by on my good looks and charm."

Miguel slapped his forehead and rolled his eyes.

Jesus laughed.

"I need some wine," Miguel declared. "And I *will* have the dining hall lighting reduced to a subdued and shadowy illumination."

"On my account?"

"Yes!" Miguel almost shouted and left the room. Jesus wasn't used to being told what to wear. Back home in Jericho, neither his mother, nor Judas, nor his house guest Berenice, *ever* commented on what he wore. He wondered if his daughter Mary would be as concerned as Miguel about his image and majesty. If she was, maybe he wouldn't be inviting her to come back with him to Jericho after all.

— ⚜ —

The royal banquet seemed a bit of a ruckus affair to Jesus, with loud talk and much laughter. Platters of roast lamb were brought out. Pork loin, ribs, and ham as well. A variety of vegetables was offered. Boiled beets, leaks, gourds, mushrooms, and truffles. There was a parade of bowls filled with olives and nuts. Salads of greens and herbs with garlic vinegar dressing. Fresh goat cheese. Hot loaves of wheat bread. And bitter or honeyed sauces for dipping.

Wine goblets were continuously refilled with wine mixed with water. Jesus noticed though that RoxAnna and her son David both drank their wine uncut. RoxAnna emptied goblets of mead as well, the Nordic drink that his beloved knight Keir had introduced to La Valdieu fifty years ago.

King David and the Queen Mother RoxAnna were seated at one end of the long oak dining table. Jesus and his daughter Mary were seated at the other end. Mary was kind, but quiet and formal, sitting quietly next to Jesus. Miguel had arranged for them to visit earlier in the day. Mary had welcomed him and they had exchanged pleasantries for most of the afternoon.

Jesus found that his daughter did not want to talk about their estrangement. And he could not find the inner strength to just apologize without excuses. So like people everywhere, they pretended that nothing had ever happened, suppressed their anger, sadness, and shame and hoped that their unspoken feelings would just dissolve with time.

The dining hall was filled with hanging banners that displayed the symbols of the houses of David's knights. They were almost a thousand noble families now, whose patriarchs and their adult sons served as the king's cavalry which had grown to three thousand men. Another seven thousand men were foot soldiers. The laborers who worked for the landowning knights. King David's military was not the largest force in Gaul. But it was significant.

In contrast, during his two years on the throne Jesus had raised an army of twenty-five thousand soldiers. Five thousand of whom were knights, supported by twenty thousand infantrymen. One legion of foot soldiers was disbursed to guard Judea's walled cities. The other legion of foot soldiers was part of the reserve forces. Once a month they gathered in small groups to practice javelin, sword, and sling. And every three months all twenty thousand infantry legionnaires and the five thousand cavalry troops came together on the vast plain of Armageddon for military exercises.

They bivouacked near the ancient Canaanite fortress city Megiddo. Destroyed by Pharaoh Thutmose fifteen hundred years earlier, it had been rebuilt by King Solomon. Then it had been destroyed again. By the Romans. Jesus had restored it with impregnable walls and gates. In the distance was Mount Gilboa where Israel's first king Saul had died in battle with his sons. His body had been beheaded and hung on the city walls of pagan Bath-Shan alongside the headless corpses of his three slain sons, Jonathan, Abinadab, and Malchisha. The city was long gone, but the humiliation done to the royal house of Judea would never fade.

Jesus and Mary had been quiet during the meal, only joining the toasts offered around the table. One toast in particular had troubled Jesus. King David had risen, invited the company to fill their wine cups and lift them high. He saluted Emperor Titus, reminding one and all of his impending visit. He declared that the fine folks of La Valdieu would celebrate his arrival with great fanfare.

The knights and their ladies drank, shouted with great enthusiasm, pounded the table with their empty goblets, and stamped the floor with their feet. RoxAnna participated quite vociferously in the antics. How was that possible? She hated Rome. She hated Titus. Yet she had cheered and stomped her feet right along with everyone else.

His daughter had not joined in with the others. He gazed at her. Mary was careful not to make eye contact. She had a pretty oval face like her mother, honey-blonde hair, and brown eyes. She was wearing a simple blue robe, but she also had on a beautiful pearl necklace, no doubt procured for her by Miguel.

"Why aren't you hollering and carrying on like everyone else?" Jesus asked.

Mary looked at him.

"Because it's a sham. Every person in this kingdom hates Titus for murdering Saul. RoxAnna would do anything to see him dead. And so would Saul's son, your grandson, David."

Jesus frowned.

"I was under the impression that David had repented of that when he became a Christian."

Mary looked at Jesus and responded slowly and deliberately.

"I think he is serious about his conversion," she said. "He is quite enamored with the story of your life. In no small part because he is your grandson and your divine blood flows in his body. However, he makes it no secret that he still harbors hatred deep in his heart for the empire, and for the emperor in particular.

"RoxAnna fanned the first embers of vengeance during his childhood, turning it into the raging fire that consumes him as an adult.

When she received word from you that Titus would be visiting, she had her Druid priest toss his magic bones. He predicted that a great ruler would be killed in La Valdieu. I am not privy to any discussions she may consequently have had with David. But I fear that they may be planning an attempt on the emperor's life. I have witnessed unusual military exercises from the manor house. Soldiers line both sides of the road and as a mounted group passes in between they come together."

"And why would that make you suspicious?" Jesus asked.

"Because the soldiers *absorb* the mounted group."

Jesus frowned. He beckoned to Miguel who was standing in a corner of the hall. He
came and knelt by Jesus' seat immediately.

"Were you aware of the military exercises being practiced on the road in front of the manor?" he asked.

Miguel shook his head.

"But military training is always happening," he answered. "And mock fights are constantly staged inside and outside the castle. I believe they are a preparation for the time King David sets out to unify the kingdoms of Gaul."

"The military maneuvers Mary observed seem more to be designed to greet the emperor with murder most foul," Jesus replied.

Miguel frowned deeply.

"I'm not sure who in La Valdieu would see Titus' death as foul."

"That's not my point," Jesus snapped. "The *consequences* of his murder are what I fear. If he is attacked in La Valdieu, this kingdom will be wiped from the face of the earth. Do you think RoxAnna and David's desire for revenge is worth the death of every living soul here?"

"Of course not," Miguel replied.

"Then for the sake of this kingdom, we must confront them about the evil they are planning against Titus."

As if he had somehow heard Jesus, King David stood and raised his goblet again.

"Fair Ladies and Genteel Men, friends all," he began. "I wish to acknowledge and honor the presence of my grandfather Jesus with us tonight."

David looked at Jesus and extended his goblet toward him. Jesus stood and raised his goblet, returning his grandson's gaze. The knights and their spouses stood and raised their goblets as well.

"I admire my grandfather," David began, "although he raises an army to fight Roman wars." The room suddenly went completely still. David's face looked benign, but the words that proceeded out of his mouth were harsh. "I respect my grandfather, though his response to Titus' massacre of Judea has been to become his vassal. I even *love* my grandfather, a man who surely is the Son of God. But notwithstanding the Star of David his soldiers bear on their shields, I've come to believe that a *Latin* god is his father. Apollo, Mars, or Jupiter!"

Every person in the room looked at Jesus. David's mocking accusations cut into all of their hearts, not just that of Jesus. Faces were grim, and many of the knights felt that David had gone too far. His own mother RoxAnna was surprised at the hardness of his words towards Jesus. Her face was a mask of detachment. But her heart was pounding.

"I have no answers that will satisfy you, King of La Valdieu," Jesus responded. "Other than to remind you that I pioneered this land. I established this royal seat. And it was I who gave the throne to your father who abdicated to you choosing to give his life trying to free Judea. I am following his very path, though that is something to which you appear to be blind. I will take my leave this night."

David set his goblet on the table, then beckoned one of his knights to rise. The man stood instantly, holding a rolled-up parchment.

"Grandfather, if you do indeed depart tonight, you will miss the arrival of the emperor. Just today I received a missive from Titus. He sent word that he plans to be here *tomorrow*. Listen to its contents."

David gestured to the knight holding the scroll. He unrolled it and read its contents in a clear strong voice.

To: David, Son Of Saul, Son Of Jesus, King Of La Valdieu
From: Titus Flavius Vespasianus Augustus,Emperor Of Rome

Greetings, Sovereign Lord of La Valdieu.

Peace be to you, my respected acquaintance, who by the will of the emperor and the Senate of Rome reigns over your subjects with good will and benevolent intentions. Be assured of the continuing support of myself and the people of Rome.

I embarked from Britannia and have landed safely on the shores of Gaul. Your grandfather left Judea some months ago to meet with me, and I hope to see him and you in your kingdom on the twenty-first day of this month, the solstice that marks the beginning of summer. I will require only one day's time with Jesus, and request the provisioning of my entourage—a Praetorian century—its officers, and myself, before we will depart for Italy. Accept my thanks for your gracious kindness.

Your respectful servant,
Titus
Signed in my own hand and sealed with my personal mark.

David stared at Jesus.

Jesus stared back.

"Have you no response, Grandfather?" David challenged him.

"I will head toward the coast and halt the emperor's progress," he replied.

David shook his head.

"That would spoil the reception we have prepared for Titus, emperor of all things Roman. Who will describe to the King of the Jews the welcome planned for the Killer of the Jews?"

"Before anyone speaks," Jesus interrupted in a commanding voice. "If any man talks of treason or murder, and if anyone is sworn to perform such when Emperor Titus enters this valley, he shall be apprehended and tried. If I don't kill him first."

Fear stole the hearts of David's knights. While this assembly indeed comprised the leaders of the troops poised to meet Titus and his Praetorians, none felt that loyalty to their king required the forfeiture of their own lives at Jesus' hand. No one spoke. Until David did.

"Grandfather, you seem to have unmanned my retainers. I myself will speak the doom waiting for Emperor Titus. Tomorrow, as he approaches the castle, two hundred cavalry riders will line both sides of the road, spears held high, swords drawn in salute. Those knights will then fall on Titus and his Praetorians slaughtering them all until Titus stands alone. Then I myself will thrust a sword through his guts and spill out the rot that fills his carcass." David looked arrogant and unstoppable. "That's the plan, Jesus. What say ye?" David folded his arms and waited for Jesus to speak.

Jesus bent down and spoke softly to Mary.

"Go to my room and fetch my sword."

Mary's eyes grew huge. She nodded and waited for Jesus to respond to David. When he did, she slipped away almost unnoticed. But Miguel had overheard Jesus' whispered request to his daughter and followed Mary out of the room.

Jesus addressed David calmly, but with a hard edge to his voice.

"I think you mean to destroy this kingdom, Grandson. And for what? Revenge on Titus?

Revenge on Rome? You are young and have made clear your dream to unite all of Gaul. Will you cast aside that grand vision and sacrifice your own life? Because if you do not foreswear your intent to spill the emperor's blood, I will kill you here and now."

The entire company in the dining hall gasped, astonished at the threat that had issued from Jesus' mouth.

David had the gall to act amused.

"Are you challenging me, Grandfather?" David grinned and then laughed loudly.

"You may appear youthful, but you are an old man. When was the last time you wielded a sword? Or defended yourself against one raised against you?"

"Say whatever you wish, David," Jesus answered, his voice furious. "I promise on your father Saul's grave that you will die in this hall in front of your vassals who will then belong to me—the founder of La Valdieu—and I will be the king who once again sits upon its throne." Jesus lowered his voice, but it remained deadly serious. "My first command will be to see to your funeral. I will personally kneel beside your coffin and pray that God will not deal too harshly with your soul, Grandson."

David froze at Jesus' threats, but quickly recovered. He stripped off his robe. Standing only in his loincloth, he ordered one of the knights to fetch a sword for him, even as he watched Mary re-enter the dining hall and hand Jesus his sword. The moment Jesus took it Miguel rushed into the hall with the Judean knights. All dozen men were armed with spears, swords, and slings. The knights and ladies at table did not move as David scanned the Jewish soldiers and their weapons. He did not speak as he took his sword from his retainer.

Jesus addressed him one last time.

"You may still repent of the evil you have plotted, David," Jesus told him. "If you do so—on your honor as a Christian monarch—there will be no fight and no death. For I will absolve your sin and make you clean."

David gazed silently at Jesus for a long moment, then leapt up onto the great oak table and began to walk toward him. Knights and ladies rushed away from the table. Jesus' soldiers put stones in the pouches of their slings and watched. Whatever prowess and capability their king showed—or *failed* to show—they would not allow David to subdue Jesus under any circumstances.

David stopped six feet from Jesus. Jesus tore off his suit coat. He stood back and motioned for David to come off the table. His grandson shook his head and held out his sword. David had worked out with knights his entire life. Jesus had begun training only two years ago, but had learned to move brilliantly with his sword, and had eventually bested even the finest of his sword masters. Jesus stepped on his chair and then onto the table. He faced his grandson. Neither adversary spoke now. Their sole focus was how to fight the other man and live to talk about it.

David moved forward and opened with a slashing blow toward Jesus' chest. Jesus fended it off with his sword. David stepped closer and thrust at Jesus' midriff. Jesus turned it away. And so the fight went. David slashed and thrust again and again, while Jesus slowly backed down the length of the table parrying his blows. None of them got anywhere near Jesus' body, though David's blows were quick and powerful. Jesus defended himself, but did not offer any sword thrusts in return.

This continued for many minutes. David's blows grew less frequent, and it was clear that they were being offered with a diminishing strength. As Jesus reached the far end of the great table he suddenly leaned in toward David and shoved him violently with his free hand. David staggered and fell backwards onto the table. With lightning speed Jesus put his sword tip on David's throat. The move stunned David and he lay unmoving beneath Jesus' blade.

Jesus spoke to him.

"I offer you terms once again, Grandson. I have but one desire. To hear you repent of the wickedness you nurse in your heart against Emperor Titus. Only say that you yield and willingly turn away from those evil desires, and you shall live."

Jesus looked into his grandson's eyes. There was fear. But was there repentance?

David spoke in a loud voice for all to hear.

"I yield. I repent of my sins and ask for mercy."

Jesus pulled his sword tip away and stretched out his left hand to help his grandson rise. David supported himself on his elbow, then swung his sword and cut off Jesus' outstretched hand. Blood burst from the wound into David's face, denying him the sight of Jesus' counterblow, a downward stroke of his sword that cut David's sword arm off at the shoulder. David fell backwards onto the table clasping his sundered shoulder.

Mary pulled off her sash and tried to stop the flow of blood from Jesus' forearm. RoxAnna ripped away the bottom of her gown and held the wad of cloth against David's gushing wound. His eyes were clenched shut, covered with Jesus' blood, and he refused to utter a single word even though he knew to the core of his being that the blood flooding from his veins was emptying out his very life.

"No, no, no," RoxAnna moaned over and over, but David's blood flowed until it had quit his body. The dead king's face turned gray as lead, and his limbs sprawled loosely on the table. RoxAnna put down the blood-soaked wad of cloth. She gazed at her son's face, then turned and left the hall without uttering another word.

Jesus had watched without sorrow and without offering to help or heal. Some people deserved to die. His grandson was one of those people. A liar. A hypocrite. A cheat. And a would-be murderer. Odd that the blood of Jehovah which had flowed in David's veins had done nothing more than declare him mortal, and showed Jesus—now more than any other time in his life—that he himself had become exactly like his own Father, Jehovah. Killing his own heir to fix things that were wrong.

Jesus looked at Mary and then at Miguel.

"Miguel, dismiss the guests and fetch whatever help you need to clean this place up and prepare it for Titus' arrival tomorrow. I will talk to RoxAnna about what she wants done with David's body. And, Mary, would you please retrieve my wedding ring? Your mother gave it to me, and I would like it placed on my remaining hand."

Mary carefully picked up Jesus' severed hand. Holding it and seeing the dark hole left by the nail that had once pierced it, she began to weep. Jesus touched her cheek, then held out his right hand. Mary gently pulled off the Star of David wedding band and placed it on the ring finger of his hand. Then she put her face against his chest and wept. The Lord giveth and the Lord taketh away. And sometimes, just like Job, he taketh until there is nothing left to take.

CHAPTER ELEVEN

Mary went looking for Jesus in the great room of the manor house the next morning. She had kept it the same as when Jesus had lived there. His study still occupied a corner of the room. She knew he would be there when she found his guest bedroom empty. Indeed, her father was sitting at the mahogany desk Miguel had ordered to replace the olivewood one he'd shipped to Jericho. Jesus was reading, but glanced up instantly when he heard Mary approach.

"Hello, Father," she greeted him. "I came to check your wound and change the dressing."

Jesus rose and gave Mary a hug. He showed her his wrist where David's sword had cut away his left hand. The flesh had healed and smooth healthy skin had replaced the bloody wound of the night before.

"It's a miracle!" Mary gasped.

"No," Jesus replied gently. "A miracle would be a whole new hand. This, however, does count as a wonder. I am glad to be healed. I have no pain. Alas, I also have no left hand. Please sit, Mary. I've been enjoying some of the books I left here. You have honored me by keeping my old study intact."

"You may thank Miguel," Mary replied. "He asked if we could preserve it for you. He always believed that you would be back. He loves you so much."

Jesus nodded. He wished Mary could say that *she* loved him so much, and perhaps in time she would.

"Have you been up to the castle this morning?" he asked.

"I have. Everyone is in mourning. Because of David's death, but also because of the horrible events of last night. No one can believe that he lied, and then wounded you after yielding. Gossip among the queen's ladies-in-waiting has it that the knights rue their liege's foolishness and that they are prepared to swear fealty to you as King of La Valdieu."

"And that they will," Jesus responded in a resolute voice. "I wonder how many of those elite knights would really have joined David to assassinate Titus? A lot of lives would have been lost in such an attempt. And successful or not, everyone in the kingdom—man, woman, and child—would have been massacred by Rome."

"I don't know how many were involved," Mary said quietly.

"No one will *ever* know," Jesus replied and shook his head. No matter who was involved, he was sure that the heart of the matter had been RoxAnna's constant goading of David. Her vendetta against Titus had caused her son's conscience to become unhinged.

"What news of RoxAnna?" he asked.

"She is wearing a plain black robe and has a black veil over her face. David's body has been washed and wrapped with spices and myrrh. He lies in his casket on a platform below the church's altar. Only his face is revealed. RoxAnna is attended by her servants, but everyone knows that she has few if any friends in La Valdieu."

"And why would that be?"

"She was haughty and put on airs all the years she was the royal regent," Mary answered. "She was no less overbearing when David reigned on his own. Self-absorbed, she spent decades refusing to display any humor, appreciation, or even civility. She was verbally abusive to her servants, the court, its knights, and even to the king himself."

"My," Jesus said. "I have to say that she was a feisty enough girl when I met her. But such conduct has no excuse."

"No," Mary agreed. "She turned into a loner somewhere along the way, and with David gone now she will be ostracized. Further, word among the servants is that *she* was actually the one behind the plot to assassinate Titus."

"And now that David is dead, no one will ever remember being in favor of that mad plan," Jesus commented.

"Absolutely," Mary agreed. "There is, however, a lot of fear in the castle and whispered rumors that you have plans to investigate and punish those who supported David."

Jesus shook his head.

"I have no intention of doing any such thing. But I *am* taking and possessing the throne until I can determine who shall rule. I need to go and see RoxAnna. Titus will arrive sometime today. Is there an honor guard posted at the entrance of castle?"

"Yes. Miguel asked your knights to take that function. They control the gates as well as the towers on both the front and back entrances."

"I approve, but who ordered it?"

"I *suggested* it," Mary answered.

Jesus pondered that for a moment. Mary suggesting orders on his behalf? Well, it was the right thing to do. Score one for his daughter. He lifted his arm and looked at the wrist where he used to have a left hand. Though he wished to be brave and stoic, he was, in fact, devastated by the loss of his hand. It would not change anything about how he worked, or read, or wrote, or fought. But destined to have but a single hand for the rest of his life was unnerving. Unnatural. Off-putting. It was, however, the way it was going to be. He stood up.

"Thank you for your kindness last night," he told Mary gratefully. "Before and after the royal fiasco. God willing, I shall live to deserve your love."

Mary hugged her father.

"Whatever shall be, shall be," she said softly.

"You sound like a Druid," Jesus teased gently.

"No," Mary said quickly. "The farthest thing from it. I'm a Jewess who loves Jehovah."

Jesus took her hand and smiled at her gently.

"You would favor your father greatly if you would consider coming to Jericho with me and abiding in my palace. It would balance out things a little." Jesus smiled faintly. "I have two Christian women living with me, and an ancient, unrepentant Zealot who's still mad at Rome.

"My home is set in the heart of Judea, the land of a bruised and suspicious people, still in shock from the revolt, and about to be wake up to a new batch of twenty-five thousand army recruits from Africa, Europe, and Asia who variously believe in just about every god you could list."

Jesus' eyes twinkled at the thought of that new blood mixing with the bruised and weary Judeans.

"And you?" Mary asked directly. "Who do you serve?"

"I do what I do in the name and to the glory of Jehovah."

Mary smiled relieved to hear her father's words.

"If he's there," Jesus added.

Mary's eyebrows shot up.

Jesus winked and whispered to his daughter.

"It would be nice if you didn't repeat that to anybody."

Jesus entered a place where he had never been before. A Christian church. The one in

La Valdieu's castle had been built into a corner of an inner wall. It was small and windowless. Bronze oil lamps on tall stands provided the only light. There were no seats. There was a wooden podium and a marble altar with golden emblems fastened to its front. A man riding a donkey. Three crosses on a hill. A tomb with the stone rolled back.

Jesus looked down at the floor. He was standing on a carved tile. He stepped back and saw that it bore a memorial to Lazarus, his generous friend and mentor.

Honoring the memory of

LAZARUS OF BETHANY

I am the resurrection and the life.
He that believeth in me, though he
die, yet shall he live, and whosoever
believeth in me shall never die.

Just below those words from the Gospel of John was Lazarus' response.

I do believe blessed Lord Jesus.
Live long. Live well. I look forward
to seeing you again at the end of time.
I never admired a man more than you.
Your eternal friend, Lazarus.

Jesus looked up from the marker. He knew that Lazarus was dead and that his bones lay in a box in La Valdieu's royal tomb. But he chose not to dwell on that sad truth, preferring to remember his friend's smile, his laugh, and their happy conversations. Lazarus had given Jesus his future in Gaul, funding everything with no consideration of being repaid. What a rare and wonderful friend he had been. Rest in Peace, brother, Jesus thought. Until the last day when I wake you up myself.

In front of the altar was the open casket of King David. It was set on a raised wooden bier covered in black satin. The body of the dead man was swathed in strips of white linen wound around his body and his head, leaving only an opening for his face. His expression was stern and irritated. He had died before his time, and he knew it. A large golden crucifix had been placed on his chest. A faithless traitor who would still receive Christian rites. Truly a theology for sinners.

"He's not quite so formidable dead, is he?" a female voice asked behind Jesus. He turned and saw RoxAnna walking toward him. She wore a black silk robe and a black linen cap with its veil drawn down over her face. She stopped next to Jesus, pulled the veil up over her head and stared at him. RoxAnna's face was stern and she had not been crying.

"Notice the crucifix?" she asked. "It's from his room. I thought it should be buried with him. A Christian both killed *and* saved by his redeemer. Pretty efficient religion."

"Do you want something, RoxAnna?" Jesus asked without politeness.

"I *do* want something, Jesus," she affirmed. "The truth is I always hated David. He was selfish, petulant, demanding, egotistical—and worst of all—he was king. How could the same womb that bore an angel like Arduous spit out a devil like David? I feel cursed."

"I am truly sorry, RoxAnna," Jesus told her and meant it. "You have always been ambitious, but not perverse or wicked. You hate the Romans with all your heart. But I don't believe that you could have been a part of David's plan to murder Titus."

RoxAnna nodded.

"The castle gossip accuses me of instigating David's hatred for the empire, but it was a masterpiece of his own perverse imagination. I couldn't talk David out of trying to assassinate the emperor which would have signed death warrants for every citizen in La Valdieu. Turns out that *you* spared us all."

"I didn't want to fight David," Jesus protested. "And I never intended to kill him. Both of our bad luck."

"No. It was good luck," RoxAnna disagreed. "The man was too vain to rule and too wicked to live." RoxAnna reached for Jesus' hand. "How unjust that my son cut off your other hand." RoxAnna put her lips on Jesus' hand and kissed it.

Jesus pulled his hand away.

"What are you doing?" he asked upset.

"Preparing you for my demand." RoxAnna's face turned hard and calculating. "Under Jewish law, you must provide me with an heir. That I may keep what is mine and raise a child to inherit it when I am gone. I have no desire for you. But sleep with me, you shall. And even in my middle age, I will bear a son to rule La Valdieu. A champion and a King of Kings. The son of man *and* the Son of God."

Jesus stared at RoxAnna. Rebuttals were not coming to mind. Didn't matter. She didn't look to be in the mood to listen to any of them.

— ⚜ —

Titus arrived at La Valdieu without fanfare. He and Jesus were drinking in the study at the manor house. Titus' escort of one hundred Praetorian guards was being fed and quartered in the castle. The emperor was dressed in short black pants and a long-sleeved white cotton shirt. Jesus wore a lightweight blue cotton robe. Both men were in their bare feet, having slipped their sandals off. Jesus looked at Titus' costume.

"Never saw you in an outfit like that before," he commented. "Short pants?"

Titus shrugged and grinned.

"All I care is that it's comfortable."

"Why not short sleeves, too?"

"Didn't think of that." Titus pulled at one of his sleeves. "I kind of like that thought though. The bastard who sold me this shirt in Londonium had the balls to tell me that both the cotton *and* the weave were Egyptian and therefore not only infinitely superior to any Roman product, but also three times as expensive. Shit howdy!" Titus exclaimed. "Can you believe that?"

Jesus reached out and touched Titus' shirt.

"But you bought it anyway?"

"I bought two dozen. Liked 'em and I can afford to be cheated."

Jesus arched an eye.

"You're a character," he said.

Titus laughed.

"I did put my foot down on one thing. The tailor wanted to put a little symbol on each shirt just above the nipple on the left side. A cavalry legionnaire sitting on a horse."

"What?"

"I know. A truly stupid idea. He said it was his *mark*. I told him he could stick his mark up his arse."

Jesus laughed delightedly.

"Let one guy get started with that shit," Titus said, "and then everybody has to have *his* mark, too. Horses, eagles, boobs, dicks, and who knows what all? You'd probably find little crosses on your stuff."

"And you could have a tongue thrust out between a pair of lips."

Titus looked surprised.

"For wine?" he asked puzzled.

Jesus shook his head.

"I was remembering our trip to Rome with Saul. Remember the Cunnus Lingus Inn?"

Titus smiled.

"I was a naughty boy."

"Not really. Just a man of many appetites."

"Back then," Titus remarked. "At forty, I am feeling old and jaded. The one woman I want to be with declined to be here."

"It's not you. Berenice has become a Christian and believes that sex should be reserved for the marriage bed."

"Really?" Titus looked mystified. "That from our old friend Paul?"

"No," Jesus replied. "It's actually courtesy of *my* old disciples."

"Bunch of virgins?"

"Pretty much. But I think their real intent was to prevent men from taking advantage of women. Not just sexually, but an effort to end their age-old habit of abandoning the women they make pregnant."

"That's sort of new thinking."

"Yes," Jesus agreed. "I don't like rules in general, but I am becoming somewhat sympathetic to ones enacted to protect women. Jews have thousands of rules concerning faith, conduct, charity, cleanliness, work, pleasure, life, death, and on and on and on. I just reduce them all to let your conscience be your guide."

"You mean God?"

"You heard what I said, friend," Jesus rebutted. "People have good hearts and, if left to their own devices, will do the right thing. Of course, there are exceptions. But in general, folks don't need Scriptures, commandments, or rules. What they need is to do is listen to the inner voice placed in their hearts. Do good. Be generous. Love and forgive."

Titus nodded and drank from his wine.

"Do unto others as you would have them do unto you," he said.

Jesus was surprised.

"Where did you get that?" he asked.

"Gospel of Luke."

Jesus' face lit up.

"I'm impressed."

Titus grinned.

"Learned it in the days when I was reading all the scrolls that Paul kept sending me. I'm glad I did. Christians seem to be popping up all over the empire now."

"That's true," Jesus agreed. "Not only is Berenice a Christian, so is my mother Mary. She even saved the crown of thorns from my crucifixion and the board Pilatus ordered nailed to the cross above my head."

"Jesus of Nazareth, King of the Jews," Titus said remembering.

"Yes."

"I'll buy those tokens off of her," Titus said. "Can you imagine what they'll be worth when the whole bloody empire has converted to Christianity?"

"Give me a break," Jesus groaned.

Titus opened his arms wide to show his willingness to embrace the future.

"I know I'm right. Ask her for me. Really. I'll leave them to my heirs."

"Domitian?" Jesus said unkindly.

Titus scowled.

"That was low," he growled. "That little prick is still trying to knock me off." Titus pointed at Jesus' amputated forearm. "I heard about that when I got here," he said. "I guess we can all get saddled with shit relatives, eh?"

"Who told you?"

"Miguel was seeing to my troops and he took me aside." Titus shook his head slowly. "You killed your own grandson. How do you feel about that?"

"I don't regret it. But I would strenuously try to avoid it if I had a do over."

"Miguel said you were trying to prevent an assassination attempt on my life."

"Sad to say, that's true," Jesus admitted. "I warned David off, and he challenged me. Even then he could have lived if he hadn't used his sword *after* yielding."

Titus nodded.

"Let me see your arm," he told Jesus.

Jesus held out his forearm. Titus rested it on his palm and studied it.

"It is completely healed," he said stunned.

"Yes."

"And it happened last night?"

"Yes."

Titus released Jesus' arm.

"This—as much as anything else I know about you—witnesses to the fact that you are truly the Son of your God."

Jesus nodded. Yet God seemed so far away these days. And he himself had become some wholly other person than the young preacher who had declared, "Love the Lord your God with all your heart, and all your soul, and all your mind." His Father—the Deus Absconditus hiding out who knew where—dwelt in his blood veins yet seemed completely absent from his heart, his soul, and his mind.

"You're a bit of a specter these days," Titus said bluntly. "The white locks. The missing hand. Not to mention that at your size you look more like a Viking god than a Hebrew one."

Jesus laughed.

"I'm past being vain," he said.

"That's good," Titus shot back. "Because you sure aren't pretty."

Jesus shook his head and laughed again.

"And I don't mind telling you," he responded to Titus, "that you're not all that impressive in your little boy pants."

Titus raised his wine goblet and drank.

"And you have really hairy legs," Jesus added.

"Sign of manhood," Titus grunted.

"More like animalhood."

Titus stretched out his bare legs and looked at them. Hairy they were. He undid the drawstring on top of his shirt and showed Jesus his chest hair. It was a matt that totally covered his skin. Jesus stared.

"I rest my case," he told Titus.

"Well, the ladies love it," was the emperor's response. "I tell them it harks all the way back to Romulus and Remus, the founders of Rome themselves. Baby orphans who suckled at the teats of a she-wolf."

"And you think that's a true story?" Jesus asked in a mocking tone.

"How can you ask me that when you just saw my chest?" Titus responded.

Both men laughed hard. When Miguel asked Jesus later what he and Titus had chatted about, he answered, "Affairs of state."

— ⚜ —

Titus left to take an afternoon nap. The campaign in Britannia had depleted his robust strength. He had led most of the charges against the wild Celts. At forty years old, the endless fighting had taken its toll. Plus, he'd drunk a lot of wine chatting with Jesus, and that guaranteed he'd be lying down for a couple of hours.

Jesus remained in his study reading a papyrus scroll entitled The Revelation of Jesus Christ. His mother Mary had sent it to him with a message explaining that the visions and exhortations it contained had been delivered to his disciple John by an angel. Jesus began reading. It was elegant Greek and moved him with its very first words.

> *The revelation of Jesus Christ, which God gave unto him, to show unto his servants, things which must shortly come to pass; and he sent and signified it by his angel unto his servant John.*
>
> *Who bore record of the word of God, and of the testimony of Jesus Christ, and of all things that he saw.*
>
> *Blessed is he that readeth, and they that hear the words of this prophecy, and keep those things which are written therein: for the time is at hand.*
>
> *John to the seven churches which are in Asia: Grace be unto you, and peace, from him which is, and which was, and which is to come, and from the Seven Spirits which are before his throne;*

And from Jesus Christ, who is the faithful witness, and the first begotten of the dead, and the prince of the kings of the earth. Unto him that loved us, and washed us from our sins in his own blood,

And hath made us kings and priests unto God and his Father; to him be glory and dominion, forever and ever. Amen.

Jesus put the scroll down. The majestic Greek language made it unlikely that the author was actually John, the youngest of his original disciples. In fact, John did not know Greek. And as a fisherman from a family of fishermen his own native Aramaic had been as elegant as a raw board full of splinters. The genuine author of The Revelation of Jesus Christ had to be another person cloaking himself in John's respectability.

Posing as the last of the Twelve, the writer claimed that he had received messages from angels, God, and Jesus himself. His writing style was contemporary, and his audience was the worldwide assembly of Christian believers, who he awarded status as kings and priests. Quite a promotion for folk who were actually slaves, laborers, unmarried maidens, and unappreciated wives. Were those titles meant to function as eternal rewards? Granted in advance?

Jesus would still read the book, if only to understand current popular thinking in Christendom. He suspected the tome would include few, if any, of his teachings about the challenges and rewards of discipleship. Focusing instead on don't worry. Be happy. Your sins are washed away.

Miguel entered the great room.

"Come in," Jesus welcomed him. "Seat yourself."

Miguel was wearing a black silk robe in official mourning for the late king.

Jesus was still wearing the plain blue robe he had put on before breakfast. He was not in mourning. Officially *or* unofficially. The king was dead. Long live the king.

Miguel took a chair across the desk from Jesus.

"Lord, RoxAnna would like to know if you will attend the funeral service for David tonight."

"Did she express a desire that I do so?"

"She told me that protocol required the king—namely you—to participate."

"So, she dodged expressing whether that was her desire as well?"

"Yes. But I think we can assume that she wants you at the funeral," Miguel responded.

"Your logic?" Jesus asked

"My *deduction*," Miguel replied. "RoxAnna wants you to request that Titus attend as well."

Jesus was stunned.

"The man her son planned to assassinate?"

"Is that a rhetorical question?"

"Yes. I apologize."

"RoxAnna wants both king *and* emperor to attend."

"Tell her that I'll attend and that I will ask Titus. I can't imagine why he'd go though." Jesus looked at Miguel and changed subjects. "Dear friend, would you consider returning to Judea if Mary decides to come with me?"

Miquel bowed his head. Then he lifted it and answered softly.

"I will be eight-one years old this summer, Lord. I would be honored to spend whatever time I have left with you and your sweet daughter."

"It is I who would be honored, Miguel," Jesus told him. "I must request, however, that you remain here long enough to recruit one last company of the younger sons of La Valdieu to migrate to Judea. I also want you to call in the aureuses you have loaned out and bring them to Judea, minus your tithe. How long do you think you will need to accomplish these two tasks?"

"Probably three months to call in the loans, and at least that long to vet additional young men who want to emigrate to Judea. Once we're off, it will be five or six months more before we arrive in Judea."

"So, Mary and I will greet you in Jericho in a year," Jesus responded. "I will ask Titus to provide a safe passage guarantee to smooth your way," Jesus promised.

Miguel nodded his thanks.

"What time is David's funeral? Jesus asked.

"After dark. Nine o'clock I would guess."

"Please have the kitchen staff serve a light meal for Titus and me at seven, and I'll see if Rome's emperor will accompany me to the service. Neither he nor I have been to a Christian funeral. Should be an interesting experience. At least for those of us still breathing."

Miguel bowed.

"I will have dinner sent at seven. May I assist you prior to that in selecting appropriate apparel for the royal funeral?"

"I was going to wear a simple black robe."

"You could," Miguel agreed. "But everyone else will be dressed in sumptuous clothing—both men and women—as a state funeral calls for royalty and landed gentry to display pomp and circumstance."

"Pomp and circumstance?"

"Expensive clothes and big jewelry."

"To impress the cadaver?"

Miguel shook his head.

"They have no regard for the dead king. They dress to impress each other. Do you remember the silver pants, sapphire-colored blouse, and silver sandals that I wore to the banquet?"

"How could I forget?"

"I had a set duplicated for you."

Jesus raised his eyebrows.

"Since last night?"

"But of course." Miguel allowed himself a small smile. "Shall I have the outfit sent down?"

"How can I say no?"

"And may I retire the Persian suit from your wardrobe?"

Jesus held up his amputated left forearm for Miguel to see.

"Touch it and you'll walk around like this for the rest of your days."

Miguel grinned, bowed, and left the great room.

Jesus got up, walked over to a side table, and poured himself a goblet of wine. Then he sat down to read more of fake John's vision of The Revelation of Jesus Christ. There were worse things for a king to do before donning silver pants, a sapphire blouse, and silver sandals for a family funeral. Gossiping servants would have a heyday talking about his new outfit. Though David probably wouldn't notice. If he did, he would most likely not care.

— ⚜ —

Much to Jesus' amazement, Titus accepted RoxAnna's invitation to attend David's funeral mass.

"It's going to be a Christian funeral," Jesus told Titus and arched an eyebrow. "In a Christian church. You know that, right?"

"They're holding a Christian funeral in a Christian church?" Titus responded jovially. "What are they thinking?"

"*They* is RoxAnna. She is not a Christian. And would rather do other things in that building. Like have *your* insides pulled out."

"Wouldn't be a pretty sight."

"No," Jesus agreed. "Neither is David by the way. His face has turned black and it's clearly showing his disappointment about being dead."

"I won't be watching him. I'll be watching everybody else. What should I expect?"

"I understand that the service will be very much like Jewish synagogue worship. Songs. Homily. Prayers. In the Christian service there is also a sharing of bread and wine to memorialize my last meal with my followers."

"Sounds simple and straightforward. What happens to the body afterwards? Is it cremated?"

"No. It is delivered to the royal family tomb where it will be allowed to decay. After a year the bare bones will be transferred to a limestone box."

"Did you have Saul's remains brought here?" Titus asked.

"No. He remains entombed in Jerusalem. I have asked Miguel, however, to bring the box with his bones back here. Judea was his homeland. But LaValdieu was his home."

"Where will *you* be buried?"

"Here. A limestone box has already been ordered to receive my bones."

Titus' face grew pensive.

"The chief reason I wanted to speak with you here in La Valdieu," he said in a very serious tone, "was to request that you allow my ashes to be interred in your family's tomb."

Jesus' face showed his surprise.

"Why, Titus?"

"I have always admired you," the emperor responded. "Above all other men. You are the only man I ever met who is so honest, so transparent, and so accepting. In death, I want to reside in the place where you rest."

Jesus gazed at Titus. The man had no wife. No family. No one who would join him in the grave.

"I grant your request," Jesus told Titus. "You do honor to me and my family."

Titus smiled gratefully.

"I will have to bribe the priests in Rome charged with my cremation to get my ashes delivered to you. As such, the officiants will direct that they be brought to you in a plain metal urn which will bear no name. My remains will be inside, and their disposition will be your burden."

"*Not* a burden, Titus. It will be my privileged task."

There was silence between the two men. Then Titus spoke again.

"My spies in Rome tell me that Domitian plots to kill me when I return. So, it may not be all that long before my leftovers arrive in Jericho."

Jesus shook his head.

"If you know this, why don't you have him arrested?" he asked showing his frustration.

"It is his destiny to be emperor," Titus answered without emotion.

"And how do you know *that*?"

"Before my father died, he told me that he would give me the throne for the decades I had faithfully served him. But he said that the people were afraid of my violent nature. And Domitian—being somewhat bland and pliable—would be preferred by the Senate as the wearer the purple. He was so obsessed with tradition and order, he'd simply be the biggest bureaucrat of them all. I had been good for war. But Domitian would be good for peace. I'd be elevated to the throne to celebrate Rome's triumphs. But Domitian would be crowned to pursue its stability."

"Well," Jesus responded, "your rationalization brings to mind what my father Joseph said when he saw a misshapen stool leg I had just carved. 'Wow,' he said. 'That's a real piece of donkey shit.'"

Titus laughed hard. Vespasian's jinx on Titus' future was causing him to stand down from the throne for a lesser man. Titus' plight was not fate. It was donkey duty.

"So, you'll address this?" Jesus asked.

"I will address it," Titus said. "But I make no promises."

Jesus stood and so did Titus. Without any embarrassment, they hugged long and affectionately. An odd couple, to be sure. But partners in a union that had been blessed—despite all the trials and tragedies they had faced apart and together—and forged into an enduring friendship by Jehovah himself. Or Jupiter.

— ⚜ —

The church interior was almost as dark as the night outside. Candles were lit and shadows flickered on David's face as the worshippers gathered to bid farewell to La Valdieu's deceased king. As Miguel had predicted, the knights and their wives wore extravagant robes and gowns, lined with fur and laden with golden chains dangling giant rubies, pearls, and diamonds. Some wore crosses or crucifixes. Golden declarations of their Christian faith.

Jesus wore the silver pants, sapphire-colored blouse, and silver sandals that Miguel had brought to the manor house. Titus wore an elegantly tailored purple toga and a gold chain around his neck bearing a round golden medallion embossed with the face of Medusa, the snake-haired goddesses of Greek mythology. When Jesus saw that, he looked at Titus and asked who it was. RoxAnna Titus answered.

Jesus, Titus, and Mary sat in the front pew with the queen mother. Miguel sat in the back somewhere, his value unheralded. There was no honor guard placed by David's casket. Jesus had told RoxAnna that any such guard had to be unarmed. He wasn't going to take any chances on the emperor being attacked during the service. RoxAnna had a note delivered to him after his imperative. It was crude and suggestive.

"Fine. No honor guard. Fuck you now. Fuck me later."

The service began. A small choir of men sang Christian hymns acapella. A clergyman wearing a black robe and a silver cross on a chain delivered a brief homily on David's life asking God's grace and forgiveness for his soul. Jesus noticed that he didn't say David had gone to Christian heaven. Must be an honest preacher, Jesus decided. Who would probably get a beating later from RoxAnna's stooges as a reward for that character flaw.

Then the priest blessed bread on a silver plate and wine in a silver chalice and offered them to any Christian worshipper who wished to commemorate Jesus' sacrifice by partaking in a remembrance his last supper. Most of the knights and ladies rose to take part, returning to their places humbly and silently.

At the end of the service everyone stood, and the priest began to chant in a low monotone. Within moments many of the worshippers joined in, singing softly and harmoniously together. Jesus was astonished when he realized that each man and woman was actually singing in a different language. How strange. And yet how beautiful. Sounding like angels, the Christians sang in Latin, Hebrew, Egyptian, Greek, Persian and many other tongues Jesus couldn't identify.

Then—on top of Jesus' surprise at the congregational singing—Titus began to sing softly as well. He had a gentle tenor voice which blended pleasingly with the other voices. Gradually the singing died away and the priest raised his arms and blessed the worshippers with words Jesus recognized as originating from the ever-optimistic Paul. "Blessed be the God and Father of our Lord Jesus Christ, who has blessed us with every spiritual blessing in the heavenly places." That was nice, Jesus thought, though he had no idea what it meant. On the way out of church every knight and every lady bowed to Jesus and Titus. Jesus asked Titus about his singing.

"Did you know that you were singing in Aramaic?"

"I did not," Titus admitted. "Just enjoyed singing along. Really a nice experience."

"You were singing a children's ditty about pee and poop."

Titus stopped and stared at Jesus as lords and ladies bowed and moved on.

"Are you shitting me?" he asked Jesus amazed.

"No."

Titus thought about that for a moment.

"Had to be your God who did that!" he said beginning to laugh. "Pulling one on the old pagan." Titus laughed harder. Then looked at Jesus. "Good for him!"

CHAPTER TWELVE

Jesus got up before dawn to visit the family crypt again. There was a large iron door shut and locked. Outside life. Inside death. He did not go into the vault, but he thought again of its inhabitants. The first burial had been his wonderful friend and RoxAnna's first husband, Alejandro. He had built the castle to protect his kin, yet he had died with his youngest son Arduous in a Gypsy ambush. The same treacherous event that had taken the life of Jesus' own young son David. The boys were interred with Alejandro.

Inside lay his beloved Mary—who snorted when she laughed—slain by Alejandro's youngest son Vercingetorix. His disgraced bones had been gathered by his executioner Saul, Mary's oldest son, and thrown onto the dung heap in his mother's hometown of Magdala. A grotesque homage to her life and death.

There were newly carved-out shelves for bodies yet to be delivered. One for his grandson, David. Another one for RoxAnna. He had ordered his son Saul's limestone bone box to be brought here. It would be placed on the floor near his brother David's box. Eventually there would be boxes for John the Baptist's skull and for his mother

Mary and his daughter. Titus would rest here. And perhaps Berenice. And, of course, someday he would lie here as well, interred next to Mary.

Jesus laid a bouquet of red roses at the entrance for Mary and left a blue bottle of valley wine for Alejandro. So much death, Jesus thought, and so much violence. The Lord giveth and the Lord taketh away. Never had that verse hit Jesus so hard as here and now, standing on the threshold of his decayed loved ones. He didn't bother to add the final part of the verse.

"Hello, Father," Mary's voice greeted him.

Jesus turned and saw his daughter.

"How did you know I was here?" he asked.

"Miguel saw you leave. He asked my servants to wake me that I might keep you company. I am happy to do so."

Jesus gave his daughter a tender hug.

"Why did you think you had to come here alone?" she asked.

"Miquel offered to accompany me, but I wanted to do it by myself. I've grown used it. And frankly I prefer it. Even when I'm dining with guests, or sitting on the throne, I feel alone. I learned after your mother died that it was best to live this solitary existence within myself. Everyone I know will die. Everyone I *love* will die. I cannot bear all that death and loneliness, Mary. So, I don't. I remove myself. Present, but absent. Surrounded, but alone."

Mary hugged Jesus again.

"That's the saddest thing I have ever heard," she said softly.

"I'm sorry," Jesus said. "But I promise that I will be the best person I can be if you come with me."

Mary took Jesus' hand. She turned it over and looked at his palm. The ancient nail hole had scars and a ring of thickened skin. But it still pierced his hand all the way through, and it would be that way forever. Mary touched the scarred wound and then spoke.

"Tell me what you thought about while you were nailed to the cross."

Jesus looked at her questioningly. No one had ever asked him that question in the fifty years since his crucifixion. He gazed at Mary's face and then answered her.

"First there was the simple realization that I was going to die. It was a welcome feeling. My life, my suffering, and my plight were finally ending. I had tried to be worthy of the role of the Messiah, but it didn't seem that there was much about my life to make me worthy of being Jehovah's Anointed One. So, what had been the point of my life, I wondered? And what really was the point of my death?

"There were moments of intense pain on the cross, both physically and emotionally. I watched my mother observing me, as dumbstruck by my circumstance as I. She kept gazing beyond my cross at the hills rising behind Jerusalem. I realized she was clinging to the ancient promise, 'I will lift up mine eyes to the hills, from whence cometh my help. My help cometh from the Lord who made heaven and earth.'

"She did that all the while I hung dying. She only stopped looking when she heard me cry out in despair, 'My God, my God, why hast thou forsaken me?' Images of my life ruled my thoughts. Uncontrolled remembrances of my past. Somewhere, somehow, I knew that I had made a mistake—or a *host* of mistakes—that had led to this failure. To this foul end. *But what were they?*

"I had no idea. I focused on my mother. The first and last face I ever saw. She had encouraged me to believe that I was God's Son from the very beginning of my life. But for what purpose was all I could ask as I hung on the cross? When my time came at last, I looked into her eyes and told her, 'It is finished.' Then I gazed at the heavens above and told Jehovah with my last breath, "Father, into your hands I commend my spirit."

"So, you died—" Mary started to speak and then stopped. What was there to say? Her father had lived his life in obedience to Jehovah and had not given up trying, *even with his final act,* to somehow please him.

"Yes, I died," Jesus responded. "Without honor. Without comprehension. Without approval." Jesus looked deeply into Mary's eyes. "Hard way to die, daughter. Then I awoke. I opened my eyes. What was happening my spirit cried out? But I was not spirit. I was *flesh*. My life was *not* done. My work had not yet been completed.

"For decades I didn't know what that calling would be. I moved to Gaul. Married your mother. Had a family. I was happy. But God was not finished with me. He put Titus in my life and led me on a route that opened my heart and mind to accept that I truly *was* the Messiah. Chosen to protect, cherish, and establish the Hebrews forever as Jehovah's Chosen People. So, it is that I now sit on the throne entrusted to me—the King of the Jews—placed there by the King of the Universe, who raised me from dead to rule until the day that he resurrects everyone from the dead, of which I am the first."

"That sounds really formal," Mary commented, trying to understand her father's long and serpentine reminiscence.

"Well, maybe that's just how I presented it," Jesus told her humbly. "The down-to-earth fact is that I have been brought back from the dead to serve God and man as best I can. But I don't pray. I don't worship. I don't have a relationship with Jehovah. And I don't mind. And he doesn't seem to care."

Jesus looked at the huge iron door standing in front of his family tomb. Feeling the nihilistic thrust of his words, Jesus took out his unhappiness on his own dead.

"I know we tell ourselves that by locking the dead inside it allows them to rest undisturbed," he said. "I also kind of think, though, that it makes us feel better shutting them away."

Mary was hurt to hear her father's words.

"The people in there are our loved ones," she reminded him.

Jesus shook his head.

"No, Mary. What is in there is corruption and decay. No one really likes to say it, but that's what it is."

"*I* don't think that way," Mary responded. "*You* didn't used to think that way either. Jews respect the remains of their deceased loved ones. Honoring the stage in which they lie suspended. Anticipating the resurrection on the last day you just confessed to."

Jesus nodded.

"Is that really what you believe?" Jesus asked.

Mary nodded.

"Yes. So, when you bury me, father, don't regret my demise. And make sure that my bone box is handy, if you please."

"You make it sound blessed, daughter," Jesus said and shook his head. "But it is a forlorn fate."

"*No, it's not*," Mary protested. "It is faith and trust placed in the promises of the Almighty. My bones will eagerly climb out of that box and greet him face to face on judgment day."

Jesus smiled, pleased at his daughter's pluck.

"Do you think about death a lot?" Mary asked.

"Have to say that I do," Jesus admitted. "Caught in the web of what appears to be an endless life makes me view death solely from the perspective of all the people I will lose. It makes me upset."

"So, you feel sorry for yourself a lot?"

Jesus felt like Mary had slapped his face. He looked at her. Begrudgingly, he slowly understood why Mary would say that.

"I will feel less sorry for myself if you reside in my house."

"Cooking, cleaning, and straightening up?" Mary said and smiled wickedly.

Jesus let himself smile, too.

"You're like your mother, you know. Happy to mix things up a little. What I actually had in mind was crowning you Princess in the royal lines of King David and King Saul both of which flow in your flesh."

"And what about the cooking, cleaning, and straightening up?" Mary asked teasing.

"There are servants for those things. And once Miguel arrives he can take over managing them and—when he thinks the time is right—train his replacement."

"Something *you* as king won't have to be concerned about?" Mary asked.

Jesus arched an eyebrow.

"My replacement? No, I still think about it. I don't know the future. Circumstances may make it necessary to pick an heir whose offspring can ascend the throne if the occasion demands it. Or..." Jesus looked his daughter in the eyes. "If you marry and bear a child, he or she will rule in my stead."

"I am too old, Father," Mary said.

"If you marry a man you care for, who knows what can happen? You are comely and bright. You will have a wonderful dowry. And as a royal princess, you will be a great match for some handsome, intelligent man. Granted, you are a bit cheeky, but I think that will diminish as you mature." Jesus smiled a little smile of satisfaction.

Mary blushed. Score one for her father. She looked at him, a smile on his face. Pleased with himself. She hoped he enjoyed it. If she indeed returned to Judea with him, who knew if he'd ever best her again?

— ⚜ —

"Would you like a formal banquet before you depart?" Jesus asked Titus. They were alone together one last time in Jesus' study.

"Lovely setting, this," Titus said, sweeping his arm around the sumptuous room that Jesus' wife had happily created so long ago.

"As I recall, *your* Praetorian apartment was rather sumptuous," Jesus said.

"Ay," Titus agreed. "But lacking a woman's touch."

"You mean the tchotchkes?"

Titus wrinkled his forehead and squinted at Jesus.

"The what's?"

"Tchotchkes. It's a word we Jews have adopted from the fur traders of Sarmatia. It means trinkets, or baubles." Jesus pointed at a small cabinet his wife had filled with silk flowers, ivory animals, and silver figurines.

"Merchants come all the way from the far north to sell their furs in Judea?" Titus asked with surprise.

"Yes. Wealthy women like them on cold nights."

"You should have those traders come back in the summer and sell ice cream to those same ladies."

"Which is?" Jesus asked.

"A desert made from sugar, flavoring, and snow."

"What's snow?"

"It's what's on top of mountains."

"Never seen it."

Titus stared at Jesus for a moment. The King of the Jews had been everywhere in the empire and had never seen snow?

"Snow is rain that freezes into soft fluff. Where it's *cold*. Like the north. Or on the top of a mountain."

"Then I have seen it!" Jesus popped up. "It fell in Nazareth one time when I was little. My mother taught me how to make snow angels. Only time she ever played with me."

"Too busy?"

"Too focused. Teaching me to be the Messiah."

"My mother was older," Titus said. "And she was pretty serious, even when she played with me. Her favorite game was called Snakes in a Basket."

"Card game?"

"No, snake game. She learned it from a Hungarian knight she had lived with before she met my father. She'd fill a basket with snakes, all defanged save one. Trick was to get the coins she'd drop on the bottom of the basket without getting bit by the one with fangs."

"How did you do?"

"Always got the coins."

"*And* got bit to shit.'

"Yep. How'd you guess?"

"Didn't guess. You're the kind of man who gets what he wants no matter the cost."

"I am honored," Titus said and bowed his head in acknowledgment. "Thank you."

"Were you ever wounded during the Jewish War?" Jesus asked.

Titus shook his head.

"Not a scratch."

"Praise Jupiter."

"Damn straight. I was always kind of surprised that Jehovah didn't put a few arrows in my ass. When I got to know him better and I saw that he mainly put arrows in Jewish butts."

Titus and Jesus both laughed.

"Jehovah pretty much does what he wants," Jesus said. "He once told Moses, one of our ancient heroes, that his name was, 'I am that I am.' Pretty non-committal, eh? That Aramaic phrase *also* means 'I will be who I will be.' Icing on the cake."

"Well, that justifies just about everything he ever decides to do," was Titus' take. "Your god should have been a lawyer."

"He's a judge. And believe me, that's a lot worse."

"I can tell by how you look."

"The white hair and chopped off hand?"

"Doesn't take a diviner to figure out that Jehovah is *your* god."

Jesus laughed, entertained. He *was* a wreck. Whereas Titus, the middle-aged ruler of the Empire of Evil, looked as handsome as ever.

"May I ask what's with the hair?" Titus asked. "You wear it long and twisted into braids. Sort of strange."

"What?" Jesus cried. "They're called cornrows!"

"I don't like them."

"Well, *I* do. They look..." Jesus paused to pick the right word.

"Wild," Titus offered.

"Yes, a little, maybe," Jesus agreed. "I'll toss a lock into your funeral urn when it arrives."

Titus laughed.

"By all means! A delightful act of friendship!"

Jesus asked Titus one more time about a farewell feast.

"So, do you want me to have a banquet in your honor before you leave?"

"No. I am sick of banquets. I'd like a meal with you and Mary. And maybe Miguel. And I want you to serve ice cream."

"I don't have snow."

"You can have it fetched from mountains that divide Spain from Gaul."

"I'd have to send people hundreds of miles."

"Perfect," Titus grinned. "Have them seal the snow inside leather wineskins and wrap those skins in more skins."

"You like ice cream that much?"

"I do. It's better than sex," Titus said. "*You'll* love it."

"I'll have an expedition leave tonight."

— ⚜ —

Jesus took advantage of the lateness of the evening to sit alone at his desk and continue to make his way through the elegant and powerful apocryphal letter, The Revelation of Jesus Christ. It actually didn't seem very Christian. Its vindictive style imitated apocalyptic Jewish Scriptures, filled with terrible end-of-days horrors. Jehovah's faithful would ultimately be saved. But everyone else would be agonizingly punished. The faithful were, of course, the Christians. And everyone else was *literally* everyone else.

The Book of Revelation's prophecies of retribution and punishment were meted out by a furious Jesus Christ. There was no love in

Revelation. Little forgiveness. And lots of revenge. Nearing the end of the scroll, Jesus looked up to see RoxAnna approaching his desk.

"Can't sleep?" he asked.

RoxAnna slid into a chair next to Jesus' desk and looked at him.

"Is there any wine?" she asked.

Jesus nodded toward a nearby side table set with goblets and a flagon. RoxAnna rose and poured wine into two goblets. She put one in front of Jesus and sat down with the other. Jesus laid his scroll down and watched her.

"Are we starting negotiations?" he asked.

"No. We're starting foreplay."

Jesus shook his head and reached for his wine.

"You killed my son," RoxAnna told him. "And now I have no heir. No king to unite the Franks. No Holy Emperor to sit on the throne a thousand years from now and rule the world as a Son of God."

"I remember when you came here as a young woman," Jesus said wistfully. "You were beautiful and bold. I thought you were utterly charming."

"And I thought that you looked like someone worth fucking. Now, not so much."

Jesus smiled.

"However," RoxAnna went on, "it's not your icy specter I care about. It's your seed."

"You are aware," Jesus replied, "that any child you might wring from my body will still be mortal?"

"I'm not thinking of a one off. I aim to create a dynasty built over future generations."

"You won't be around to see that."

"No, but *you* will. What a perverse switch, that I, the progenitor, has to bag the one true God. And you, the unwilling deity, has to watch how it all works out."

"Your brain is on fire," Jesus commented.

"So what?" RoxAnna cried out. "The parts of me that need to be productive are waiting and willing."

RoxAnna drank her wine and refilled her goblet.

"You owe me a boy, Jesus," RoxAnna told him. "I am here to have you pay your debt."

"This is my wife's house, and I will not defile her bed."

"Then we will mate outside, on the grass, witnessed by the universe and *its* king."

Jesus stood up, took his goblet, and walked toward the front door. RoxAnna followed, grabbing her goblet *and* the flagon. Jesus knew that Jewish law required that he provide RoxAnna with an heir. She wanted a boy. She might have to settle for a girl. If he honored her request, whoever she conceived would be who she got. He was in no mood to give a refund.

"I'm pregnant."

"That was fast."

"*You* were fast."

Jesus and RoxAnna lay on their backs on the grass fronting the manor house. It was the middle of the night, and both of them had kept all of their clothes on. Procreation had been nothing more than sticking a key in a lock and opening it.

"How can you tell that you're pregnant already?" Jesus asked.

"A woman knows," RoxAnna answered mysteriously.

"Boy or girl?"

"Boy. He will be named Christian."

"Gosh, that's just great," Jesus said. "I think I have to go now."

"You don't like the name?" RoxAnna asked.

"No, I don't. And I'm covered with ants."

"When will I see you again?"

"I don't know. In the meanwhile, I appoint you Steward of the

Kingdom of La Valdieu. Rule it well."

"I'll be faithful."

"I'll be watching."

Jesus stood and helped RoxAnna to stand.

"Go with your God," she told him.

"If he's available," was Jesus' response.

"Oh, ye of little faith."

"Afraid so."

Jesus started walking towards the manor house. RoxAnna called after him.

"He won't let you go, you know. Jehovah *never* lets go."

RoxAnna's words echoed in Jesus' mind. How he wished that was true. He walked slowly. His robe was wet from the night dew. His amputated stump ached. He was ashamed of his union with RoxAnna. His faith had grown pathetic and weak. If there ever was a time for Jehovah to show that he *hadn't* let go him go it was now. Jesus felt like he was in freefall. Unmoored from the divine, he feared that he was going to crash hard if something didn't change. Soon.

— ⚜ —

Miguel whispered Jesus' name.

"Majesty, I have news."

Jesus opened his eyes. He was sitting at his desk, having fallen asleep reading The Revelation of Jesus Christ. Ferocious nighttime reading, but it kept his mind off having slept with RoxAnna. And not just the physical act, but having to face the fact that he would live to not only see the birth of his son Christian, but would endure to watch the entire future of that king and his house. Talk about reaping what you sewed. He sat up and looked at Miguel.

"Pardon me, Lord," his friend said. "It is mid-morning, and Titus has just received a message from General Septimus. Apparently, he left Judea only a few weeks after we did, escorting Princess Berenice.

He is hoping to reach Titus' family estate in Italy by the time the emperor does.

"Septimus also forwarded a missive for you." Miguel extended his hand. He held out a leather bag. Its drawstrings were sealed in wax with the Greek letter B impressed upon it. Jesus did not recognize the mark. He broke the seal and took out the parchment scroll.

> Dear Lord Jesus,
>
> I have dreamed in the Spirit of the Lord and feel compelled to journey from Caesarea to join Titus at his family's home in Aquae Cutiliae. I hope to give him love and consolation at a time when he sorely needs both. I offer them freely, given without any need or hope of reciprocation. If the emperor will have me, I do not know when or if I will return to Israel.
>
> You have been so very kind to me, my Lord. There is no way to adequately thank you. You welcomed me as a sister. And as a Christian I received your lovingkindness like a balm of forgiveness.
>
> Your mother is well, and your big cats like to chase Judas. He takes off at a run when he spots Alpha and Omega roaming the halls of your palace. Then it's just a matter of time before they run him down and lick his face.
>
> May God bless you all the days of your life. If it is possible, when my life is finished, I would like to have my ashes interred wherever Titus is laid to rest.
>
> Your eternal admirer,
>
> Berenice

"Are you awake at last sleepyhead?" Titus cried.

The emperor walked in radiating absolute happiness. He gave Jesus the once over sitting at his desk, then shook his head making disapproving clicking noises with his tongue. He and Jesus stared at each other. The emperor was freshly bathed and wearing his armor. Jesus looked like Titus had ridden him over with his horse.

Jesus waved Miquel closer.

"Bread and wine for both of us, please."

"And some bacon if you have any," Titus added. "Fried potatoes would be good, too."

Miguel bowed to both men, hiding his smile as he left. Titus sat in a chair across the desk from Jesus. He waved a parchment scroll in front of Jesus' face.

"You're the Son of God," he said teasingly. "Omniscient like your Father. What do I have here?"

"A letter from General Septimus telling you that he is escorting Berenice to your family's home in Tuscany."

"By Jupiter!" Titus cried clearly amazed and impressed.

"By Berenice, actually," Jesus corrected him, then waved the scroll he had received from her. Titus reached out his hand and Jesus gave it to him. Titus read it while Jesus watched. He rolled it back up and laid it on Jesus' desk.

"What do you suppose made her change her mind?" Titus asked.

"She didn't spell it out exactly, but I think she had a foreshadowing of your death."

Titus nodded as though it matched his own premonitions.

"You don't seem disturbed by that," Jesus remarked.

"I'm not," Titus replied simply. "I've had terrible headaches and hugely negative moods ever since I was crowned emperor. War is one thing—and the one thing that I'm good at—but governing the empire has been backbreaking. In the two years I've ruled, Mount Vesuvius erupted, murdering scores of Rome's elite in Pompeii and killing thousands of farm families as far as its poisonous gases and ash could travel.

"While I was organizing rescue efforts, Rome itself caught on fire. Four days of sweeping flames eradicated hundreds of square blocks of the city. It not only required heroic efforts to put it out, but an exhaustive clean-up followed by the development of painstakingly detailed reconstruction plans demanded by the Senate as to how and when the city would be rebuilt.

"My father could have handled all that. Domitian, too. But I think I aged twenty years managing those two crises. I am weary, and I am not happy with the thought of enduring this burden, this punishment, for the rest of my life."

"Then resign," Jesus replied straightforwardly.

Titus flipped his head back as though Jesus' suggestion had knocked him silly.

"Emperors don't resign."

"Yes? Well, Messiahs don't resign either, and look what it got me."

"Ha!" Titus barked, appreciating Jesus' self-deprecatory humor. Fact was, Titus thought that Jesus was the bravest man he had ever met. Exceeding even his son Saul's courage. Jesus had carried his burden, accepted his fate, and had not shirked God's terrible demand that he suffer and die. He had risen from the dead, of course, but the fact that such cruelty was required by Jehovah to ratify Jesus' work was unsurpassed.

Titus looked at Jesus. His friend's hair was white, his long cornrows unkempt and wild. His left hand was cut away. He bore eternal wounds in his remaining hand and in both of his feet. Jesus looked worn out. Exactly like Titus felt. But Messiahs didn't resign. And neither did emperors. For all that, both men possessed a wellspring of resilience which the next few moments would prove.

Mary ran into the room.

"There are soldiers outside the house!" she cried. "I can see a half dozen Roman legionnaires through the front windows!"

Titus jumped out of his chair and ran to the entry hall where the windows faced the front gardens and lawn. There were six men on horses wearing Praetorian armor. Two of them were senior officers who the emperor recognized. The others were unknown to him. In a moment Jesus was at his side.

"So," Titus said. "Six legionnaires on horses. All with spears. Not five yards from the house. Are there swords here?"

"No," Mary answered.

"I have my sling," Jesus told Titus.

"Then let's kill five of them," Titus proposed. "And find out from the sixth who sent them." The emperor scowled. "Although I think I can guess." He looked at Jesus. "I will go out and speak to them. You follow me and take out the nearest one. I'll grab his sword, and we'll kill the rest."

"Spears are pretty serious," Jesus reminded him.

"No, they're not," Titus countered. "Wait until you see a Praetorian throw. Then move right or left. It's easy."

Jesus looked at Titus' face. He was focused and intense. Jesus turned and ran to get his sling and bag of stones. Titus waited for him to return, then opened the manor door and stepped outside. Immediately three soldiers tossed their spears. Titus stepped lightly and dodged them all.

"What, ho, Brutus, son of Ovid?" he hollered at one of them. "You throw your weapon before there is even a word exchanged? You are a shame to your tribune rank."

"Say whatever you wish, Titus—"

Titus cut the man off.

"—Emperor Titus, you traitor," he roared in a ferocious voice.

"For some little while longer then, *Emperor*," the Praetorian sneered. "Your title is about to expire."

"At whose command?" Titus shouted.

"Dead men don't need explanations," Brutus shouted back. In that moment Jesus stepped out of the manor door and slung a stone the size of a robin's egg at the loud Praetorian. It hit his cheekbone with such force that it shattered the bone and drove splinters into his brain killing him instantly. The tribune fell off his horse without realizing what had happened. Didn't matter. Dead men don't need explanations.

Titus sprinted toward the dead legionnaire. Two more javelins were tossed, and he dodged them easily. He pulled Brutus' sword from its scabbard and swung up onto the dead man's horse. With a sharp kick Titus drove the horse toward the nearest legionnaire. The Praetorian raised his sword. Titus drove his blade into the soldier's underarm piercing his lungs and heart.

Titus turned his horse around and watched as another Praetorian took a rock to the front of his jaw from Jesus' sling. His chin shattered. Teeth flew in every direction. The horseman sat stunned for a moment, then screamed in pain. A second stone entered his open mouth and exited out the back of his head stopped by his helmet. He slumped forward, dead.

Titus rode his horse toward another legionnaire. The Praetorian lifted his sword and charged at the emperor. Titus taunted him as they raced toward each other.

"Farewell, Gaius, son of Adolphus! I shall personally console your lovely Helena in the best way I know!"

Gaius cried out in fury and slashed his sword at Titus' torso as they passed each other. His blow missed. Titus spun in his saddle and cleaved the back of the Praetorian's neck with his blade. The soldier once known as Gaius tumbled to the ground. Jesus ran up to Titus. The final two horsemen turned their horses to flee. Jesus put a stone to the base of one man's neck directly below his helmet which shattered the top of his spine. He fell as the last Praetorian fled in the distance.

Titus wiped his face with the back of his hand and got down off his horse.

"Let that son of a bitch explain to Domitian that six Praetorians could not best Emperor Titus and Jesus of Nazareth." Titus panted from his exertions.

"You're sure Domitian sent them?" Jesus asked.

"Praetorians? Who else? They're *my* private guard. Sworn to protect me. Disloyal scum." Titus looked at Jesus. "Thank you, partner.

I'm too old to learn how to use a sling, but it's one hell of a weapon in *your* hand."

"That it is. Ancient machinery of death."

"Yep," Titus agreed. "Just like you and me."

Titus and Jesus laughed long and hard standing in the midst of five dead Roman Praetorians sprawled out on the manor house lawn. Jesus asked Mary to fetch Miguel and have the dead legionnaires cast into an unmarked grave. Titus heard him and asked if instead a bronze sign could be mounted that read:

> *HERE LIE FIVE PRAETORIANS WHO CAME UP AGAINST TITUS, EMPEROR OF ROME, SON OF VESPASIAN, AND HI BROTHER, JESUS, KING OF JUDEA, SON OF THE HEBREW GOD. IT WASN'T A GOOD DECISION.*

Jesus accepted the honor Titus intended and bowed his head. Titus gazed at him for a moment. Then winked and bowed his own head. Jesus wondered if his epic relationship with Titus had at this very moment achieved its zenith, fate now poised to intervene and end the strange, bloody, and symbiotic partnership the two had shared for twenty years. It was. Titus was dead within the month.

CHAPTER THIRTEEN

JESUS DEPARTED LA VALDIEU A week after Titus left. Alas, they had never shared the ice cream the emperor had been promised. But Titus had literally bolted, happy that he was going to meet Berenice on his return home. The group Jesus was leading was small. His dozen legionnaires. And perhaps his daughter Mary.

"She's never actually said that she is coming," Jesus told Miguel.

Miguel had smiled.

"I think the odds are in your favor."

Jesus nodded, but felt anxious, unsure of Mary's company.

"My mother told me ages ago," he replied, "not to come back to Judea unless I had grandchildren for her. I think she will be quite happy with her namesake. I am not sure, however, how my daughter will deal with a cranky, bossy, old—very old—grandmother."

"I suspect she will handle your mother with love and kindness," Miguel answered. "It goes a long way with everyone."

"Everyone," Jesus agreed. "Except maybe RoxAnna. I am glad, however, that she is allowing you to recruit another century of young nobles for Judea. Try to spare me too many Christians, however.

They're kind and all that, but so self-righteous. They will be living in Judea after all, and very likely marrying Jewish girls."

"And having Christian babies," Miguel commented.

Jesus frowned.

"Hadn't thought about that. As long as they love and support their fellow citizens, there shouldn't be any issues."

"Right," Miguel agreed. "Especially if you are careful to maintain a majority of Hebrew believers in the government and the military."

Jesus nodded and gazed at Miguel.

"I will look forward to you joining us next year. You realize that by choosing to come and live in my home, you will probably die in Judea?"

"Do you remember when I first met you at Lazarus' house?" Miguel responded. "Since that time, I have traveled to Judea to buy and sell so many times I can't count them all. I will die happy when the day comes that I *don't* have to leave again."

Jesus laughed. It probably *would* take death to finally slow Miguel down.

"When you arrive in Jericho you can use as much gold as you want to refurbish the palace again. Any way that you like. If your own quarters don't wind up being more posh, more artistic, and more flamboyant than Titus' palace in Rome, I'll be banishing you back here to RoxAnna."

Miguel chuckled, and as he had done for eighty years, put his hand over his mouth to cover his crooked teeth. Jesus noticed his gesture, having grown so used to it that he usually missed Miguel's embarrassed action.

"My mother had a problem with her teeth and I was able to help her," Jesus told him. "Maybe I can help you as well?"

"What would be the point?" Miguel asked and spread his hands wide. "Straight teeth are for men who are ready to propose to their brides."

"Ha!" Jesus chortled. "If we fix them now, who knows what may happen in Judea? The country is full of widows who pray for a husband every day."

Miguel blushed and laughed.

"What should I do?" he asked.

"Open your mouth and close your eyes."

"I would feel better closing my mouth and opening my eyes."

Jesus arched an eyebrow.

"Fine," Miguel conceded.

Jesus touched Miguel's face, then lifted up his hand towards heaven and spoke "Father, not my will, but thine."

"Oh, my!" Miguel exclaimed and grabbed his jaw with both of his hands. "I can feel the teeth pressing against the bone!"

"It won't last long," Jesus assured him.

It didn't. Within minutes the pressure subsided. Miguel tasted blood in his mouth and spat it into his handkerchief. He walked to a polished silver mirror in the great room and opened his mouth wide. He couldn't believe what he saw. His teeth were straight and perfect. He put his face right up to his reflection and stared at it. He turned around and faced Jesus. "Why didn't you offer to do this fifty years ago?"

"Oops," Jesus said.

Miguel laughed and looked in the mirror again.

The day of Jesus' departure dawned hot and humid. He was surprised when Miguel told him that the first dozen of La Valdieu's new recruits had already assembled without being asked, ready to begin their journey to Judea. The young men were lined up in their armor—spears and swords strapped to their horses—their saddlebags packed with toiletries and extra clothing.

The men were exchanging farewells with their parents and friends and there was much excited chatter and laughter. Mary was scurrying everywhere with Miguel at her side. They had arranged for several covered wagons to join the enlarged expedition, packed with travel supplies, food, beer, wine, and water, and they were now lined up behind the young nobles.

The Judean legionnaires who had journeyed with Jesus from Jericho divided up to ride at the front and the rear of the caravan as scouts and guards. They were charged with watching for bandits, mercenaries, and Roman troops on the move. With his enlarged company, Jesus suspected that the travelers would be left alone. He hoped so. The plain fact was that the young men from La Valdieu might be good combatants individually, but they had not yet served in La Valdieu's army, and therefore had no training on how to fight together.

Miguel popped by and handed Jesus a cup of chilled spiced wine.

"Did you get breakfast, Lord?" he asked.

"This will do."

Miguel ignored Jesus' comment and offered him his choice of rolls and pastries from a basket he held out. Jesus took two cinnamon rolls spread with sugary frosting.

"Thanks, Miguel," he said graciously. Jesus looked down the line of recruits ready to mount and depart. "Do you know if these men have a commander?"

"There is no commander, my Lord. But the men have asked Harald, son of Keir, to act as their liaison with you."

"Keir, the former captain of the knights of the castle?"

"One and the same. His son is gentle, but don't let that fool you. The men's Nordic nickname for him is Magnus."

"Which means?"

"Giant."

Jesus raised his eyebrows.

"Giant?"

"Or Almighty. Take your pick."

"Ha!" Jesus laughed. "Must be some chap."

Miguel looked down the road.

"See for yourself," he told Jesus and pointed. "He's coming to meet you."

Miguel ran off to catch up with Mary while Jesus watched a very tall soldier approach wearing a square Roman-style helmet and a steel chestplate affixed with a large gold crucifix. He was indeed a giant, at least as tall as Jesus at six-foot-six. He was broad-shouldered and heavy with muscle. Jesus suspected it had been a breeze for him to earn his nickname. Almighty. When he drew within a few feet of Jesus, he stretched out his arm in a salute and greeted him.

"Hail, Lord Jesus, King of Judea."

At that he pulled off his helmet and went down on both knees, head bowed. Jesus touched his shoulder and asked him to stand.

"Harald, son of Keir, rise and let me embrace you."

Harald stood, a handsome young man with blue eyes and long braided blonde hair trailing down his back. He looked Jesus straight in the eyes, then grinned with enthusiasm.

"I remember meeting you when you were just a little boy, Harald," Jesus told him. "You were holding your father's hand. He and I had many adventures together. Those were praiseworthy times, if not altogether happy ones. I grieved when I heard that he had fallen. I loved him very much."

"And he loved you, Lord," Harald said gently.

Jesus stepped forward and gave the Almighty giant a hug.

"Why are you and the others wearing chestplates in this heat?" Jesus asked.

"We'd rather be hot than skewered by some outlander's javelin or spear."

"Looking at you, I can't imagine the man who could accomplish that."

Harald nodded appreciatively.

"And you, my liege, why are you *not* wearing a chestplate?"

Jesus had on a light cotton robe. His sword and spear were strapped to his horse by the saddle cinch and his shield with its golden star hung from his leather saddlebag. His sling was in his belt. He pulled it out for Harald to see.

"Know ye this weapon?"

Harald nodded.

"Then you know that it is deadly. I can use it long before javelins or swords can threaten me."

"I would gladly learn to use such a weapon."

"And you will, lad. Every soldier in the Judean army learns to use it with skill."

Jesus looked at the prominent crucifix on Harald's chestplate.

"You are a Christian, like your father?" he asked.

"Yes, Lord."

"And you know that I am a practicing Hebrew?"

"Yes, Lord."

"Do you have any issue with that?"

"None, my Lord. Save that I will earnestly desire the day when the shields your soldiers carry bear a cross joined to the star. Judea under your sovereign rule will not only be a mighty Hebrew nation, it will be loved and hallowed by tens of thousands of Christian soldiers and their families as well."

"I will remember your words, Harald, son of Keir," Jesus told him. "Your vision recognizes that men of both faiths may live and fight as equals in God's Holy Land. United stars and crosses on the warriors' shields would be a potent emblem for the world to see."

"Thank you, Majesty."

Harald bowed and walked back to his place in line. Jesus mounted his horse and smiled as Mary rode up on her horse and stopped beside him.

"Good morning, daughter," he said happily. "Where are you off to?"

"Wherever you are going, Father," she replied tenderly.

Jesus felt tears come into his eyes and he choked up. Mary saw it and reached over to take his hand. She squeezed it and then let go.

Jesus nodded, his heart full of gratitude. But he would have to wait to speak of it until later.

RoxAnna suddenly appeared walking by herself. Jesus watched the woman—by her own claim pregnant with his child—draw near.

"Farewell, Jesus," she said. "You have pledged to come again to LaValdieu. I will count on that day."

Jesus looked down at RoxAnna. Her still comely face was flushed, a pregnancy glow giving legitimacy to her expectations.

"Rule well, RoxAnna," he told her. "Steward of La Valdieu and faithful vassal. I will be back. Grant me a pleasant return by providing this kingdom with an heir I can be proud of."

"You may take that as my true intent, my king," RoxAnna responded joyfully.

She blew Jesus a kiss with her hand and was gone.

Jesus' raised his arm high and commanded the train of knights and wagons to proceed. He and Mary started down the road.

Mary looked at her father.

"May I ask what that conversation was about?" she asked having listened to every word.

"One laden with portents better left undiscussed," Jesus answered. "Time itself will unseal its truths, whatever they may be."

— ⚜ —

Jesus' journey to Judea was long, but without incident. The Roman roads from Marseilles to Jericho were wide and sturdy. Built for the ages. Mary invited different recruits to dine with Jesus every night until everyone had met the King of the Jews and had a chance to share the stories of their lives.

Harald was the great prize of the batch, being genteel yet brave. He was courteous to all the men and universally regarded with respect and awe. He could read and write both the local Frank dialect and Latin. And he expressed interest in learning Aramaic, the language of Judea, as soon as possible. He believed that it was important that the mix of soldiers in Jesus' army should all speak the same language.

After one evening meal when the guests had gone, Mary asked Jesus who commanded the Judean army. Jesus told her that it was a general named Aias—Aramaic for Ajax—an orphan who had grown up in Judea after his Greek parents had been killed by Zealots at the beginning of the revolt. As a young man he had gone to Roman Africa to fight as a gladiator and had returned wealthy and famous before he was thirty.

Judas had recruited Aias into the army at the very beginning. He had quickly displayed the leadership talents necessary to rise through the officer's ranks and become a general. He had subsequently been given control of the army with the responsibilities of training and promoting officers as well as absorbing the masses of new recruits that arrived every year.

Mary spent a lot of hours learning how Jesus had organized his army, his government, and his own personal staff. Her conclusion was that her father possessed a thorough knowledge of the requirements and duties of his government and army leaders, but had little awareness of—or connection to—those who actually performed the tasks associated with running his kingdom and military.

Jesus didn't protest her findings. He liked to delegate, and he trusted those who had been given significant roles in his administration. Mary believed that he should develop personal relationships with all of his senior officials. Learning their names, families, and aspirations, just as he had done with the La Valdieu recruits on the trip back to Jericho.

"You are the one constant in the lives of these army officers and government administrators," Mary told him. "Use your person, your reputation, and your interest in those who serve you to build a loyal network of agents who will not only take care of your kingdom, but will watch and listen to everything that goes on, privately supplementing the information you receive through official channels."

Jesus nodded and looked at Mary.

"Daughter, I suspect that you could rule Judea better than me." Mary flushed, but listened. "Therefore, I would like you to take on the overall management of the government and military establishments. I will meet and forge bonds with whoever you bring to me. But the day-to-day affairs of those organizations will be directed to *you*. I'll make this role public when I declare you the Crown Princess and my successor."

Mary remained silent for a moment. Her father was offering her the opportunity not just to manage, but to shape the fledging entities of his government and military. To actively set in place roles and models that would direct the growth and shape the stability of Jesus' kingdom far into the future. It was a unique offer.

"I accept with humility and resolve, Father,' she answered humbly. "And I thank you for this opportunity. I will do everything in my power to avoid disappointing you."

Jesus smiled at his daughter's seriousness.

"I can't imagine that you will fail me, Mary. And, lest you wonder, there will still be time enough for love and marriage if you choose such a future."

Mary bowed her head.

"Come, come," Jesus said to her. "Who knows what bright and handsome soldier or civil servant will catch your eye?"

Mary smiled, but did not speak. She was middle-aged, but still pretty. She was a virgin, but had taken no oath of chastity. She would have no regrets giving herself to the right man. In the meanwhile, she had the momentous task of organizing Jesus' kingdom and making him intimate with its movers and shakers. With a little luck though she might find someone to move and shake *her*. She suddenly laughed out loud at her own thoughts and snorted, trying to stop.

"Your mother made that exact same sound when she laughed," Jesus remarked and smiled happily at the memory. "Maybe when she was thinking the same thoughts as you were just now."

Mary laughed again, snorted again, and resolved not to be filling her head with thoughts about sex when she was around her father. Jesus just shook his head and smiled.

— ⚜ —

Jesus' mother Mary was waiting outside the palace doors. She stood with a cane and a smile. Jesus was familiar with the cane. Not the smile. He beckoned his daughter to walk with him. They were both wearing robes and sandals. His mother was dressed in a dark blue robe with a light blue scarf covering her hair. Jesus had sent a courier from the road telling Mary that her granddaughter was in the returning company. Now as they approached, his mother tossed aside her cane and came out to embrace the child of Jesus and Mary Magdalene who she had never seen.

"Mary, Mary," she cried holding her close. She was tiny compared to Jesus' daughter. She stepped back and took Mary's face in her hands.

"Welcome, sweet Mary," she crooned. "Have you come to live with us?"

"At Father's kind bidding, I have come to dwell in Judea with you and him," she answered softly.

Mary's grandmother studied her face.

"You are quite beautiful, lass. Why are you not married and carting children around with you?"

"It was not God's will," Mary answered.

"Oh, nonsense," her grandmother replied. "Getting a man to marry you is more a matter of snagging them than praying for them."

Jesus arched an eyebrow, and his daughter grinned with surprise.

"I am serious, dear girl," Mary almost scolded. "Mary Magdalene had Jesus twirled around her little finger and 'followed' him all the way to Gaul. And if I may speak for only a moment about my own circumstances, I managed to get Joseph to marry me despite the fact that I already had a loaf baking in my oven. Namely your dad."

Jesus shook his head and Mary stood stock-still, having no idea whether her grandmother was serious or not. Jesus spoke to his mother.

"Stop teasing your granddaughter, Mom. A better use of your time would be to instruct her on exactly *how* to ensnare the man of her dreams."

"Ho, ho!" his mother exclaimed. "Leave it to me!" she cried and grinned. Her mouthful of healthy white teeth was a sight to behold. Jesus could already see her demanding that Miguel open his mouth to compare their dental work when he arrived. If either of them lasted as long as their new teeth, they'd be around for another fifty years.

Jesus felt a pang of sadness. How he wished that could somehow be true. He stepped over to his mother and squeezed her tight. Mary touched his cheek and patted his face. As she withdrew, she grabbed Jesus' amputated forearm.

"This is new," she said frowning. "And not nice."

"Lost it in a fight with a barbarous king," Jesus replied. He had long practiced for this moment when he'd be required to tell his mother what happened. "I defeated him in single combat and after he yielded, I turned away. He lunged at me and cut off my hand."

Mary looked up at her son's face.

"And what did you do?"

"I cut off his sword arm," Jesus said.

"Good. Served him right. Was he a Roman bastard?"

"No. He was a Christian bastard."

Mary scowled and pondered that.

"Are you sure?" she asked slowly.

"Pretty sure. He had a Christian funeral."

Mary scowled again.

"Did he have time to pray before he died?"

"He had time while he bled out, so he might have managed to get in a last prayer, too."

"My, aren't you cold?" Mary said disapprovingly.

"My arm was shooting out blood, Mom," Jesus told her. "I was not terribly focused on last rites for the man who had just tried to kill me."

"It's all right. If he truly was a believer, then Jehovah will have sorted it out."

"Does he do that for Jews, too?" Jesus asked.

"I suppose it depends on what they've done. *And* what they say in the process of dying. But yes, I'm sure that he reaches out to both Christians and Jews."

"I'd like to think that God even extends his grace to the unsaved," Jesus told her.

"What are you thinking?" Mary cried horrified. "Christians and *maybe* Jews. Everyone else belongs to God's *unChosen* People."

Jesus shook his head.

"You're a tough old bird, Mom. Make sure that you and your believer friends avoid being exclusive and self-righteous."

"That's never going to happen," Mary responded indignant. "Christians don't think they're better than anybody else."

Jesus was incredulous.

"Have you read that book you sent me?" Jesus asked. "You know. The Revelation of Jesus Christ?"

"Yes!" Mary answered enthusiastically. "I really got into it. Good old John."

"Do you recall what the author records about the returning Messiah's criteria for salvation when he judges the peoples of earth?"

"That they repent and believe on the Lord Jesus Christ!" Mary answered triumphantly.

"No. He doesn't even talk about that."

Mary frowned and pursed her wrinkled lips. The deep lines that appeared around her eyes and mouth made it obvious that she had made that face her whole lifetime.

"Then what *did* he ask?" Mary wanted to know, obviously upset that she had not remembered correctly. Then suddenly fearful that it wasn't going to be something she wanted to hear after all, she held her hands up as though to stop Jesus. She was too late.

"Christ the Judge is ready to save all those who fed him when he was hungry, clothed him when he was naked, and visited him when he was imprisoned."

Mary frowned deeply.

"That can't be right," she protested.

Jesus looked amused.

"No?" he asked.

"*Nobody* has done any of that."

"You're exactly right, and in Revelation the people of earth respond quite defensively that not only did they *not* do any of those things for him, they had never even had the opportunity to do so. The Christ nods and agrees, but then amplifies and explains. "Whoever helped *any* hungry person, whoever dressed *any* naked person, and whoever visited *any* prisoner will be rewarded *as if they had done it to him*."

"No," Jesus' mother said again, shaking her head. "That doesn't make any sense."

"I believe it does, and I agree with all of my heart."

"Well, I don't," Mary said in a huff. "Either you're wrong, or that book is wrong. Let me read it again."

"You don't know how to read Greek, Mother."

"Someone read it to me before, and they can read it to me again. I want to hear that malarkey at the end."

Jesus smiled and watched his mother retreat back inside the palace. As she did, General Aias appeared. He was wearing a cream-colored toga—a frequent choice for him—reflecting his status as a gladiator who had survived innumerable contests and had been heralded as a hero of Rome.

He was of average height, olive-skinned, with a perfect oval face, thin lips, an aquiline nose, and black curly hair. He was trim, well-muscled, and bore no obvious scars. Jesus had once asked him how he had managed to not only survive the gladiatorial bouts, but to do so without being disfigured. Aias told him that it was because of God's grace *and* his own ability to attack his opponents as fast as lightning. Good assets, Jesus thought. Especially the fast as lightning one. General Aias saluted his king and welcomed him.

"Hail, Lord Jesus," he said. "Welcome back to your home and to your kingdom."

"Thank you, Aias. All is well, I trust?"

"All is indeed well, Majesty." Aias pointed at the line of men from La Valdieu standing by their horses outside the walled gates. "Though it looks like you have brought me another bunch of babies, my Lord."

"Yes, I have General. But they come with adventure in their hearts."

"Marriage and children?"

Jesus smiled.

"Yes. Those adventures. *And* military training as well."

Jesus looked at his daughter, put a hand on her shoulder, and introduced her.

"Aias, this is my daughter, Mary. She will be your partner and I hope your friend. She will assist me in running the affairs of the kingdom."

Aias bowed his head.

"Welcome, Princess. Welcome to your new home."

Mary nodded and smiled.

"Mary, will you take Aias to Harald? He has a dozen future knights to introduce to the general."

"Immediately," Mary responded and asked Aias to join her. As they exited the palace's walled gates and walked down the line of men, horses, and wagons, kitchen staff poured out of the palace with beer and bread to refresh the travelers, even as livery boys took their horses to be watered and fed. Suddenly Judas hurried out the front entrance of the palace. He pulled the doors closed and braced his back against them. Jesus walked over to him.

"Ho, Judas! Why are you blocking the entrance?"

"As if you didn't know," Judas snapped angrily.

Jesus laughed out loud. Of course, he knew.

"Are you hiding from Alpha and Omega?" he asked.

"Does it look like I'm hiding?" Judas answered furiously. "I'm *avoiding*. Trying to save my scrawny neck from your *pets*."

Jesus laughed again.

"Move aside and I'll save you."

Judas scowled and stepped away from the wooden doors. Jesus swung them open. Waiting there were Alpha and Omega, his magnificent lions. They stood up on their hind legs and licked his face.

"Whoa, boys!" Jesus cried. "Missed me, eh?"

The lions licked his arms and his hand and purred.

"See, Judas, they're just big kittens."

"Right," Judas responded still grumpy. "Just wait until they finish with you and see what happens."

It didn't take long for the cats to realize that Judas was still nearby. Their favorite person in Jesus' absence. With a leap Alpha bounced his muzzle against Judas knocking him over. Omega rested his front paws on Judas' chest and licked his face.

"Get off of me!" Judas cried.

Jesus walked over.

"The boys won't hurt you."

"I'm not worried about being hurt!" Judas shouted. "I don't want some big, stupid lion thinking I'm his chew toy."

"But you are," Jesus told him. "Kind of." He knelt down and tickled Judas' underarm.

"Oh, please, no!" Judas cried. "What did I ever do to deserve this?"

Jesus grinned and ordered the cats to come and stand by him. They obeyed without hesitation.

Judas got up slowly.

"That happened every day while you were gone," he said offended.

"Why didn't you take them to Mary?" Jesus asked. "These fellas can always use a little motherly love."

"Not from *her*. They're scared to death of that old bag."

"Excuse me?"

"Sorry, Lord. I know she's your mother. But she's also a terror. *Nothing* is ever right, and *somehow* it is usually my fault."

"Thank you for being patient."

"I wasn't patient!" Judas cried. "We fought all the time!"

Jesus helped Judas stand. He embraced him warmly.

"It's good to see you, my friend," he told him. "Even if you are upsetting my mother."

Judas stared at Jesus.

"That was a humorous remark, right?" he asked.

Jesus laughed.

Judas straightened his robe and tried to recover his dignity.

"The things that were *my* responsibility ran smoothly in your absence," Judas claimed.

"I heard two hundred and seventy-three petitions and I ruled on all of them."

"You *ruled* on them?" Jesus asked very surprised. "I thought you were just going to have them recorded and filed."

"There *are* some appeals," Judas admitted.

"Some?"

"One hundred and forty-six. More or less."

Jesus rolled his eyes.

"There is also a visitor waiting to see you," Judas went on. "He has lodged here two nights waiting for your arrival."

"Who is it?" Jesus asked.

"General Septimus," Judas answered. "He said he had news for your ears alone."

Jesus knew in an instant that something had happened to Titus.

CHAPTER FOURTEEN

"PLEASE TAKE WORD TO GENERAL Septimus that I have arrived," Jesus told Judas.

"Shall I have a lunch brought in?" Judas asked.

"Yes, thank you. Are there any plaintiffs waiting for you?" Judas shook his head. "Then go and join the recruits and introduce yourself to my daughter Mary. She has come to live with us and administrate Judean affairs."

"Actually, I will *re-introduce* myself, Lord," Judas replied stiffly. "I met Mary when I visited La Valdieu."

"Yes, of course, you did," Jesus said. "My oversight. Go share my message with Septimus, and give Mary a hug."

Judas hobbled off to find Septimus. Jesus walked through the palace to his public office. Alpha and Omega walked next to him, nudging his ankles with their foreheads, marking the master as their own. Jesus entered his royal office. It was elegant and Spartan. Marble desk. Marble chairs. He would savor its bare bones simplicity for as long as it took Miguel to move here. Once that happened, his dear old friend would undoubtedly *sumptuize* it.

Probably go through all his clothes too. Jesus made a mental note to hide the threadbare Persian pants suit his wife Mary had given him. He liked it. He wore it. He didn't care that his loin cloth showed through at his bottom.

Jesus noticed that Judas had left more parchment scrolls on his desk that he had procured from households whose scholar had perished in the revolt. Twelve years after the Roman destruction, folks were rebuilding towns and farms with help from Jesus' government. But books were passe. You couldn't eat them. You couldn't plant them. You couldn't even sell them unless someone like Judas appeared.

This current batch of parchment scrolls appeared to have come from the same library. They were treatises composed by a mystical splinter group of Christians that referred to themselves as Gnostics. *Those in the know*. He opened random scrolls and read the titles. The Dialogue of the Savior. The Book of Thomas the Contender. The Apocryphon of James. The Gospel of Philip. The Gospel of Thomas. Jesus was sure that they were all fakes. Falsely credited to the hands of known historical authorities on Jesus' life.

He had seen such books before. His favorite was The First Gospel of the Infancy of Jesus Christ. In that gem, adolescent Jesus turned children he didn't like into animals. And simply struck adults dead who rubbed him wrong. Junk. Amusing junk. But junk nonetheless. All of these new acquisitions would likely turn out to be junk as well. He was sure that he would enjoy reading each and every one of them.

Septimus appeared in the office doorway. Jesus walked over to him. The general fell to his knees. Jesus urged the Christian believer to rise. He did. Then Jesus offered him his hand. Septimus shook it.

"I am sorry that you had to wait," Jesus told him. Septimus' face looked deeply troubled. Jesus' heart sank, fearing the news that he dreaded most. "Do you bring tidings of the emperor?" he asked in a quiet voice.

Septimus nodded solemnly.

"The worst news, Lord Jesus. Emperor Titus is dead."

"When?" Jesus asked quietly.

"Three months ago now. As you know, he wanted to visit his family home in Aquae Cutiliae before returning to Rome. I intercepted his party on the way, escorting Berenice. Titus was delighted that she had come. I believe that she insisted that their relationship be platonic, but it did not diminish his happiness at just being with her. We traveled the last week together, but alas, the second night at his family's estate Titus fell ill after taking his evening meal and died."

Jesus frowned, puzzled.

"Poisoned?"

"Yes. Undoubtedly administered by the hand of a household servant acting on orders from Domitian."

Jesus scowled and spoke with intensity.

"You are *sure* his meal was poisoned?"

"Without a doubt," Septimus maintained. "Berenice dined with him—just the two of them—and she sickened and died alongside Titus."

Jesus' head reeled at the news of the double murder. He was overwhelmed by the tragic news. He wiped his tears away with the back of his hand and told Septimus to sit down.

"So tragic," Jesus said. "I couldn't help but love him. Such a charming rogue. I shall miss him every day for the rest of my life." Jesus wiped away his tears again. "Has Domitian been crowned?"

"Not yet. But the Senate will surely proclaim him emperor before the year is over. Domitian has bribed every senator and every Praetorian. I was at Titus' side when he died.

His final words were, "I die regretting only one mistake in my life."

Jesus remembered when Titus had shared those same words with him. He waited for Septimus to repeat what he had heard. The general choked up, unable to speak.

"Crucifying Saul," he finally whispered.

Jesus sighed.

"What happened to Titus' body?" he asked.

"The emperor was cremated immediately. As was Berenice. On the emperor's own orders their ashes and bones were mixed. They were given to me. I have them safe. They are yours whenever you command."

Jesus nodded gratefully.

"It was his wish to rest in my family tomb in La Valdieu," he told Septimus. "Thank you."

Servants appeared at the door, bearing wine and food. Jesus nodded and they entered. He pointed at his desk. The servants set down a silver wine flagon, two silver goblets, a tray of cold roast lamb, a mixed salad tossed in oil and vinegar, a platter of bread, and an herb dip. Wine was poured into the goblets and given to Jesus and his guest.

"Septimus. Please eat and drink while we plan."

"Plan what, Lord?"

"We know that the emperor's brother murdered him. While there is nothing we can do about that, you and I are going to return to Aquae Cutiliae and find out which persons administered the poison to Titus and Berenice." Jesus locked eyes with Septimus. "Then one by one, we will cut their throats."

— ⚜ —

They rode all day everyday sleeping only a few hours a night at inns along the way. They did not force their horses to move faster than a steady walk, but they did not halt until well into the night. Even with such long travel hours, it would take close to a hundred such days to reach their destination of Aquae Cutiliae, fifty miles north-east of Rome.

Septimus and Jesus did not talk much while riding, often because winter rain and wind encompassed them almost every travel day.

They did not talk much at night either, sharing a late dinner in the inns where they stayed. Jesus carried enough gold to cover any expenses. Used generously, there was no difficulty having their horses cared for at odd hours, or having late dinners prepared.

Near noon on the ninety-fourth day of their journey, Jesus and Septimus saw the foothills that rose behind Aquae Cutiliae, home of natural hot springs where many Roman families came to soak away their stresses and strains. Titus' father Vespasian had purchased land here when he was serving in the Praetorian Guard and had built a large villa. Titus grew up savoring the times he got to be in the country. Riding. Hiking. Swimming. Banging swords with Domitian.

The villa had been maintained by slaves who kept it in a state of readiness for Vespasian's visits. And then for Titus. How he must have anticipated spending time with Berenice here on his last trip, before forcing himself to set his face towards the capital once again. Only, that never happened.

Jesus was sure Titus had worked diligently to bed Berenice during that final visit. Instead death had bedded him. Likely not as pleasurable. So long, breath and appetite. So long, laughter and kisses. So long, Titus.

Jesus and Septimus stopped within fifty paces of the villa. It was constructed in typical Roman fashion. Three stone wings with a mosaic courtyard in the center of the u-shaped building.

"How many slaves would you say there are?" Jesus asked.

"At least twenty inside," Septimus estimated. "Probably twice that outside."

"Soldiers?"

"None now. Though Titus had ridden with a hundred Praetorians."

"Who served Titus his food?"

"The night of his death, he ate alone with Berenice in a private dining room adjacent to the royal bed chamber. I posted two legionnaires at the dining room entrance and two more at the bedroom's entrance. I stood with the soldiers outside the dining room, noting which slave took each course into the couple."

"You experienced a foreboding of Titus' death?"

"In a way, yes. Vespasian died in this summer house, too.Three years ago. He was old, but vital. And then one day, he couldn't get out of bed. He insisted on being helped to his feet commenting that a real man died on his feet. Alas for him, he did not die, and had to lie down again. When at last he did speak his final words, he did so with some jocularity. 'I think I'm becoming a god,' he said, taking a shot at the Senate's habit of deifying emperors."

"But he wasn't murdered?"

"Who knows?" Septimas replied and shrugged. "We wouldn't have known that Titus died of poisoning if Berenice had not had the misfortune to dine with him."

"Will you recognize the kitchen manager?" Jesus asked.

The general nodded.

"The service manager?"

Septimus nodded again.

"We have to believe that one of them—or both—were involved in dousing the food with poison," Jesus said. "We'll see who feels like confessing. I am not going to identify myself. You may be recognized, but I suggest you not acknowledge it if anyone uses your name."

"I agree."

"Let's do this."

Jesus and Septimus drew their swords and rode up to the villa's entrance. No one appeared. Jesus looked at Septimus.

"Do you want to roust them," Jesus asked. "Or watch the front of the villa?"

Septimus dismounted and put his sword in his scabbard.

"You're going in with your sword sheathed?" Jesus asked surprised.

"Yes. I'm not going to kill anyone by accident."

Septimus tried the front doors. They were not locked. He pulled them open and entered. Jesus watched and waited. In minutes, a steady stream of young men and women poured out the entrance and stood huddled together in front of the villa. Two older men dressed in wool robes came out last, followed closely by Septimus. One was thin and bald and walked confidently. The other was very short and very fat with graying curly hair. Jesus was pretty sure that he was looking at the staff manager and the service manager. Septimus told them to step forward to where Jesus sat on his horse. Jesus' noted that the general had his sword in hand now.

"My Lord," Septimus spoke up. "These two men are the prime suspects in Titus' poisoning." He pointed his sword at the thin bald man. "This is Felix, responsible for the serving staff." Then he pointed at the rotund man. "This is Cato, head cook and manager of the kitchen workers."

Septimus came around and faced the two men.

"There is a quick death for the man who admits that he carried out Domitian's orders to murder his brother," Septimus spoke in a stern voice. "What say ye?"

Neither man spoke up.

"Kill them both," Jesus said.

"No, sir, please!" the cook suddenly cried out. "I did not poison my dear Lord Titus."

"You are innocent," Septimus told him. "Step aside."

Felix, the service manager, scowled when he heard Septimus' words. Cato stepped away from him rather nimbly.

"Confess, so innocent people don't die," Septimus told Felix. He stood close to him sword in hand. "If you poisoned your lord and master for money, then don't speak.

But if you did it for Rome, or for love of Domitian, then say so and go to your eternity proudly."

Felix folded his arms and spoke.

"Titus was a vain buffoon. Domitian is a Roman. The likes of his father Vespasian. Sturdy. Level-headed. A man who can sustain the empire with wisdom, not by threats and violence, and who will now have the opportunity—"

Before Felix could finish Septimus plunged his sword into his chest. The slaves screamed in terror. Jesus got down from his horse and walked over to the cowering servants.

"Which of you was the taster for the emperor?" he asked.

A man in his thirties stepped forward, dressed in a linen robe with a long black ponytail.

"What's your name?" Jesus asked.

"Otho, son of Andreas," he answered in an even voice, apparently unafraid of what could happen next.

"You didn't taste the food that was served to Emperor Titus, or his lady guest, did you?"

"I was warned not to by the man who was just killed."

"So, you knew that it was very likely poisoned and you did nothing?" Jesus asked.

Otho dropped to his knees and bowed his head. Jesus waited for him to cry out for mercy. He did not. He would die without regrets. Jesus looked at Septimus. The general stepped over and raised his sword. He cut the head off the conspirator who had earned his doom. His body fell silently to the ground.

"No one else needs to die," Jesus told the stricken slaves. "Except for the servers who carried the untested food to Titus and Berenice. Step forward on your own, or I will have you identified."

Two teenage girls walked forward together holding hands. Both were thin and very young, wearing shifts made from cheap material. One had curly red hair and a pretty freckled face. The other girl had a plain pale face and brown hair. Neither girl was more than twelve or thirteen. Jesus walked up to them.

"You served the food?"

"Yes, Lord," the red-haired girl answered. She began to sob. "It was handed to us by our master, Felix. We always served the emperor. He felt safe and happy around us."

"Because you were harmless?"

"Because we are Christians and would hurt no one."

"Well, you killed a man who did not deserve to die. And I will clean the slate of his murderer by doing the same to you."

Septimus stepped forward in protest.

"Lord, these are but children!" he cried. "Killing them is madness."

Jesus looked at Septimus, his face dismayed.

"They served Emperor Titus the food without having the taster do his duty," Jesus said angrily. "They killed him as surely as the dead men on the ground."

"You're wrong!" Septimus answered upset. "The guilty have been punished. Our work here is done. If you harm these children, it would be better that you had a millstone hung around your neck and be cast into the sea, rather than face the wrath of God for such a sin."

Jesus stared at Septimus.

"I'm the one who said that," he murmured.

"A long time ago," Septimus said. "When you were yourself."

Jesus looked into Septimus' eyes. What the general said had cut him to the heart. Because it was true.

"Thank you, brother," he told Septimus. Jesus felt shocked and dazed.

The general began giving orders for the disposition of the bodies. Jesus removed a handful of gold sesterses from his saddlebag. He gestured for Cato the kitchen manager to take them. "This to bury the dead," he said.

Septimus looked at Jesus and then mounted his horse. Jesus did as well. It was time to go home.

— ⚜ —

There was no talking on the return journey. Jesus thought again and again about the two children he had almost killed. What had he been thinking? Titus had probably loved those two little girls. Neither he, nor they, knew that the meal they served him and his guest was filled with death. Yet he had been ready to have them cut down as quickly as the guilty serving master and food taster.

Jesus understood in his heart that he had become a harder and more demanding man in his role as King of Judea. But up until now he hadn't really questioned if that was a bad thing. God had sent him to protect and save the Jews from persecution and extinction. And *whatever* it took to carry out that mission, he would do.

He also knew that despite his acknowledgment that Jehovah was up there somewhere, he didn't feel close to, or in touch with God's person, plans, or desires. He had become hard-hearted because he was alone. Relying on his own strength and his own wisdom to get things done.

His old antagonist the Apostle Paul had once declared, 'When I was a child I spoke as a child, I understood as a child, I thought as a child; but when I became a man, I put away childish things.' Jesus had put away his love for God. Had put away his own gentleness and forgiveness. He *wanted* to feel hard and powerful. Respected and feared. He was an adult done with childish things. He was the King of the Jews. Yet after the journey to Aquae Cutiliae, Jesus began doubt the wisdom of this choice. Was there indeed another way?

"Father, you don't look well," his daughter Mary told him. Jesus had been back for several days, and was having trouble eating and sleeping. He was wrestling with his dreams and his fears. He and his daughter were walking together along the Jordan River accompanied by Judas. Two bodyguards followed. Jesus was surveying the new greenery that Mary had ordered planted along the river. Thousands of flowers, bushes, and palms. He wore a light cotton robe. Mary wore a red sheath made of linen. Judas wore short black pants and a short-sleeve gray cotton shirt.

Judas walked carefully, but had no difficulty keeping up with Jesus and Mary. Mary told Jesus again—as she had every time she had seen him since his return—that he didn't look well. He didn't respond, choosing to focus on the lush beauty of the full-grown palms planted along the Jordan.

"This is a wonderful, Mary," Jesus remarked. "I like the palms and the wide promenade for pedestrians. It's so quiet! Have you banned commercial traffic?"

"Yes," Mary answered somewhat adamantly. "Including delivery boys all in a rush."

"Thereby allowing you, me, and Judas to exemplify a vaunted Roman paradigm," Jesus remarked. "The family out together."

"Rome should be so lucky," Mary told him. "The empire's birth-rate continues to decline. Too much wine and too few marriages."

Jesus turned his head and looked at Mary.

"Is that true?"

"Of course, it's true. Official census reports suggest that by the year 400, there will not be enough Roman soldiers to defend even the capital city itself against the Franks, the Goths, or the Huns."

Jesus shook his head surprised. He'd think about that. As Rome's vassal, he didn't want to consider that a future day could come when a Hebrew army largely composed of the descendants of Jewish men who had been slain in the great revolt would be called upon to save Rome. That was beyond ironic. It was nauseating.

Mary saw Jesus blanch and asked him again if he felt ill.

"Jesus! Answer your daughter already," said Judas irritably. "Also, may I remind everyone that Roman mothers have access to herbs and potions that can prevent pregnancies or even abort the little Caesars inside of them. One more reason the goddamn empire will fall."

Jesus stopped and stared at Judas.

"That's nonsense. Your mother took those herbs and look what happened."

"Lucky me!" Judas cried and waved his remaining arm in the air.

"Also," Jesus asked, "did you just swear?"

Judas craned his head toward Jesus. His hair was mussed, and his face was lined, but his eyes still burned intensely when he talked about the hated Roman Empire.

"Don't think I did," he answered.

"You did," Jesus contradicted him.

"Mary?" Judas appealed.

"You did."

"Does it count if I can't remember?"

"Yes, it does," Jesus told him. "Good thing you're not in my court charged with swearing."

"Is *that* against the law now?" Judas asked, uncertain whether he was really in trouble.

"Not yet."

"Whew," Judas said. "I'd hate to be in the throne room on the wrong side of the throne."

Jesus smiled and started walking again. Not far ahead on the pedestrian walk, two girls were approaching. They were dressed in blue cotton shifts and wore white headscarves. Maybe age eleven or twelve. Each carried a large bouquet of long-stemmed calla lilies. As they drew near, Judas stepped in front of Jesus and stood between him and the girls. He muttered that the bouquets were so big. Jesus had no idea what that meant, but he stopped and let Judas talk to the girls. Both of his bodyguards stepped forward and flanked Judas.

"Hello, young ladies," Judas said. The girls stopped and stared at him. Had a golem escaped from the graveyard? They glanced at its forehead, searching for the magic words of life, aleph, mem, and tav. They were not there. So, this was just an old ugly man.

"Are those flowers for the king?" Judas asked.

The girls nodded.

"Why are your bouquets so very, very big?" Judas questioned. Neither girl spoke or moved. "They must be heavy," Judas continued. "Why don't I help you carry them?"

The girls stood frozen in their steps. When Judas leaned down to look at one girl's bouquet, she pulled a dagger out of the lilies and stabbed him in the throat. Stricken, Judas collapsed. One of the bodyguards knocked the knife out of the girl's hand with his shield, even as the other girl threw her flowers down, leapt over Judas' prone figure, and lunged toward Jesus with a knife in her hand. The other bodyguard tripped her with his spear. Down she went, the knife flying out of her hand.

The two soldiers held the girls at sword point as Jesus and Mary knelt by Judas. Blood was gushing out of his neck. Jesus put his hand on Judas' cheek and Mary tore a sleeve off of her robe trying to staunch the gush of blood from Judas' neck.

Judas looked at Jesus.

"Don't heal me," he whispered.

Jesus pulled back stunned.

"I am sorry not to see you restore Judea to greatness," Judas said breathing hard. "Maybe on Judgment Day I'll get to see it in all of its glory."

Mary began to weep, still holding the cloth against Judas' wound. The flow of blood had diminished and Judas' skin was turning gray.

"Are you referring to the end of time as predicted in The Revelation of Jesus Christ?" Jesus asked him.

"Why not?" Judas whispered, then chuckled softly. "Don't tell your mother, but I was the one who wrote that and delivered it to her saying I had received it from John."

Judas closed his eyes.

"Is that really true?" Jesus asked dumbfounded.

Judas opened his eyes and smiled.

"Who will ever know?" he said in a quiet voice, almost impossible to hear. "I always wanted to have some mysterious last words."

"Goodbye, Judas," Jesus said.

The old betrayer did not answer. He looked at Jesus for a long moment and then closed his eyes for the last time.

Jesus stood up and spoke to the knights.

"Take the two girls to General Aias and report what happened. I want their parents found and charged with murder. Neither child struggled as the knights took their hands and walked toward Jesus' palace. Jesus looked at Mary. Her hand was wet with Judas' blood and her dress was stained.

"Go wash in the river," Jesus told her. "Then find Aias. Have him send a wagon for Judas' body. Then we'll find your grandmother and tell her what happened. She loved this old troublemaker, no matter what she says. He's gone to his rest, but his last act was to save my life a second time. Double payback for the one he took when he betrayed me."

Mary glanced a last time at Judas, then left. Jesus looked at Judas' lifeless form and waited. Did you really write The Revelation of Jesus Christ, he wondered? If so, that trick would likely dupe the gullible far into the future. And indeed, it did. Kings, nobles, popes, and clergy would all refuse to believe that Judas wrote the Church's favorite apocryphal text when Jesus told them centuries later. Judas had died with a smile on his face. Maybe he'd been counting on that.

CHAPTER FIFTEEN

TIME PASSED, AND A BOUNTIFUL ten years had prospered Judea in every way. The country's farms and orchards had been restored and expanded and were producing an abundance of food. In fact, the port of Joppa, which once exported mostly salt, fabrics, and semi-precious stones, was now loaded with ships carrying fresh oranges to all parts of the empire. Salt was still important and remained the most valuable export. Its harvesting and exportation had become a state industry run by Princess Mary. She also managed the nation's collection of taxes and the distribution of land to newly created knights.

General Aias had married. So had General Harald. Mary had not. But she had built herself a brilliant social circle of rabbis and teachers—both male and female—who regularly dined with her. She also hosted a dinner for a dozen different knights every week and included both Jesus and his top generals. These occasions allowed the king and his commanders to meet and talk with their soldiers.

Aias managed the active armed forces and Harald was responsible for the nation's reserves. Aias was a proud convert to Judaism, and Harald was a devout Christian. Every citizen of Judea was allowed to worship with his or her family—including soldiers on active duty—receiving the Sabbath off to return home.

Hebrews worshipped in new synagogues built by Jesus in every Judean city or town. And Christians worshipped in new churches erected by him wherever populations had requested one. The country was at peace. And during this last decade of plenty its people had seemed at last to accept Jesus as their rightful king. Jesus had rescued Judea from the destructive aftermath of the Jewish revolt. The people hadn't done it. Rome hadn't done it. Jesus had done it. And no one other than him could have made it happen.

Jesus had a formal relationship with Emperor Domitian, exchanging letters once a year when Jewish taxes were delivered to Rome along with an exact accounting of their sources. At the beginning of his reign, Domitian had asked Jesus to renew his oath as the emperor's vassal. In turn the emperor offered the throne of Judea to him and his heirs in perpetuity. Jesus sent Domitian his pledge of loyalty, and a letter confirming his reign over Judea was delivered to him, signed by both the emperor and the rulers of the Senate.

As Vespasian had predicted—and Titus had confirmed—the youngest Flavian served the empire well, expanding the imperial treasury, rebuilding the city of Rome, and running an efficient bureaucracy across the entire empire. Officials were honest. Soldiers were well paid. And no one was gouged by unfair taxation.

Domitian was not a charmer like Titus, but he was respected, appreciated, and lauded as a grounded man who practiced traditional Roman values. He did not have the gifts of the great Augustus, but neither did he bear the dark impulses of the demented Nero. Everyone quietly gossiped that Domitian had killed his brother Titus. But as the gods seemed all right with it, so were the people of Rome.

Jesus had invited John, the last living disciple of his original twelve followers, to come and visit him and his mother Mary. John was close to eighty now and Jesus' mother was cracking a hundred and nine. John wrote back that regretfully he was too infirm to visit.

In that letter, John also responded to Jesus' question as to whether he was the author of The Revelation of Jesus Christ. John said that he had not written it. He was very critical of the book's strident tone and vengeful prophecies. He said it inappropriately harked back to the "old days" when Jehovah seemed to be perpetually upset.

Yes, Jesus thought. Jehovah had never been seen as a God of love by the authors of the Hebrew Scriptures. Not that he was all that full of loving kindness now. Actually, Jehovah was sort of missing in action, though ingenious vitriolic books like The Revelation of Jesus Christ were cram-packed with all the things God was *going to do* when he showed up again at the end of time. Most of them were awful.

Mary shook her head after Jesus read John's denial of authorship to her.

"If he didn't write it," his mother asked, "then who did?"

Jesus watched her stew about it and kept silent. He actually had other things he'd rather do than discuss who was responsible for Revelation. Miquel was visiting and Jesus was anxious to see him. He had never moved here, but he always seemed to be in and out. During each of Miguel's visits, Jesus invited him to share as many private meals as Miquel had time for, where they could speak about the happenings at La Valdieu.

RoxAnna had given birth to a lovely boy and had indeed named him Christian. He was a winsome lad, resembling his mother when she was young and full of happiness. He liked to hunt and play war-games. But most of all he loved to sit by himself and read. RoxAnna was ruling the country well, and it was prosperous. She continually schooled Christian on the rules of kingship, and told him that the blood of kings flowed in his body. She mesmerized him with tales that his sons and grandsons would be the foundation of a golden age to come when Frankish monarchs ruled all of Europe.

Interestingly enough, though everyone in La Valdieu whispered about Jesus' role in Christian's life, Miguel did not know if RoxAnna had told the young man himself who his father was. Jesus didn't press her on it, but he still planned to visit Christian, King of La Valdieu, when his right to rule occurred at his majority. It would be good to behold an heir who might actually be the good sovereign that La Valdieu had yearned for since the death of Alejandro so long ago.

At one of their meals, Jesus enjoyed hearing Miguel describe with both wisdom and humor what it was like to be old. In his nineties now, he had aches, pains, diminished functions, vanished desires, deep regrets, lost opportunities, and mourned friends. It made for quite a catalogue. But Miguel claimed that life's blessings had outweighed its burdens and sorrows.

"Imagine how many hugs and kisses I have received," Miguel told Jesus. "And handshakes! And salutes! Good food and good company. Decade after decade full of music, dance, and laughter. It all adds up, you know," Miguel said and his old eyes sparkled. "A greater treasure than the all those aureuses you hoard."

Miguel winked and Jesus smiled.

"Of all that I've experienced and learned," Miguel went on, "I think my greatest insight into the art of living is that we are required above all else to take care of ourselves and to protect—even unto to death—the family and the village of which we are a part."

"Really?" Jesus responded surprised. "That narrow?"

"Not narrow," Miguel gently corrected Jesus. "Local."

"So, doing good is meant for your closest relatives and neighbors?"

"Yes!" Miguel declared. "Changing the world is the concern of folks like you. And Titus. And Saul. Doing good—as you've pointed out so many times—is at the heart of every religion, but most of us have only a small place to practice it. What could be more important than being loving and kind to our families and our neighbors? I am proud to say that I have fulfilled such a calling. Everything else doesn't matter."

Jesus' take away from that conversation was that Miguel was preparing to die. He professed that he had done what life had been required of him and was ready to depart. There had been no talk of sin. Or forgiveness. Or sacrifice. Or falling short of God's expectations. Just a simple declaration that he had lived his life in the manner that had been required of him. Taking care of his family and friends. At the end of their conversation Jesus asked where he had learned such a philosophy.

"From observing animals," was Miguel's unexpected answer. "They take care of themselves and their own. If that is what life is all about for them, then why would I be so different? I didn't really need to check in with God. I did what was in my heart. What is in the hearts of all living beings. Animals *and* people."

"Do you think that maybe there isn't any God?"

"No, no, no," Miguel protested. "I believe in the Creator God. I just don't think that he expects to have a lot of interaction with me. Or with any of us. I believe that he is content when we just live our lives the way we were created to do."

"I don't know, Miguel," Jesus answered doubting his portrayal of a mellow Jehovah. "The God in the Hebrew Scriptures is very demanding. Full of criticism and righteous anger."

"Yes, I know *that* God," Miguel responded. "Made up by a bunch of old, bitter Jewish men. I don't believe in that God. You don't either. Your God is a loving Father. A comforter.

A friend. He raised you from the dead so that your ministry of love and healing could continue forever. *That's* the God I want. And who knows? Maybe that's exactly who I'll meet when I die."

Jesus smiled and gently nodded his head. But Miguel was wrong. He hadn't believed in a God of love for a long time. He had become convinced instead that the God of blood and violence portrayed in the Jewish Scriptures *was the real God after all.* But who actually knew? He no longer claimed to have any insights about which divinity might be living up in heaven. And Miguel was going to find out whoever that God was a lot sooner than he would.

Days after Miguel's ninetieth-second birthday, he passed away in his sleep. RoxAnna had dispatched the news to Jesus, simply sharing that Miguel had gone to bed and had never risen again. Jesus remembered the great love and vitality of his friend and appreciated RoxAnna's last words saying that as per Miguel's stated desire he had been cremated and his ashes dug into the rose beds in the front of Jesus and Mary's manor house in La Valdieu.

Jesus felt numb. Miguel was gone. There would be a sad spot in his heart for a long time. Maybe forever. In the meanwhile, he knew that he had no choice but to accept it, and get on with his own life.

— ⚜ —

Mary briefed Jesus on kingdom affairs every morning at breakfast. She reviewed general topics concerning the nation, and focused on specific issues that needed the king's response. Over mulled wine, bread, cheese, and honey, the bits of grit causing problems in Judea's bureaucratic machine were examined and extricated.

At one particular breakfast they had a lengthy discussion regarding a plea sent from Jews living in Susa. It was one of the ancient capitals of Persia, controlled the last two centuries by Parthia. The Parthian Jews had been forced by the ruler King Arsaces to move into urban ghettos. Butchers, bakers, wrights, and smiths—along with most other trades—were forbidden to do business with anyone other than Jews. Food sources were reduced, and medicine was denied. What else was this but an effort by the pagan monarch to destroy the Jewish citizens in his own country?

Jesus told Mary to have a missive drawn up to the Parthian requesting his permission for a Judean mission to enter his lands with food and medicine for the Jewish residents of Susa. As the King of the Jews in Israel he also requested permission to pay a royal bounty to the Parthian treasury of 100,000 gold aureuses as a recompense for allowing his emissaries to carry out their charitable activity.

"How long will it take to get that letter to the king?" he asked.

"His capital is Ctesiphon," Mary answered. "Significantly closer to us than Susa. A courier could make it in ten days. I can also have a wagon of gold with an escort ready to leave tomorrow. Hopefully Arsaces will not be angry if we embark without his formal approval. How many knights should accompany it?"

"Any more than a dozen will raise alarms," Jesus said. "Any less will jeopardize their safety. Ask Aias to select a dozen men and appoint an officer to lead them."

Mary told Jesus she'd return with the letter for King Arsaces. Additionally, she would draw up a request for safe passage for Jesus to sign. Parthia was no friend of Rome. Nor of the empire's client kingdoms. The Parthians had warred against Rome for hundreds of years, managing to successfully fend off its repeated attempts at conquest.

The Parthian Empire had little resemblance to ancient Babylon or Persia. It had thoroughly adopted Hellenistic culture, and its elite families spoke Greek as well as Parthian. Jesus did not personally know the reigning monarch, King Arsaces, but the Jews of Parthia had historically been granted equal rights with all other Parthians. Now something had drastically changed. And many Jews—even skilled hcraftsmen and artisans—were being persecuted. It was perplexing. Why now? Would obstacles be thrown up against humanitarian aid from Judea? He would see soon enough.

— ⚜ —

"I got a letter from John today," Mary told Jesus at dinner one night. Jesus' mother was quite old now, but she was healthy, feisty, and got around well. Jesus never told her, but at night when she was sleeping he visited her, blessing her and willing vitality from the founts of his own immorality to keep her robust and alert. If she suspected that her great old age might be due to her son, she never mentioned it.

"You already know that he's not coming from Ephesus to visit," Mary told Jesus. "But it's not really because he feels too old to travel. He's worried that if he comes, the only thing you two will do is argue."

"What?" Jesus was hurt. His mother was drinking water and eating roast lamb. She was wearing her traditional dark blue gown with a light blue sash and matching scarf. She was thin and her face was etched with lines. But she was still sharp and argumentative. She responded to Jesus' unhappy reaction.

"John says that you have turned into someone he does not recognize. The Jesus he remembers died on the cross for the sins of the world."

Jesus bit into his bread and tried not to get angry. John had only been twelve years old then—the little brother of James—the sons of Zebedee. John had been the only disciple to witness his crucifixion. He'd held Mary's hand and cried the whole time. He had been a loving boy, and Jesus had missed him. But what was this sins of the world stuff? John had clearly become deeply entrenched in Christian mythology, and Jesus remembered that it was John who had converted his mother.

"Why does he think I'd argue with him?" Jesus asked. "*You're* the one who likes to argue."

Mary didn't disagree.

"Maybe *he'd* be the one putting up a fuss," she said. "I don't know."

Jesus ate his dinner and stewed. John didn't want to see him. John thought they wouldn't get along. Jesus was sad and upset. He had become somewhat inured to criticisms aimed at him as king, and at home he just ignored his daughter or his mother if their issues seemed petty. But the fact that the last living disciple of the Twelve didn't want to see him again was unexpectedly painful.

His daughter entered, kissed Mary on the cheek, and then reminded Jesus that he had a case to judge. Two brothers had been charged with assault and rape. They were servants of a knight in

Hebron whose daughter they had savaged. He had pressed charges, asking for the execution of both men.

Mary sat down at the table. Jesus poured some spiced wine into a goblet for her.

"I read the documents," Jesus told her. "This is the case put forward by Uldin, son of Balamber."

"Yes."

"What kind of names are those?"

"His ancestors were Huns."

"Christians?"

"Yes. Uldin immigrated here six years ago. He owns a well-run estate and serves in the reserve infantry. He is well thought of by his neighbors and his commanding officer. The servants are two young men who got drunk and intercepted Uldin's daughter—a fourteen-year-old girl named Ildico—outside of Uldin's house and dragged her into the fields."

"How old are the boys?"

"Octar is eighteen and Rugila is sixteen."

Jesus rested his chin on his palm.

"Do you think Uldin would be amenable to dual castrations?"

Mary raised her hands. Who knows?

"Maybe if you cut off their members, too," she ventured.

"Really?" Jesus asked.

"Eunuchs can still get erections," she replied, "And who knows what Octar and Rugila might do the next time they get drunk."

"All right. I'll change and head to the throne room."

Jesus went to his quarters followed by his two bodyguards and found his pet lions Alpha and Omega sleeping on his bed. They woke, and required a lot attention before they allowed him to change into the new scarlet gown that Miguel had brought on his last trip to Judea. A toga. Jesus shook his head every time he put it on, but he had to admit that it was magnificent. Fit for a king. And best of all, it was a present from dear Miguel.

He set his formal crown on his head. The one wrought in gold with Stars of David around the top rim. In his life, he had been a carpenter and a construction worker. He'd been a rabbi and a counselor. He'd been a criminal and a fugitive. All in all, Jesus had to admit that his current job was the best one. King. It even sounded nice to say. King.

Hearing legal cases, however, was his least favorite part of the role, but one did what one had to do. Meeting the good and the not-so-good were just part of the job. He himself had been forced to appear before King Herod Antipas. But that clever fox had just shipped him off to Pontius Pilatus. Here, it was only him. Just as well. He was fair. He was fast. And he'd live long enough to see the results of all of his verdicts. For better or for worse.

He walked down the hall to the throne room. Alpha and Omega followed him. He entered through a private side door that would be guarded by his two bodyguards after he entered. Legionnaires also stood on either side of his throne and there were two more at the front entrance. The courtroom had been redesigned by Miguel twice. Jesus' marble throne was now set back against a marble wall. Pillars of white marble were erected in a semi-circle around it leaving floor space in front for litigants and defendants. Miguel hadn't allowed any chairs inside the throne room. Jesus sat on his throne. Everyone else stood. Except for his lions. Alpha and Omega laid down by his feet, as if daring anyone to try to get closer to Jesus.

Jesus studied the people in the room. The tall man of confident bearing was likely Uldin, son of Balamber. He was wearing a fine damask robe and a chain around his neck that held a golden medallion struck with his family coat of arms. He bowed when he saw Jesus looking at him.

There were two young men standing together, nervous, shifting foot to foot. Both were of a good height and build. Likely Uldin's outside servants Octar and Rugila. There were no others. Neither the noble's wife nor daughter was present. Not unusual, considering the upcoming testimony about the young girl's violation.

Jesus began the session.

"Greetings Uldin, son of Balamber," he said in a commanding voice.

Uldin bowed again.

"Hail, your Majesty," he said respectfully.

"Tell your story," Jesus ordered.

Uldin did, sharing in detail the wicked behavior of the two drunken servants who had assaulted and raped his daughter. His tone was angry and urgent. He had employed these young men ever since they had been young boys. Hardworking sons from a good local family. But they had hurt his daughter. And they had hurt him.

Jesus looked at the young men. They bowed and identified themselves.

"What say ye to these charges?" Jesus asked them.

Neither young man offered a defense. But Octar spoke up and asked for the king's mercy on them both.

"My Lord, we sinned while under the influence of too much wine, and we grieve for the carnal sins we committed. We plead for our master's forgiveness and for that of his daughter, Ildico."

Jesus looked at Uldin. The knight's face looked stern.

"King Jesus," he said. "Both Ildico and I forgive these men. However, the Holy Scriptures declare that the wages of sin is death, and I ask that they be executed for their crime against my daughter."

"I have heard the accusation and the response," Jesus stated. "Uldin, I offer you two choices. First, the guilty men will be emasculated *and* their manhoods cut off. Second, they will become your indentured laborers for life. Alternatively, they will be executed for their sins against your daughter and you. What say ye?"

Uldin frowned and didn't answer immediately. Both choices were severe, but having indentured workers seemed an awful lot like slavery, and that had been banned by King Jesus himself. He did not want to be the only landowner who had slaves. Plus, neither Ildico nor he desired to see the rapists around their family ever again.

Uldin answered.

"My king, I ask that they be executed for their crimes."

Jesus looked at the young men. They both burst into tears. One fell down on his knees, his face in his hands. A feeling of sadness weighed on Jesus. Nonetheless he passed judgment according to the choices he had given Uldin.

"I command that Uldin's servants, Octar and Rugila," Jesus spoke firmly as a court clerk recorded his ruling on a parchment skin, "be taken into custody by the court's military personnel and executed by the appropriate members of the king's army." Immediately the two guards standing by his throne took the sentenced men into custody, leading one and dragging the other. Jesus watched Uldin's reaction. The accuser's face was hard.

"You might have shown mercy, Uldin," Jesus told him when the prisoners were gone. "You are a knight who has been granted land and wealth. You could have spared those men the only possession they had. Their lives."

Uldin looked at Jesus.

"May I speak?" he asked.

Jesus nodded.

"What would you have done in my place, great king?"

Jesus thought about that. What indeed would he have done if his own daughter Mary had been treated in such a vile and cruel manner? He looked directly at Uldin.

"I would have chosen execution."

Uldin nodded his head.

"You may leave," Jesus told him. "Comfort your daughter."

Jesus sat alone in the throne room for a long time afterwards. How odd to bear the right to declare who would live and who would die. He looked at his pierced hand, then gazed at his left forearm where his other hand had been cut off. His back was marked forever by Latin whips. And his chest was a mass of scars where a Roman sword had been plunged into his heart. His wife and sons had been murdered, and he'd had to fight and kill his own grandson. Those were all terrible things. Horrendous physical and emotional wounds. But they were also evidence. Proof that he by his suffering he had *earned* the right to sit on this throne and exercise the wisdom to declare lives saved or forfeit. No one deserved that privilege more than him.

"Father!" Mary cried as she ran into the throne room. "I found Grandmother on the floor of her bedroom, and she is unresponsive!"

"Quickly!" Jesus cried and followed her.

Mary led her father to his mother's private room, furnished with only a bed, a lampstand, a wooden table and two chairs. Mary said the plainer her room was, the better. It would prepare her for lying in the tomb at La Valdieu.

Saul had been laid to rest there now. His remains had been taken by Miguel and interred in Gaul. Judas was the only one buried in the Jerusalem tomb, his bones resting in a limestone box. Jesus had retrieved them a year after his death and burial and placed them in the box himself. With the tip of his knife he had cut Aramaic words on one side of the box. "Judas, the betrayer of Jesus of Nazareth, lies inside." Jesus had long ago forgiven Judas. But he had never forgotten.

Mary had lifted her grandmother and put her on the bed when she had first found her. Jesus knelt at her side. She breaths were shallow. Her eyes were shut. Her fists were clenched. He took one of her hands.

"Mother?" he said in a worried voice.

Mary slowly opened her eyes

"Hello, son," she said very softly. "I think I fell down."

"You did, Mother. Mary found you and put you on your bed. Then she fetched me."

Mary grasped her hanging crucifix with her free hand and clutched it to her breast.

"I'm thirsty."

Mary filled a ceramic mug with water from a clay pitcher on the table and held it to her grandmother's lips.

"I am ready to die," Mary told Jesus after she had sipped at the water.

"God is your witness," he said quietly.

"And I would like *you* to honor my last wish, son. Open your heart to Christians. In the way you love the Jews, you should also love Christians."

"I do the will of Jehovah who sent me," Jesus replied. "If it his desire that I honor your request, then I will gladly do so."

Mary smiled. She closed her eyes. In a moment she opened them again.

"I hope to meet Jehovah soon," she said. "Hard old guy. And *such* an absentee father." Mary looked Jesus in the eyes. "But you turned out okay. You are the son that every mother wishes she had."

Jesus put his face on his mother's hands and wept. It had taken Mary her whole life to tell him that. And it had come only just in time. His daughter offered her another drink of water. She turned her face away.

"It is time to go now, son," Mary whispered. She looked tenderly at Jesus. "Say your prayer for me while I close my eyes."

Jesus held on to his mother's hand and recited the prayer he had taught his followers in the days of his earthly ministry. Mary said it with him, her lips moving silently.

Our Father, which art in heaven,
Hallowed be thy name.

Thy Kingdom come, Thy will be done,
on Earth as it is in Heaven.
Give us this day our daily bread,

And forgive us our trespasses
as we forgive those who trespass against us.

And lead us not into temptation,
but deliver us from evil.

Mary's eyes opened gently at the end, but Jesus knew that she had died. After more than a century of service to her God, to her family, and to him, she had gone as quickly as a candle blown out by the wind.

— ⚜ —

Late that night Jesus changed into a light cotton robe for sleeping and walked from his dressing area to his bed. His mother Mary was sitting on the edge of his bed. He stopped and stared.

"It's only me, son," she told him. "Come sit here." Mary patted the bed by her side.

Jesus walked over and sat next to her.

"Why are you here?" he asked.

"I have a few things to tell you that I didn't want to say in front of your daughter. I've observed your behavior as king, and I've talked to those who care about you. Septimus. Harald. Aias. Sweet old Miguel. Not-so-sweet old Judas. And your daughter, Mary. Here's what they've observed.

"You don't pray. You don't ask God for guidance. You don't even request a blessing. No one believes that you have any kind of relationship with God. Are you a non-believer now, my son? Or have you simply given up on Jehovah?"

Jesus looked at Mary, but he didn't answer.

"You are so unapproachable now," his mother went on. "The walls of your cities are more vulnerable than your heart."

"I am the way I am," Jesus responded without emotion.

"I've heard others before you say that. Unhappy persons who walked paths of solitude and darkness. Have you learned to despair of life? Or just *your* life?"

"I wouldn't know."

"You're being stubborn," Mary chided. "Jehovah raised you from the dead for a sign and a blessing to the world. He gave you wealth beyond measure *and* the throne of your fathers. Do you think you did any of that by yourself?"

Jesus clenched his teeth, but kept a civil tongue.

"I worked hard and faithfully with the talents I was given."

"Yet you *never* acknowledge those as gifts from God, and you don't offer him thanks or praise."

Jesus stared at his mother.

"What would you have me do?" he asked tersely.

"I'm not done. Jehovah—who is not a patient God—is not a patient father, either," she said. "He warns that your mission to the Parthian Jews will *fail* and that any action you take to avenge them will result in a great tragedy. Almighty God has *already* laid his destruction on Parthia, and he exhorts you to desist from your ambitions to punish that people yourself."

Jesus sat on the bed and looked at his mother. Just as countless Byzantine icons would portray her a thousand years hence, she sat stoically in her blue robe, light blue sash, and headscarf. She wore her long chain with the golden crucifix hanging from it.

"Is that all?" he asked her.

"No. Jehovah says he wishes to bless you for a hundred generations, but calls you back to obedience and humility before his heavenly throne."

Jesus chafed under the punishing words of his mother. And the irony of being *lectured* by the notoriously silent Jehovah was particularly galling.

"And next you're going to tell me," he addressed his mother curtly, "that if I don't listen to you, Jehovah is going to kill me."

Mary gazed at Jesus, then replied.

"Yes."

"Is this a dream?" Jesus asked.

"It is."

"But real enough to know that God will still kill me if I don't respond the way he wants?" Jesus asked.

"Yes."

Jesus woke in a sweat. His room was dark and quiet. But he remembered everything his dead mother had told him. And obeyed none of it.

CHAPTER SIXTEEN

General Aias requested an audience with the king. It had been six weeks since Jesus' mother had died. That same day his daughter had dispatched a military courier to carry the king's appeal to the Parthian ruler. And the following day Mary had authorized a hundred thousand aureuses from Judea's treasury to be loaded into a wagon destined to be delivered to King Arsaces for allowing Jesus to aid the destitute Jews in Susa.

Today Aias entered the palace early in the morning to meet with the king. Two legionnaires posted at Jesus' private dining room stepped aside to allow him to enter. Jesus was at breakfast with his daughter Mary. He stood and greeted Aias. The swarthy, well-built officer bowed deeply. He was wearing a long-sleeve white shirt and a red leather pleated skirt. Jesus and Mary were both wearing white cotton robes.

"Have you broken your fast, General?" Jesus asked.

"No, my Lord."

"Then sit."

Jesus pointed at an empty seat on the stone bench that circled the round marble table. Not so very long ago, Judas had sat there.

Berenice in the spot next to him. And his mother Mary by her. Judas had been killed saving Jesus' life. Berenice had been poisoned comforting Titus. And Mary had turned into a ghost who had visited him after she died.

He was sure that his encounter with the spirit of his mother was likely just a figment of his sorrowful dreams. Yet it disturbed him that Mary hadn't spoken sympathetically to his broken heart. Rather, like an oracle sent from the God of Abraham, Isaac, and Jacob, she had beckoned Jesus to return to the Almighty's iron embrace. Don't interfere with my will for Parthia, Jehovah had warned Jesus. Get on your knees and tell me you're sorry for neglecting the One who gave you life, wealth, and the throne of your fathers.

Job had called out God on his cruelty after Jehovah had killed his wife and his children, stolen his prosperity, and broken his health. Jehovah had gotten so angry at Job's protestations that he came down and verbally assaulted the man who he had stripped of everything. Job was terrified by God's ferocious incarnations as wind, typhoon, and flood, and threw himself to the ground afraid and overwhelmed.

It was in *that* moment of Job's total humiliation and utter defeat that he uttered the famous words of his capitulation, "The Lord giveth. And the Lord taketh away. Blessed be the name of the Lord." Job might still have wanted to curse—not bless—Jehovah. But he didn't. God had broken him.

"Don't interfere with my will for Parthia," Jehovah had told Jesus. "Get on your knees and tell me that you're sorry."

Jesus' son Saul had believed that the King of the Universe couldn't fix anything. So, instead he banished or destroyed the people who failed him. Now he was threatening to kill Jesus over Parthia. Thanks, Abba.

Jesus told General Aias to help himself to breakfast. Wine, bread, eggs, bacon, applesauce, butter, and jam. The kitchen servants brought a dining service for the general. There was a small, but vocal Hebrew group in Judea that observed all the archaic health laws demanded by the Jewish Scriptures and promoted lists of foods that observant believers could and could not eat. Jesus helped himself to some bacon. He didn't care about anybody's lists.

Aias did not eat, but did accept a goblet of wine. He waited for the king to call upon him to speak. After a moment Jesus did.

"It probably bodes ill that you are here so early in the morning, General," Jesus told him.

Aias nodded solemnly. Jesus gazed at his top military officer and told him to proceed.

"We have received a reply from King Arsaces in response to your request to aid the Parthian Jews."

"I don't see a document in your hands," Jesus observed.

Aias shook his head no.

"His reply is not written. He has communicated by means of a grisly and evil deed."

Jesus put down his wine goblet and waited. "Would you prefer a report or behold the deed with your own eyes?" Aias asked.

Jesus stood up.

"Lead on, General."

Aias preceded Jesus out the main doors of the palace, and then out the massive gates of its protective walls. The king's two bodyguards followed. General Harald and several legionnaires were waiting outside. Two donkey-drawn commercial wagons were parked in front of the gates. Each one was flanked by a driver wearing traditional Parthian garb. Purple pants, white shirts, long scarlet coats, and brown turbans on their heads. One wagon bed was covered by a tarp. The other held a large round clay jar at least four feet tall and four feet in diameter. It was held in place by ropes tied to the wagon.

Everyone bowed as Jesus approached. The Parthian drivers needed no introduction to the legendary white-haired giant. He was the King of Judea. Jesus saw them standing by their wagons. He walked up to the waggoneers and spoke to them in Greek.

"Who are you?"

One of the men handed Jesus a parchment scroll that he had already shown many times during the journey to Jericho. Jesus unrolled it and read the Greek text. "To Whom It May Concern. I am requesting safe passage for these men and their cargo. They bear gifts for Jesus of Nazareth, King of Judea. Signed and sealed by my own hand, Arsaces, King of Kings, seated on the hallowed throne of Ctesiphon." Below the text was a wax seal impressed with the image of a griffin and below it the signature of the king. Jesus rolled up the scroll and handed it back.

Jesus looked at General Aias.

"You've been informed about the contents of these wagons?"

"Yes, Lord."

"What is in the wagon covered with the tarp?"

Aias walked over to the wagon and pulled back a flap that he himself had untied. Jesus saw that the wagon was filled with the bags of gold Mary had sent for King Arsaces.

Jesus nodded towards the large clay jug other wagon.

"And the contents of that vessel?" he asked.

General Aias answered.

"The drivers said they only know that the vase is filled with wine."

"Cut the ropes and open it," Jesus ordered.

Aias climbed into the wagon and Harald stepped up and joined him. Aias pulled out his sword and cut through the ropes. They were as thick as a man's forearm. Harald used his sword tip to chip away the hardened clay that sealed the wooden lid to the huge jar. He and Aias lifted the heavy top and eased it over the side of the wagon into the hands of waiting soldiers.

Then Aias and Harald looked inside. Neither general blanched nor pulled back at what they saw, but there weren't many men—citizens or soldiers—who could have shown such discipline in the face of the gruesome sight they witnessed. Aais turned and spoke to Jesus. His face had turned ashen.

"My Lord, the vessel contains the head of the courier you sent to King Arsaces. And the heads of the legionnaires who escorted the gold to his capital."

Jesus gazed at the two teamsters who had brought the grisly cargo. They had been stoic at at the beginning. Now they were terrified.

"Knew ye of this atrocity?" Jesus demanded.

"We are only wagon drivers, Great Lord," one answered his voice quivering. "Hired and paid by agents of King Arsaces. We were not privy to the contents of this cargo."

Jesus spoke to the driver slowly, word by word.

"You are to carry this message back to Parthia, speaking it into King Arsaces' own ears. 'A great wind will blow out of the Negev and utterly destroy your kingdom. As you have done to the men who faithfully served the King of the Jews, so shall it be done unto you. This man returned to you is a harbinger of the day when Jesus shall cause you to perish from the face of the earth and have your corpse plunged into a vat of wine and buried without a marker.'" Jesus stopped and looked at the waggoneer. "Do you understand?"

The man nodded, his face a mask of fear. Jesus turned and looked at Aias.

"Kill the man who has not spoken."

Aias bowed his head. He walked over to the man whose life was doomed. A stern and brave man, the driver knelt and closed his eyes. General Aias pulled his sword and swung it down hard on the man's neck. His head dropped. Blood shot out of his torso. A true fountain of death. His headless body collapsed on the ground.

Jesus nodded at Aias.

"After the remains of our legionnaires are taken away, disburse messengers to summon their families. Put the dead Parthian's head and body into the jar, fill it with new wine, and send it off with his companion."

Aias nodded, speechless at the brutality of his King. Jesus stepped up into the wagon and looked for a long time at the soldiers' heads sitting in the wine. Then he got down from the wagon and walked back to the palace. Aias watched, sure that the shaking shoulders of the vanishing king revealed a monarch hiding his grief.

— ⚜ —

Jesus returned to his dining room. His guards stopped at the door and he entered. Mary was still there, working her way through a stack of official scrolls. She looked up at her father. He looked spent. He sat down at the table and stared at her.

"That bad?" she asked.

Jesus nodded.

"King Arsaces sent back the heads of our men in a jar."

Mary groaned and covered her mouth with her hand.

"Aias will have the men identified," Jesus told her. "I want you to work with him to make sure their families are notified as soon as possible. I want each head preserved in a vessel of honey, and I want each family to be receive ten aureuses to make up for the loss of the dead man's earnings."

"That's generous," Mary commented.

"You think so?" Jesus snapped. "Ten gold pieces for the life of a son, a husband, or a father?"

Mary flushed at Jesus' sharp rebuke.

Jesus filled his wine goblet. He drank it down and filled it again.

"I want to meet with the families. I cannot bring their men folk back, but I can embrace their grief. Will you help me draft a letter to Emperor Domitian requesting permission to launch a punitive expedition against Parthia?" Mary gazed at her father's face. He was distressed and angry, but was he really willing to sacrifice the lives of countless more Judean soldiers because of a barbaric insult from King Arsaces?

"May I ask if your desire to punish Arsaces is based solely on the murders of our soldiers?"

Jesus looked at Mary.

"What else would it be?" he asked her.

"You feel immense sorrow and shame for the betrayed and murdered legionnaires," she said. "I am just wondering how you will feel when a thousand more of your soldiers perish? Or ten thousand more? Win or lose, attempting to punish the Parthian king will require a great loss of life."

Jesus looked at his daughter, but he did not answer.

She went on.

"I honor you, Father. I admire you. And I will obey whatever your final decision is. But I ask you to first ponder the cost to your country, its people, and your own heart before you decide to set out against Parthia."

"I hear your words, daughter," Jesus finally replied and stood up. "I need to think."

With that the king left and walked down the long palace hall, out the front doors, and through the gates of the outer wall. He stopped where the Parthian wagons stood and watched as palace servants under Aias' supervision carefully lifted the severed heads of the murdered soldiers out of the jar—one by one—dried them off and handed them to other servants who washed and cleaned the faces and the hair of the dead men.

The general recognized the face of every legionnaire. He dictated their names and the names of their families to a scribe. Some men were married with wives and children. Some were owners of their family's estates. Others were youngest sons not yet betrothed. Jesus watched, remembering how his heart had ached for his sons David and Saul when fate had stolen them from him.

General Aias had to sit down on the side of the wagon when the next head was brought out. He motioned that it be handed to him. He held it on his lap and asked for a clean cloth. He carefully wiped the dead face. Forehead. Eyes. Nose. Mouth. As he gazed at it tears formed in his eyes.

Jesus stepped inside the wagon and went to Aias' side. He looked at the face of the dead man. He could not have been more than twenty years old. He had a surprised expression on his face and his eyes were sprung open in wonder.

"Your kin?" Jesus asked gently.

Aias nodded and wiped his tears away.

"Aeschylus was his name. The son of my sister and her Greek husband," Aias replied. "He begged me to go on this mission, and I found that I could not deny him." Tears came into Aias' eyes again. "I would not deny him even now—despite seeing his doom—but alas, the price of his bravery and loyalty was indeed unto the death."

Jesus looked into the dead eyes of the once handsome and courageous man. He glanced back at Aias' grieving face. Indeed, the price of goodness and freedom was often paid with the lives of young soldiers. But if they did not fight and die, the whole world would be absorbed by the wickedness of such men as Arsaces of Parthia.

He believed that he had no choice but to levy a punishment on that king. He would pursue the very course of action that both his mother's apparition and his daughter Mary had spoken against. Even if it cost him his army. Even if it cost him his life. He looked upon Aeschylus' face a last time and put his hand on Aias' shoulder.

"I am sorry, dear friend. You and I will break down the very gates of Ctesiphon to put our hands on Arsaces and avenge your nephew's death. May God grant you solace."

Aias bowed his head and wept. Jesus stood back and watched the rest of the severed heads as they were retrieved from the depths of the clay jar. The heads felt nothing. Sorrow was an experience for the living. If he invaded Parthia and lost, *his* sorrows would be done. But if he was victorious—despite Jehovah's threats—he would bring back the blood of the Parthian king and pour it out on Aeschylus' tomb.

Jesus rejoined Mary inside the palace. She had finished her work and was waiting for him. He didn't sit, but stood beside the marble dining table and issued his orders.

"Draft a letter to Emperor Domitian. Describe what happened to our envoys to Parthia and tell him that I am requesting official permission to launch a punitive expedition comprised of two full Judean legions numbering twenty thousand troops. Send two copies to the emperor by couriers on separate ships. I want the letters to arrive within ten days. And I desire a return response in no more time than that."

Mary nodded and rose.

"Also," Jesus went on, "Aias says that the slain soldiers were both Christian and Jews."

"You mean that they were of both Christian and Hebrew beliefs. They were *all* Jews, sons of Judea."

"Of course, Mary," Jesus responded gently. "That is a better and truer way to say it. My hope is to hold a joint service for all of the martyred men. Do you see any issue with that?"

Mary shook her head.

"There is no enmity between their faiths," she pointed out.

"Do you know rabbis or pastors who would perform a joint service?"

"I know of both," Mary answered. "Would you like to state your desires for the rubrics of such a service?"

"I want Scripture readings, songs, prayers, and not a lot of Christ stuff."

"There will inevitably be some of that."

"*Some* is acceptable."

"Your capacity at the service?"

"Attendance as king. Limit the service to immediate families and legionnaires who were close to their deceased comrades. Provide a simple altar, a podium, and seating in the courtyard in front of the palace." Jesus looked at Mary's face. "I will leave for Parthia next spring pending the emperor's permission. I will be gone on the campaign six months to a year. I want you to govern in my stead."

"I am truly honored, my Lord," Mary answered and bowed her head. "But I am accompanying you on your mission."

"For what reason?" Jesus asked vexed by her refusal.

"If God above grants you a victory, then my role will be to serve you by seeking and saving Jews in need. If you fail, then my job will be to bring you back to Jericho. Dead or alive."

Jesus just stared at Mary.

"Which do think it will be daughter?" he finally asked.

Mary did not reply to her father's question.

Jesus did not ask it again.

The memorial for the murdered soldiers was held on Sunday evening at dusk.

Wooden chairs from the military barracks had been set up in the tiled courtyard of the palace. More than a hundred seats were filled by grieving families. Behind them stood legionnaires who had lost comrades. A bare marble altar and a marble podium lent by a local church had been placed at the front of the courtyard. A copy of the Hebrew Book of Psalms sat on the top of the podium. Beside it was a copy of the Christian Gospel of Luke.

Jesus and his daughter Mary sat in the front seats, along with General Harald, General Aias, the guest rabbi Akiva ben Joseph, and the guest pastor, Ignatius of Antioch. Jesus had talked to Akiva, a well-known Hebrew scholar, for over two hours earlier in the day. He was older, with a gentle face, white hair, and a white beard. He was a respected authority who had contributed to both the Midrash and the Mishnah, Hebrew commentaries on the ancient Scriptures. Jesus liked Akiva and hoped in his heart to meet him again.

Afterwards he had met with Ignatius, the Christian bishop and head pastor of the churches in the rich and famous Roman city of Antioch. A renowned preacher, he had coined the term Catholic Church for the universal Christian church. He was a very vocal critic of the pagan Roman Empire and had often been threatened with arrest and punishment by Antioch's Roman governor.

Meeting Jesus, Ignatius launched into an immediate attack on the king for practicing the Hebrew faith instead of confessing his role as Christian savior. Ignatius' exact and rather offensive words were: "If you are still practicing Judaism, it's an admission that you have failed to receive the very gift of grace that you yourself offer others by your death on the cross. To profess to be Jesus Christ and still follow Jewish beliefs is an absurdity. The Christian faith does not look to Judaism. Rather Judaism looks to Christianity."

Ignatius was robust man in his late middle age, wearing a purple robe and a white stole with an embroidered gold cross on each end. He appeared to be full of himself, or at least full of his authoritative position as the spiritual leader of the Antioch Christians.

"And where did you learn this truth?" Jesus asked him, having encountered this diatribe many times before in Christian letters and sermons.

"From my reading of the Gospels and the Epistles of Paul," Ignatius answered.

"Thank you," Jesus told him. "You may leave now."

Igntius' face showed his surprise.

"But you spent two hours with Rabbi Akiva!" he protested.

"I did. And I learned much. There would no such benefit in spending more time with you."

Ignatius was insulted.

"Say what you will, King Jesus. My only wish is to serve God and—if attainable—yield my life as a Christian martyr in Rome."

"I hope you get your wish," Jesus told him.

Ignatius smiled, bowed, and said, "Thank you, Lord!"

The service itself was modest and dignified. There were prayers, readings, Hebrew and Christian hymns. Then Rabbi Akiva led those faithful to Judaism in reciting the Kaddish for the dead soldiers who were sons of the Torah. After, Bishop Ignatius led the rest of the congregants in a traditional confession called the Apostles' Creed and the Lord's Prayer on behalf of the deceased Christian soldiers. General Aias read the names of all the dead, ending with his nephew, Aeschylus, son of Kratos.

At the conclusion of the service Jesus walked to the front and waited as the congregation stood up in respect for the king. He raised his right hand and blessed them with Jehovah's own ancient words of comfort.

The Lord bless thee, and keep thee:
The Lord make his face shine upon thee,
And be gracious unto thee:

The Lord lift up his countenance upon thee,
And give thee peace.

Many of the people at the service made their way to the front of the church to pay homage to Jesus of Nazareth, King of the Jews. Or to Jesus Christ, Son of God, Savior. He embraced those of Hebrew faith, and put his hand on the heads of those who knelt professing Christian beliefs. Rabbi Akiva kissed Jesus on both cheeks, and Ignatius knelt and received a personal blessing wherein Jesus prayed that God Almighty would help him discern truth wherever it might be found. Afterwards, Jesus sat with Mary in his study.

"How do you think it went?" he asked.

"I'd say it was a loving and gentle coming together of the family of believers who live in your kingdom."

"Thank you, Mary," Jesus said. "I found it comforting. There wasn't a lot of pontificating, except, of course, for Ignatius. I am beginning to really dislike the man. Abrupt and arrogant, he's just a—" Jesus paused searching for the right word, "—just a—"

"—just a prick," Mary finished for him.

"Thank you for that," he told his daughter. "And for everything else tonight."

Unspoken was their mutual fear that Ignatius' dogmatic assertion claiming it was monstrous to talk of Christ in the same breath as Judaism presaged a future where the kind of fellowship and tolerance seen at the memorial service would be swept away by intolerance and condemnation.

They did not know it then, but Bishop Ignatius' inflammatory words of judgment would indeed be seeded by his blood in the Colosseum itself. His body ripped asunder by wild beasts. After his martyr's death, a new wave of bigotry flowed across the empire like a tidal wave. Not just between Christians and Rome, but also between Christians and Jews. This early wave of bias would grow over the centuries into hatred, revulsion, and genocide, recorded in Jewish blood in Medieval Spain, Renaissance France, and twentieth century Germany. Christians in those coming ages would single out Jews for torture and death. Onward Christian soldiers, marching as to war, with the cross of Jesus going on before.

Emperor Domitian's reply arrived in the late autumn, three weeks after Jesus' message had been sent. The scroll was delivered by a Praetorian when Jesus was in the throne room hearing a case. Mary accepted it, holding it for Jesus until he finished. He gave Mary a kiss on the cheek and took the parchment scroll she held out. He opened it as he walked to his royal office.

To: Jesus, King Of The Jews
From: Caesar Domitianus Augustus, Emperor Of Rome

Greetings Faithful Servant,

Peace be to you, who by the will of the emperor and the Senate of Rome, rules the Roman Kingdom of Judea. We thank the gods for your loyalty and pray for your success and longevity.

I and the Senate authorize your use of deadly force to deal with King Arsaces' bitter insult to the citizens of the empire. I will commit twenty thousand Roman legionnaires to match yours. This army will be composed of one hundred and fifty centuries of cavalry and fifty centuries of infantry. I am sending engineers as well to design and supervise the construction of siege engines if needed.

My troops will be under the command of General Rubrius Gallus.

He will confer with you and your senior commanders on travel, attack, and punishment strategies. It will take some weeks to prepare the caravan of wagons that will carry food, emergency water rations, extra weapons and the materials to forge more. Accompanying this vast train will be priests, coopers, wheelwrights, carpenters, blacksmiths, leather workers, cooks, barbers, tailors, servants, slaves, merchants who purchase the soldiers' battlefield trophies, and women to service the legions.

Under no circumstance will any officer or soldier use Parthian women for sexual gratification. I will not have local women abused. I and the gods are defenders of decency and family solidarity. I regret that King Arsaces will cause the deaths of so many of his men by insulting the eternal Kingdom of Rome. But be that as it may, General Gallus' orders include the execution of all Parthian males over the age of twelve. Rome has warred against Parthia for three hundred years. This expedition will end this conflict once and for all. Parthia will at last show obedience to the empire.

Expect our legionnaires and wagons to arrive in six months. Prepare your own troops in the meanwhile. Couriers will arrive on the Friday of each week hereafter appraising you of our progress.

Master and God,

Domitianus

Signed in my own hand and sealed with my personal mark.

Jesus handed the scroll to Mary.

"We have six months before we march to war," he told her. "Will you oversee the preparations?"

Mary nodded.

"I am not sure, however," she responded, "that I will be able to find *any* women willing to service our troops."

Jesus frowned.

"You're not serious, are you?" he asked.

"What do you think?" Mary asked and laughed. "It's the only thing humorous about this whole enterprise."

Jesus looked at his daughter, handed her his crown, and sat down at his desk. Then he smiled.

CHAPTER SEVENTEEN

EMPEROR DOMITIAN SENT RUBRIUS GALLUS, the general who would lead the Roman army marching on Parthia, and six additional Roman officers who would function as military planners, aiding Judea in the gathering, assembling, and transporting of goods for the expedition. They also drilled Jesus' legions on Roman battle formations and tactics. The planners met with Jesus, Mary, and the Jewish generals Aias and Harald every morning to schedule the day's activities. Then again at the end of the day to discuss progress.

General Gallus and his men were polite, professional, and eager to take on Parthia, one of Rome's oldest and most recalcitrant enemies. All of them had campaigned extensively in the two recent Roman wars to conquer Dacia in eastern Europe. They had participated in significant battles against marauding Parthian armies, and executed punitive excursions against Parthian cities. They understood *exactly* what would be required of an invading army desiring to destroy the Parthians, whether engaging them in open battle, or facing them barricaded inside their fortified cities.

"The clash of cavalries will likely be one of the largest mounted forces ever to meet in battle," Gallus said. The grizzled old general's once bright red hair had now turned rust-colored, and his face was lined and covered with black moles—badges from the sun he told everyone—earned by his years of service in the eastern empire. "More men and horses are destined to fight in this conflict than any other in history," he predicted.

One of the general's officers nodded vigorously. His name was Lapius Maximus. He was tall and patrician with a pale narrow face and brown curly hair. Whereas Gallus was one of Domitian's oldest generals, Maximus was one of his youngest, having just been promoted to that rank by the emperor himself. He had long functioned as a spy for Domitian among the army officers and the Praetorian guards. In keeping with that kind of role, he now suggested that any Parthian nationals in Jesus' army who had immigrated to Judea be called upon to enter that land as spies.

Aias and Harald screened their troops for such candidates and it turned out that more than two dozen soldiers had emigrated from Parthia. All of them volunteered for the reconnaissance mission. The two men selected were cavalry officers in their twenties, single, intimate with Parthia, and spoke the country's language.

Their names were Phraates, son of Antiochus, and Tiridates, son of Daha. They were mature confident officers. One had short-cropped, brown hair, and the other shaved his head. They left their spears behind, but took their short swords, slings, and stones. They hid the slings inside their robes as those would be instantly identified by the Parthians who were well aware of the infamous weapons wielded by the Judeans. The two officers wore white cotton robes, red linen jackets, and brown turbans to protect their heads from the sun. They left in the winter, aware that they had to be back in twelve weeks or less before the spring campaign against Parthia began.

One afternoon, Jesus and Mary were watching the cavalry units train. The men wore light cotton shirts and leather skirts. They executed maneuvers that taught their horses to veer right or left, lunge ahead full speed, or stop precipitously if their riders commanded it.

The cavalry preceded the infantry in battles, smashing the opposing cavalry and breaking the lines of the enemy infantry.

General Gallus left the training session after ordering his centurions to have the men and horses rested and refreshed before another maneuver. He wore a white shirt and white short pants. He was deeply tanned and at ease, looking for all the world like he had done this kind of thing every day of his life. Which was actually pretty close to the reality. He rode up to Jesus and Mary, dismounted, bowed his head, and then extended his greeting.

"Hail, King!" the old general almost shouted. "Your soldiers learn quickly and ride with a ferocity that I have not seen in the empire's horsemen for a long time."

"Thank you, General," Jesus replied. "The men are young and anxious to be tested. Over the last weeks they have taken to you like a father. You have taught the horsemen to ride together as one. What enemy will be able to resist them?"

"They perform brilliantly," Gallus replied. "Which is critical. Their lives and the lives of their mates will depend on it. The next great lesson they will learn is how to fight against *other* men on horseback. Trust me, that is the worst fighting they will ever experience."

"How so?" Mary asked.

Gallus shook his head recalling such slaughters.

"Cavalrymen do not attack other riders at first. They wound and kill their horses, creating a sea of blood and guts enveloping the stricken horses and fallen riders. Only when one side has managed to destroy most of the opposite cavalry's horses do they ride their enemies down and slay them. Keep in mind *that is also the very moment* when foot soldiers enter the battle, attacking the enemy riders whose horses have been killed, as well as going head-to-head with the opposition's own attacking infantry."

"You've seen this?" Jesus asked.

"More times than I can number," Gallus answered. "And with seventy thousand horsemen taking the battlefield in this conflict, I will see it again in Parthia. If we haven't talked about it, each man in your cavalry corps should have two or three additional horses that are battle trained, used to his style and smell, and ready to ride into war."

Mary was incredulous.

"So, the Roman and Judean cavalrymen will be training, riding, and bringing as many as a hundred and thousand horses on this mission?"

"That number is correct. But half of those horses will be brought from Rome by *their* cavalry riders."

Mary was still in awe.

"And how many wagons will accompany the Roman army of twenty thousand men?" she asked.

Gallus responded, totally intimate with how the empire prepared for war.

"Figure half a wagon per man filled with food and water, supplemented by cavalry raids for meat and produce from Parthian farms. The other half of the wagon will carry camping gear, food preparation items like pots and pans, and materials for wheelwrights and smiths along with other miscellaneous supplies. We will allow an additional two thousand wagons for merchants who buy the soldiers' spoils and courtesans who help them spend it. All in all Rome will march with twelve thousand wagons.

"We will pack enough food for the Jewish legionnaires to last *twelve* months," Mary responded. "It is eight weeks' march to the Parthian capital of Ctesiphon, and Jewish soldiers *will not* be taking anything from the Parthian people."

"Noble," Gallus replied wryly. "Wars kill far more citizens than soldiers."

"We know that all too well," Jesus said emphatically. "Anyone in Judea older than age twenty-five remembers how many elderly men and women, and mothers and children were killed in the Jewish revolt." He looked at Gallus who met his gaze without flinching. "That will not happen to the people of Parthia who encounter my legions on this campaign."

Gallus raised his eyebrows as though he just heard the impossible, and believed that Jesus must be forgetting that the emperor had ordered the extermination of all Parthian males twelve and older. But he didn't argue. We'll all just wait and see, he thought. Noble ideals don't last long when blood flows and soldiers die.

Mary turned back to the planning required for the great trek to Parthia.

"So, we are looking at some twelve thousand wagons and mules to support the needs of twenty thousand Roman soldiers. Horses will be watered and fed from the land along the way?"

"Yes."

"We will need a wagon filled with food and emergency water rations for each Judean soldier. And perhaps as many as two hundred wagons for smiths, artisans, and their supplies. So that is twenty thousand, two hundred wagons to support the Jewish legions. We will not be allowing any commercial vehicles or wagons filled with harlots to accompany us."

Gallus threw his head back and laughed.

"Are you setting off to war with angels?" he asked.

Jesus smiled.

"For the most part, yes," the king answered.

Gallus nodded a bit stunned at Jesus' reply.

"Well, should any of your *angels* desire to share in what the devils enjoy, send them over to the Roman ranks."

"I suspect that those who wish to indulge," Jesus replied, "will find their way without either permission or directions from me."

Gallus roared with laughter.

"Fine then, my Lord," he said. "But if you yourself wish a bit of *innocent* refreshment during the trek I will have sparkling Cava wine from Spain ready for your enjoyment."

Jesus nodded, and then once again Mary took the conversation back to army preparations.

"So, our combined forces will need thirty-two thousand wagons," she told Gallus. "And upwards of sixty thousand additional cavalry horses. I can hardly believe that employing these kinds of numbers we will be able to stay organized and unified."

Gallus nodded. It was a gargantuan enterprise.

"The wagons will travel ten abreast and will stretch out five miles," he told Mary. "Cavalry will escort them front and back, and the infantry will protect both sides. Scouts will search for enemy movement from any direction, giving us plenty of time to prepare for a Parthian assault. This kind of formation has worked for Rome since the Republic, and it will work this time as well."

Jesus and Mary both stared at the general impressed.

Jesus spoke up.

"General Gallus?"

"Yes."

"Whatever we accomplish in this war, my hope is that any Parthian Jews who so desire may return with us to Judea."

"And what about King Arsaces?" Gallus asked.

"Arsaces' fate can await Emperor Domitian's decision," Jesus answered. "My vengeance for the thirteen men he murdered in cold blood will be to free Parthian Jews from bondage and persecution."

"So, the Parthian king's fate falls to Roman hands?" Gallus asked.

Jesus nodded.

"I would think that a trip for Arsaces to the great city of Rome would be in order," he told Gallus. "Should be an eye-opening experience for the Parthian king."

"Especially the Colosseum," the general suggested.

"Indeed," Jesus agreed. "But please make sure that he gets to do some sightseeing first. Most captive kings don't seem to manage their way alive out of the Flavian man-eater."

Gallus laughed and winked at Jesus.

"Neither will he."

— ⚜ —

The advance into Parthia was without incident. It was late spring and abundant rains had made the forests green and the prairies thick with grass. There were countless streams and rivers which provided water for the cavalry horses and the legionnaires. Mary was somewhat amused to find that the men in the Judean army washed as often as the opportunity arose, whereas the Roman soldiers did not.

As the Jewish troops were composed of soldiers practicing both Judaism and Christianity, there was a lot of banter and rude teasing about circumcision or the lack of it. It didn't seem to matter how old the men were, their boyish enthusiasm for off-color humor manifested itself every time the soldiers stripped and wadded into the rivers. Apparently, the only time the Jewish soldiers observed any kind of decorum was when either General Aias or General Harald joined them. Or more rarely, when Roman generals Rubrius Gallus or Lapius Maximus came with their servants for a good soap down.

It was all polite business as usual until one time when General Gallus commented to some Hebrew officers bathing near him that at last he understood why Judean men didn't participate in the Greek Olympics where athletes competed naked. That brought a cloudburst of teasing back from the Jew soldiers that actually made the bond between the Hebrew officers and the Roman general stronger and more cordial. Go figure.

Seven weeks into the journey—and no more than two days march from the Parthian capital city of Ctesiphon—the invasion force still had not met any resistance. Jesus and Mary were both very concerned that the two spies who had been sent into Parthia months ago had not returned, yet the Roman scouts scouring the countryside ahead brought no reports of *any* Parthian military presence.

"Something is drastically wrong," Gallus told Jesus. "Not only have we not faced any forces defending Parthia, there are no troops anywhere ahead of us. None."

"It may be a subterfuge," Maximus spoke up. "The Parthians rarely engage in open battle, preferring to safeguard themselves inside their cities."

"But they do have armies and cavalries?" Mary asked.

"Well-trained armies and brilliant horsemen," Gallus answered. "They have skilled archers as well, able to ride and shoot simultaneously to devastating effect. They use them to harass moving armies, splitting away before the armies can react."

"Or they sit in their cities and wait," Maximus repeated. "Three times in the last three centuries Rome has invaded Parthia, and there was not a single battle. The generals and their armies stayed inside their fortified cities. We besieged them and took them. But Rome could not hold them as Parthian irregulars waged constant warfare until they forced the undermanned occupiers to withdraw."

"Odd to take a country's cities and not hold them," General Harald remarked.

"Brilliant armies, but poor kingdom builders," Maximus conceded. "Rome had the same issues in Judea. It took a rebellion and the loss of two full legions numbering twenty thousand men before the Senate finally invested ten additional legions to keep it in the empire. In the case of Parthia, they refused to pay the price."

"Then why keep conquering its cities?" Mary asked.

"To be plain," Maximus replied, "this punitive expedition differs from earlier ones which intended conquest. This mission sharpens the fighting skills of both the foot and mounted soldiers. It also redounds to the glory and fame of Emperor Domitian who would like nothing more than to say we burned Parthia's cities, took its crops, and brought the king back to Rome for execution.

"Last and most important, the mission will provide significant revenues for the empire's treasury. The wealth taken from the conquered king and the tons of booty the soldiers will loot are taxed up front and the proceeds reserved for Rome. There are eight hundred tax collectors on this trip, did I mention that? So, the soldiers are enriched, the empire's purse is fattened, and the Parthians can starve to death after we're gone."

"So, this is nothing more than an exercise in pillage?" Mary asked somewhat offended.

Gallus arched an eyebrow.

Maximus shook his head and answered.

"It is a punitive venture first and foremost, dear Princess. Mounted to retaliate against the barbaric and insulting actions of King Arsaces toward Rome's envoys."

"Judea's envoys," Mary amended.

"Rome's envoys," Jesus corrected her. "Judea is a client state of Rome and therefore *is* Rome in all of its political, military, or economic dealings."

Gallus spoke up again.

"I suggest that I take a legion of cavalrymen and investigate the conditions regarding Ctesiphon. I'll send back word as to what we find in the Parthian capital. Approaching it with a full legion I imagine there won't be any surprise attacks."

"I agree with Gallus," Harald said. "I have to admit that I am almost struck speechless by the fact that we have ridden this far into Parthia without any contact. Not only have there been no scouts or military, no one protests when we cross their land or graze our horses. No one tries to prevent soldiers from cutting down their wheat and harvesting their olives. The land has been denuded in a swath ten miles wide as we have marched, but not one Parthian lord, knight, or farmer has appeared to say cease and desist."

What else was there to say? Yet the mystery of these strange circumstances was suddenly solved within the hour when one of the two original Judean spies sent into Parthia returned and was brought to Jesus' tent. He was escorted inside by two Jewish legionnaires. He walked slowly and bowed before Jesus. He was thin and pale and his robe was filthy. His eyes looked feverish and he had hundreds of small red marks on his face, his hands, his arms, and legs. He stood at attention and waited for permission to speak.

"Welcome back," Jesus told him gravely concerned for his condition. "What is your name, brave soldier?"

"I am Phraates, son of Antiochus," the man said. "Tiridates, son of Daha, is no more." "Will you sit?" Jesus asked.

The man nodded. Servants immediately pulled up camp chairs for Jesus, Mary, and the spy.

"Thank you, Lord Jesus," Phraates spoke accepting a goblet of wine from a servant.

"Speak now of what you have seen," Jesus told him.

"The land is cursed," he began. "The grain is ready to harvest, but there are no men to bring it in. The Parthians have been aware for weeks that you and Rome are approaching, yet no army stands to protect them. The people are sick, Majesty. Sick unto death. We entered Ctesiphon posing as merchants. They were no guards at the city gate. There was no market. The city was barely populated. Most of its people had been struck down, sick and dying."

"You saw this with your own eyes?" Jesus asked.

"We saw the dead everywhere. Endless numbers of bodies were being carried from the city and burned outside its walls. All the remaining able-bodied men were occupied with this task. Tiridates got sick after three days in Ctesiphon, and shortly thereafter so did I. At first, there was fever and nausea. Then small red boils appeared all over our faces and arms, chests and legs. That is when most people die. Tiridates died. I did not. I have pits where the boils were. But I am alive, if not recovered."

"Did you see any military presence?"

"None. People said that the sickness had been brought into the city by the king and his court after a visit to Babylon a month earlier. It is a tropical city often subjected to diseases and ailments. Alexander the Great caught a fever there that killed him, but no fever has ever destroyed an entire city before."

"What news of the king?"

"No one spoke of him. He was isolated in his palace."

"So, he may be dead as well?"

"No one knows. He may be alive, or he may have died weeks ago."

Jesus gazed at Phraates. He had red pits on his face, his hands, and all over his body. If this disease was so virulent that it could kill and maim most everyone in Ctesiphon, it would certainly kill General Gallus and the legion he would be leading to the Parthian capital.

"It sounds like fate has already dealt with King Arsaces," Jesus said.

"It felt like the hand of Jehovah," the spy said. "And I would beg you, Sire, do not allow a single soldier of ours to enter that accursed place."

Jesus stood. Phraates stood and bowed again. Mary told Jesus that she wanted to get a hot meal in the man's stomach and have his skin examined by a physician. Jesus nodded. Before Mary took the scout, Jesus had one last question for him.

"Does the sickness have a name?"

"Yes, Lord," Phraates answered. "It is called smallpox."

— ⚜ —

"This is a gift from the gods!" Gallus exclaimed when he heard the news. "Who knows what force of heaven has all but erased our enemies from the face of the earth? Ctesiphon is a city of riches beyond calculating, and now it belongs to us."

"It belongs to *you*," Jesus told him. "As I said before we left, Judea will take no prizes. I will accompany Gallus and his Roman legion to the gates of Ctesiphon with a full Jewish legion under the command of General Aias and observe what has befallen the city. If it has indeed been decimated by the smallpox disease, my soldiers will not enter Ctesiphon."

Mary spoke to General Gallus.

"What precautions will you exercise when dealing with the populace, living or dead?"

"We will avoid physical contact with the sick or the dying," Gallus answered. "I don't think we have to fear the food or drink."

Mary nodded.

"Then let us continue on to Ctesiphon," Jesus said.

Gallus and Maximus bowed and left. So did Harald and Aias. Jesus watched them leave.

Mary looked at her father.

"This is a new and deadly plague," she said.

Jesus looked at Mary. Her face was marked by anxiety.

"What would you have me do?" he asked.

Mary shook her head.

"I don't know. What worries me is that it may be a false conclusion to say that Jehovah destroyed the pagan Parthians."

Jesus narrowed his eyes.

"What are you saying?"

Mary looked into her father's questioning eyes.

"One could just as easily believe that God has led us into a trap, and that the *Romans* are the real target of his wrath." She paused and then finished speaking almost in a whisper. "*Or that we are.*"

— ⚜ —

Gallus and Aias had the Roman and Judean legions assembled for the march on Ctesiphon by eight o'clock in the evening. It was a full night's march to the city gates so this dark start would allow the legions to position themselves outside of the Parthian capital city walls before noon the next day. The supply and commercial wagons and the spare cavalry horses were left behind. The other two legions of Roman and Jewish soldiers remained behind as well.

The Roman cavalry wore armor and carried spears, swords, and bows and arrows. The infantry was armored and equipped with lances, short swords, and tall rectangular shields. The Jewish legions were armored and armed very similarly, except that the soldiers in Jesus' army also carried slings and stones.

The army reached Ctesiphon in the late morning. The city's sandstone walls rose twenty feet high and were ten feet thick. Behind them were two more identical walls. But the battlements were empty. There were no Parthian soldiers. And the city gates were open. Mighty Ctesiphon had no defenders.

Jesus addressed General Gallus next to him.

"It appears that the city is yours for the taking."

"I've seen plagues," Gallus said. "And I've seen devastation wrought by disease. But I've never seen anything like this."

"Let us enter the city with a century of men and reconnoiter," Jesus said. "If the defenders of the city have indeed been destroyed, then the battle for Ctesiphon is won."

Gallus rode back and spoke to a Roman centurion. The officer brought his hundred-strong cavalry unit forward—five across and twenty deep—accompanied by the Parthian-speaking soldier who had been assigned to his century. The centurion nodded to the general. Then he bowed his head deeply toward Jesus who saw the large gold cross affixed to his chestplate.

Jesus gestured for him to approach.

"What's your name, son?" he asked.

"Angelos, son of Hieronymos, Lord Jesus."

"Angel," Jesus translated from the Greek. "Your parents are Christians, too?"

"Yes. They reside in heaven where, by the grace of God, I will someday embrace them again."

"Maybe not today, though, okay?" Jesus asked.

The centurion flushed and then smiled, appreciating Jesus' wish for his survival.

"Bless you, Angelos," Jesus told him, then waved to Gallus that he was done. The centurion looked at Jesus, touched his cross, and rode back to the front of his unit. Gallus gave the order to move out. He led the century through the open gates of Ctesiphon with Jesus and Angelos at his sides.

The horsemen passed through the three sets of open gates—twenty-foot-tall cedar doors braced behind with thick iron sheets—and entered the city. As far as the eye could see the giant plaza they had entered was filled with wagons being filled with bodies. The men and women loading corpses paused from their task and observed the Roman Empire's soldiers entering into the heart of their city.

Gallus called a halt after the century had entered the plaza and studied the mercantile streets that emptied into the square. They were devoid of people and activity. Gallus took Angelos and five of his men and followed Jesus toward the king's fortified palace on the other side of the plaza. It sat elevated on a great stone platform with high granite walls surrounding it. It was a beautiful palace, made in the image of the marble Parthenon that crowned the Athenian acropolis. Had it become a funeral temple for King Arsaces?

The front gates of the citadel were closed. A lone Parthian soldier stood watching the party approach. He wore armor and a helmet, but had no weapon. Gallus dismounted and asked Angelos and his Parthian-speaking legionnaire to walk with him to meet the man at the gates. Gallus stopped about six feet from the Parthian and spoke to him through the interpreter.

"Hail, Master of the Gates! I am Gallus, commander of a Roman army set in an attack formation outside your city."

"Welcome!" the man called out. "I am not the master of these gates. Merely a herald posted to greet your arrival. Arsaces, King of Kings, has expected you, General Gallus of Rome. Our spies within your ranks send us daily tidings of your plans and activities."

Gallus scowled, but held his tongue.

The herald went on.

"The great king bids you and your army welcome. His royal city has perished as you can plainly see. Mighty Arsaces gives it to you as reparation for the deaths of the couriers sent to him. The gods have punished him, and he repents of the evil he did. Behold Ctesiphon," the herald said, sweeping an arm across the plaza and city. "And behold the holy place of the King of Kings himself." He raised his hand and pointed toward the citadel and palace. "They are yours."

"Where is Arsaces?" Gallus demanded.

"I do not know, my Lord. Three days ago, the king marched out of the city with his army, or what remained of it. No more than five thousand knights left this place alive."

Gallus stared at the herald and then turned away. With a sudden leap the Parthian landed on the general's back and knocked him to the ground. He plunged a knife into the Gallus's neck just below the lip of his helmet. Centurion Adeodatus pulled his sword and rushed toward the assassin. The Parthian stabbed himself in the belly, then rolled onto his back and lay on the stones of the plaza.

"Sorry, I neglected to mention that last little gift from the king," he said. He smiled a thin smile and went limp, blood gushing from his bowels. Adeodatus sheathed his sword. Jesus dismounted and knelt next to Gallus. He put his scarred hand over the wound in the general's neck and in moments it stopped hemorrhaging. He told Gallus to sit up. Gallus did. Adeodatus stared in amazement.

"I've read the Gospel stories of your healing gift," he said to Jesus stunned. "But I must admit that I thought such miracles occurred only when you walked the earth."

"I still walk the earth," Jesus replied. "And I still heal. But as always—then and now—it is God who makes up his mind about who lives and who dies. The power is in *his* will. Not in my hands. The Lord giveth. And the Lord taketh away. Today he is in the mood to give."

Jesus stood and helped Gallus get to his feet. The general reached his hand behind his neck and touched his wound.

"It is healed," he said staring at Jesus.

Jesus nodded.

"There are likely more such *heralds* in this place," he said warning the general. "Take care for yourself and for the lives of your legionnaires."

Gallus bowed his head and thanked Jesus. He told him that he would allow the legion waiting before the gates to enter the capital and plunder the city. Jesus nodded. His own legionnaires would not loot the city. And none of his soldiers would protest. Most were still possessed by nightmare memories of Roman legionnaires entering Jerusalem, slaughtering the survivors, breaking into shops and homes, and stripping the city of everything of value. Those were terrible sins, and ones which no pious Jew would ever allow to stain him. However, for all of their piety, the saintly men in Jesus' army would not be spared the plague. It was about to encompass them all.

CHAPTER EIGHTEEN

JESUS MET WITH GENERAL MAXIMUS, his own generals Aias and Harald, and his daughter Mary.

"Maximus," Jesus began. "Please inform your legions and the Roman commercial wagons that Gallus has occupied Ctesiphon. The soldiers and the merchants may advance to the city as soon as they choose. However, the population of the capital has been virtually destroyed by the smallpox disease. Tell them as forcefully as you can that if they enter Ctesiphon they will surely be infected.

"It seems foolish to me," Jesus went on, "to touch or carry away the goods of the citizens of that place. I don't know how the plague communicates itself to its victims, but anyone contemplating entering the capital must be reminded that as easily as smallpox kills a Parthian it can kill a Roman, too."

Jesus turned to Mary.

"Was Phraates, the infected scout, quarantined?"

"Yes, he was," she replied. "He keeps away from the camp. Food and water are left for him."

Maximus rose.

"I will contact the Roman officers, the merchants, and the women.

And I will warn them of the doom that infests Ctesiphon. For all that, I doubt anyone will remain behind with money to be made."

Jesus nodded and Maximus left.

Mary spoke to him.

"Father, you realize that Gallus and you—as well as the Roman escort that accompanied you into the city—have all been exposed to smallpox?"

"I do," Jesus said. "Several of the soldiers touched the soil, the stones of the plaza, and Gallus had direct physical contact with a Parthian who tried to murder him. Can stones be contaminated? Was the assassin infected with smallpox? I don't know. No one knows. What we *saw* is that Ctesiphon is full of death and that the very act of entering the city has very likely exposed us all."

Mary looked disturbed and distraught, clearly believing that a cloud of death was hovering over everyone—in the city *and* in the camp—and not believing for a moment that there was any way to stop or avoid it. Jesus shared her worry and fear. For her. For his army. For himself. What could he do except return to Judea?

But then any exposed Hebrew soldiers would carry the smallpox home. Even as the Roman legions would carry the disease to Rome itself. It could be the end of the world for all he knew. Once again, perhaps for the hundredth time, he remembered his mother's visit from beyond the grave, warning him that Jehovah wanted him to leave off his desire to punish Parthia. He had never told his daughter about it. But he all too vividly recalled Mary's warning of his own punishment and death.

Jesus looked at his daughter.

"I need to be alone."

She rose and gave her father a kiss on the cheek.

"I will return at dawn," she said.

Jesus watched her leave his tent. Then he pulled back the carpets laid over the ground, stripped off his robe, and prostrated himself face down in the dirt. He lay there for a long time before he finally confessed to God that he had disobeyed his will and mocked the only communication Jehovah had ever granted him. And why?

Because he had willfully determined to ignore God and do what he wanted to do? No. The truth was even worse. He had disobeyed because in the depths of his heart *he no longer cared what Jehovah wanted*. He had turned away from the God he had once loved. And now, that God was raising his hand to punish him. And not just him, but his army, and the Roman army as well. And who knew how many hundreds of thousands of Jews and Romans beyond that?

Was there a way to be forgiven? Was there a way to save the forty thousand soldiers in this place? To save his nation? He didn't know. But pushing his face deeper into the dirt, he was going to implore Jehovah for mercy and forgiveness. Until God answered.

Three days and nights, Jesus lay without getting up. Without taking water or sustenance. He prayed unceasingly for God to forgive his disobedience. To spare his soldiers, his land, and his people. Would Jehovah for once repent of his threats of destruction and stay his hand? On the fourth day Jesus got his answer. He saw that his hand was covered with small red pustules. His arms, his chest, his legs all testified that God had given him smallpox.

Mary brought Jesus water and saw that her father's face and his hand were covered in spots. He was sitting on the ground without moving. She offered her hand. He shook his head.

"I have smallpox," Jesus told her. "You must not touch me."

Mary took his hand.

"If God wills that I get smallpox, then I will," she replied. "Whether I help you or not."

Jesus took her hand. Mary helped him stand and walk to a camp chair. He sat with his head hanging, grieving over God's rejection, struggling to absorb the fact that he had a sentence of death written all over his body. Mary made him drink some water. Then she filled a basin with water and washed the dirt off her father's face, arms and hand, legs and feet. Jesus thanked her, feeling feverish and weak. Despite the onset of the smallpox he wanted to take his soldiers home.

"Is our army still able to evacuate?" he asked.

"Hundreds of the soldiers have come down with the disease."

Jesus groaned.

"But how?"

Mary shook her head.

"The smallpox is here. That's all anyone knows."

"Tell Aias and Harald to prepare for withdrawal. We have enough supplies to pace our retreat slowly enough to care for the infected and bury those who die."

"I will tell them immediately," Mary promised. "You will be transported in a private wagon, and I will care for you myself. If you die, I will take your body home."

Jesus locked eyes with his daughter.

"I want my body to be packed with myrrh and wrapped with linen strips. And after my bones have been harvested I want them transported back to La Valdieu and placed in the box that is reserved for me in the royal tomb."

Mary knelt and held her father's hand. She spoke to him gently.

"Do you sincerely believe that you are going to die?"

Jesus nodded.

"Look at me, dear one," he said. "As surely as these spots have appeared on my body, they declare that it is the end of my life." Jesus rubbed his eyes. He looked at Mary again. "I want you to personally scratch a new identification on my bone box.

Jesus of Nazareth.

A Savior to the Jews.

A Disappointment to his Father.

Mary wrapped her arms around her father's neck and began sobbing.

"Thank you, Mary." Tears formed in Jesus' own eyes now. Mary pulled off the sash she was wearing and dried his eyes over and over. "All I can think about now," he said softly, "*is not having to live this life of frustration and humiliation any longer.*"

"Are you so very sure that Jehovah does not appreciate your life?" she asked.

Jesus held up his only hand for her to see. It was covered with smallpox sores.

"What do *you* think?" he asked.

Mary took his hand and spoke from her heart.

"I believe that you will overcome the smallpox and recover. I believe that when God raised you from the dead it was his way of being proud of you. And by granting you long life, he allows you to excel at what you do best. Exemplifying kindness and forgiveness to his people.

"Maybe," Mary argued, "this smallpox is actually God's reminder to you yet again, *that you and he are not alike*. He is violent and judgmental, striking down both those who are evil *and* those who are good. *He doesn't need you to be like him. He doesn't want you to be like him.* This Parthian excursion should make you see yourself as a *balance* to God, *a balance that he himself created you to be.* Not by punishing the sinful. But by providing the love, hope, and comfort to his people *that he has never been able to do*. Be the Son your Father wants you to be."

Great drops of blood fell from Jesus' face onto Mary's hands which were still grasping his hand. Alarmed she raised her fingers and touched his face.

"You are burning up and your pores are sweating blood."

Jesus nodded.

"It is the omen of my death. It happened in the Garden of Gethsemane before my crucifixion."

Mary shook her head.

"Perhaps this time it is the omen of your rebirth."

Jesus didn't answer. Mary wiped the blood from his face with a damp cloth and helped him lie down on his cot. She pulled off the blankets and left a small pillow. Jesus laid on his back and fell asleep instantly. Mary kissed his feverish brow and wondered what her worried father had been thinking when fatigue overwhelmed him. Known only to himself, Jesus' last thought had been, *If for just once in my life I am lucky, I will never wake up again.*

— ⚜ —

Thousands of soldiers fell sick and died on the four-month trip back to Judea. Jesus was sick with fever and boils for almost two weeks. But he did not die. His constant dreams about God's intentions caused him to finally accept that Jehovah was sparing his life on the condition that he accept the fact that God was not love. *But that he himself was.* And that he need never again look to heaven seeking that validation.

Instead, he should teach. And preach. Heal and forgive. Proving through the ages ahead that God's greatest ambition is to have men love one another, even as his own Son loved them. Jesus felt the hatred and self-pity he had nurtured so long sink into remorse and sorrow. He understood and accepted God's will. The lonely God. The silent God. The unpredictable God. Who had, after all, warned everyone of his mercurial nature as early as the Jews' Exodus from Egypt, "I am that I am. I will be who I will be." Murderer. Monster. Bringer of death and destruction.

But he had birthed a boy in the humblest of circumstances, seeking a different and better way to deal with humankind. It had been Jesus' calling to be God's harbinger of love. But instead, he had insisted on acting like his Father—murderer, monster, bringer of death and destruction—the King of the Jews. Jesus repented of his evil and humbled his heart to accept his destiny as the mediator between God and man. He had to learn to believe again what at this moment he still couldn't speak out loud. That above everything else, God was love.

— ⚜ —

Jesus returned to Jericho with only six thousand men, and proceeded to watch the smallpox plague destroy more than a third of the population of Judea. He received word that the Roman army had fared no better. Generals Gallus and Maximus died. Centurion Adeodatus died. Sixteen thousand Roman legionnaires died. All of the merchants and all of the prostitutes died. When Domitian's army finally returned to Rome, smallpox spread from there throughout the empire killing almost half of the population.

In the late winter, three months after he had returned, Jesus resumed holding court. Those who presented themselves before his throne stared at him, stunned. Jesus himself had to force his eyes to look in a mirror. He had long white cornrows flowing down from under his crown. He had but a single hand, pierced and pitted. And his face—more than any other part of his body—was covered with holes where the smallpox pustules had eaten into his flesh. Then dried and fallen off. Jesus accepted his punished appearance, because that's exactly what it was. A sign for all to see that God had punished him, *yet had also spared him and set him once again on the path that had been ordained for him.*

Jesus felt like he had wasted a hundred years. But he would waste no more of the time remaining to him. Be it a solitary year or hundreds more. Which was good. For, in fact, Jesus would live another nineteen hundred years, loving his life, loving his mission, loving at last the God he knew in the depths of his heart could never love him back.

Jesus sat down on his throne with both lions—his full-grown beasts Alpha and Omega—at his feet, guarding his presence. He sat for a very long time.

The End of Volume 2

Acknowledgements

I would like to thank the many wonderful readers who have shared how their thinking has been affected by this alternate life of Jesus of Nazareth, King of the Jews.

I would also like to thank the professional partners who have worked with me on this book. Copy and content editor Jerry Sexton; the formatting artists at WordZWorth, London; Vincent Chong for his cover art and design, and last, my friend, publisher Lionel A. Blanchard.

www.ingramcontent.com/pod-product-compliance
Lightning Source LLC
Chambersburg PA
CBHW051849090426
42811CB00034B/2266/J

* 9 7 8 1 7 3 3 5 8 5 8 2 8 *